D1587456

700043694830

CHRIS KRAUS
AFTER KATHY ACKER

CHRIS KRAUS
AFTER KATHY ACKER

A BIOGRAPHY

ALLEN LANE
an imprint of
PENGUIN BOOKS

ALLEN LANE

UK | USA | Canada | Ireland | Australia
India | New Zealand | South Africa

Allen Lane is part of the Penguin Random House group of companies
whose addresses can be found at global.penguinrandomhouse.com.

First published in the United States of America by Semiotext(e) 2017
First published in Great Britain by Allen Lane 2017
001

Printed in Great Britain by Clays Ltd, St Ives plc

A CIP catalogue record for this book is available from the British Library

ISBN: 978–0–241–31805–8

www.greenpenguin.co.uk

MIX
Paper from
responsible sources
FSC
www.fsc.org   FSC® C018179

Penguin Random House is committed to a
sustainable future for our business, our readers
and our planet. This book is made from Forest
Stewardship Council® certified paper.

For Sabina Ott

. . . memories haunt me, increasing frequency and my sense of the obdurate. Time transforms into thing; no wonder myths of afterlife and rebirth proliferate—this is the dubious gift of reliving narratives which may never have existed, but which appear to carry the concrete weight of the world. Memories transform into inert substance, a form of hardness, as one grows distant from them. One is fashioned by the fashioning of them.

—Alan Sondheim, autobiog.txt

You realize that the past is just like everything else—it's a dream. And it's just as much of a fiction as if you were actually writing fiction and we choose to say or choose to remember or can't remember how to remember whatever it was you were trying to remember. It comes out filtered and redefined and has an envelope of fiction to it. Because we're all basically fiction.

—Rudy Wurlizer, interview
by Jonathan Dixon, *Vice* magazine

Contents

Littoral Madness   13

Politics (1971–1973)   25

The Childlike Life of the Black Tarantula (1971–1974)   66

Breaking Through Memories into Desire (1974–1975)   93

Tasting and Spitting (1975–1979)   115

A Person of Great Expectations (1979–1983)   155

Fiction (1983–1990)   199

1995 (1989–1995)   237

Fable (1996–1997)   266

Notes   281

Index   331

Acknowledgments   343

TO BEGIN . . .

As the twentieth century fades out
the nineteenth begins

                    again
it is as if nothing happened
though those who lived it thought
that everything was happening
enough to name a world for & a time
to hold it in your hand
unlimited   the last delusion
like the perfect mask of death

               — Jerome Rothenberg, for
                 Jean-Pierre Faye

LITTORAL MADNESS

Like everything in the past, everyone remembers it differently, and some of the people involved hardly remember at all. We're talking about something that happened more than seventeen years ago. But on January 23, 1998, which was a Friday, friends of the late writer Kathy Acker drove from San Francisco to Fort Funston park, about twenty-five minutes away, to scatter her ashes. She'd died two months earlier at an alternative clinic in Tijuana, where she received palliative care for late-stage, metastasized cancer.

The ash scattering—like the wake at Bob Glück's house on December 13 and the memorial reading at Slim's Bar where Michelle Handelman was booed off the stage for no reason she can recall—devolved into a kind of black comedy, the way these things often do. I remember Cookie Mueller at Jackie Curtis's memorial, standing up on the stage of La MaMa halfway through an evening of readings and monologues, blinking back tears as she faced the dark auditorium. She had no speech prepared. "I thought this was supposed to be a funeral," she said to the room. "Not a variety show." Speaking to Sylvère Lotringer, the artist Steve Brown recalled how the elegantly planned Nembutal suicide of Danceteria emcee Haoui Montaug among a small group of friends ended with a plastic bag over his head. He was a large man, in the late stages of AIDS, and whoever arranged for the pills had underestimated the dose. Before time accelerated, deaths among friends in the art world were like salt to a sting, bringing unresolved feuds to the surface. Now we care less, or are nicer.

Around this time last year, when I started working on what may or may not be a biography of Kathy Acker, I imagined beginning the book with the melee at Slim's Bar, or at the wake, where a group of friends gathered to transfer her ashes from a box to an urn, or at the scattering. To describe these proceedings would be to stage an establishing shot of a movie that uses a single protagonist to traverse an entire milieu. Although she wrote first-person fiction and gave hundreds of interviews in which she was asked to recite the facts of her life over and over again, these facts are hard to pin down in any literal way. Because in a certain sense, Acker lied all the time. She was rich, she was poor, she was the mother of twins, she'd been a stripper for years, a guest editor of *Film Comment* magazine at the age of fourteen, a graduate student of Herbert Marcuse's. She lied when it was clearly beneficial to her, and she lied even when it was not. Perceptive readers of Acker's work have observed that the lies weren't literal lies, but more a system of magical thought. As Dodie Bellamy notes in her essay "Digging Through Kathy Acker's Stuff": "Over and over, Acker tells the same tale: the mother is pregnant with the daughter, and the father leaves. The mother blames the daughter and tries to abort her. The daughter's body survives, but not her unified self. . . . Is it true? Does it matter? . . . Acker liberates libido from Freud's repressed underworld." But then again, didn't she do what all writers must do? Create a position from which to write?

Acker's life was a fable, and to describe the confusion and love and conflicting agendas behind these memorials would be to sketch an apocryphal allegory of an artistic life in the late twentieth century. *It is girls from which stories begin*, she wrote in her last notebook. And like other lives, but unlike most fables, it was created through means both within and beyond her control.

* * *

By the time Acker died, at age fifty, she'd known thousands of people. Since her divorce from her second husband, Peter Gordon, in 1979, she'd had no long-term partner. She'd lived, at different times in her life, in San Diego, San Francisco, New York, and London, a half-conscious rotation between cities familiar to her. "I think she was just always trying to find her community," the technology writer R. U. Sirius told me last year at a Mill Valley café. Michael Bracewell, who'd known her in London during the mid-1980s, concurred. She'd bought, then abandoned an apartment in Brighton. Her friend Gary Pulsifer doubts she ever spent a night there. Estranged from her remaining immediate family, she'd known poets and bikers, leather dykes, tattooists, philosophers, astrologers, renowned artists and writers, bodybuilders, psychics, promoters, and editors, and she'd slept with a great number of them. In London, she played chess with Salman Rushdie.

She'd lived in San Francisco between 1990 and 1996, teaching a class in New Genres at the Art Institute while trying to find a more stable, tenure-track job anywhere in the U.S. During those years she worked out at a Gold's Gym, published two novels, toured constantly, recorded CDs, and added an enormous, impressive tattoo across her shoulders and upper back to the series of pictographs already inscribed on her body. *Literal* madness; images written not just as words on the page, but as pictures on flesh. The tattoo—an enormous lizardlike fish overlaid with a garland of flowers that morphs into a sleek airborne bird—was done in the style of Ed Hardy and took weeks to complete. Her friend Kathy Brew recalls Acker coming into her office in the Humanities Department after each session and saying, "Honey, would you put some cream on my back?" After the last session, Brew grabbed her camera and took a much-reproduced photograph of a bare-chested Acker astride her 650cc motorcycle. "We were just playing around. It felt like two girls playing dress-up, or something." Brew was newly divorced, and during those years the two hung out a lot, talking about being single, desire, and intimacy, and then in '94 Brew moved back to New York.

By the time Acker left San Francisco for London in July '96, she'd stopped talking to a lot of her former friends in the city's literary worlds and cyberpunk scene. With some, there'd been feuds. Others couldn't handle her medical choices and denial of the cancer, which had been diagnosed in April that year. When she returned to San Francisco in September, she was no longer closely in touch with anyone from her old extensive and disparate circles. From a hotel, she called Aline Mare, an old colleague from the Art Institute, and asked for help. She'd known Mare years before in New York, but in San Francisco their friendship had been distant, at best. Mare recalls running into Acker holding court at parties and openings, looking into the middle distance beyond her old friend. "Oh c'mon, Kathy, I *know* you," Mare felt like saying. Acker told Mare she was sick, and although Mare was now working full-time and caring for a young child, within minutes of arriving at Acker's hotel room, she had a strong feeling—"I have to be there for this." Sharon Grace, another SFAI colleague, became a key part of Acker's support system in San Francisco during those weeks before her friend, the writer and artist Matias Viegener arrived from L.A. and arranged for her move from the UC San Francisco Medical Center to American Biologics, the only alternative clinic in Tijuana that would accept cancer patients at such a late stage. They arrived with a Buddhist nurse in a rental van on November 1, the Mexican Day of the Dead. By the time Viegener returned to San Francisco with her ashes, everyone knew of her illness and death. There'd been a fundraising drive for her clinic expenses, a few of her closest old friends had traveled to visit her in Tijuana, and thousands of emails about her condition had been exchanged. A strange sonnet was posted online less than two weeks after her death by the "Acker Society" of Gothenburg, Sweden:

> *These news are not for real*
> *We have nothing more to feel*
> *Death again has put us in trances*
> *But You will always be in my dances*
> *I cannot take much more*
> *What on earth are we here for?*
> *You were a prostitute, some kind of whore*
> *Kathy, You have made your final score*

* * *

Acker died a month after arriving in Tijuana. During the last weeks of her life, Matias Viegener became her constant companion, her next of kin, overseeing her treatment at the clinic, coordinating visits from friends, and acting as a clearinghouse for all the related communication.

They'd met some seven years earlier, when Acker gave a reading with Dennis Cooper at Beyond Baroque in L.A. They connected immediately. She'd just moved back to San Francisco from London. Viegener invited her to read at CalArts, where he taught. He'd see her when he was in San Francisco, and sometimes she'd ride her motorcycle down to L.A., where she'd stay at his house, and they'd drive out to the hot springs. Viegener traveled to see her in San Francisco after she underwent a mastectomy in April '96. Her boyfriend at the time, Charles Shaar Murray, had flown in from London to be with her during the surgery. When Viegener arrived, he found Acker miserable, weak, and pissed that he hadn't come sooner. She wanted to be taken care of, but not treated as if she were sick, which he found impossible. He had a strong feeling then that she was going to die. As he would write later, "I knew she was going to die and how she would die and that I would be there because I wasn't afraid of it, or if I was it was minuscule in proportion to her fear of it, so it was blotted out."

After the mastectomy she turned her back on Western medicine, a decision she'd eventually describe in an essay, "The Gift of Disease," and a libretto, *Eurydice in the Underworld*. She stayed in San Francisco for three months after the surgery, consulting psychics, astrologers, healers, nutritionists, and a past-life regressionist in Marin County. By July, her healers agreed that she was cancer-free, and as planned, she left San Francisco to live with Shaar Murray. Two of the practitioners Acker consulted would later be indicted for medical fraud in other cases. However, those closest to Acker came to agree that the claims of her healers were more metaphoric than fraudulent. Which was not unlike the extrapolations in Acker's first-person writings and interviews, which, if misread as *literal* truths, could then be dismissed as false.

Acker's domestic arrangement with Shaar Murray didn't last long. Two months after arriving, she bought an apartment in Islington and continued the work of self-healing. Living in a temporary one-bedroom apartment in Roanoke, Virginia, for a visiting writer job at Hollins University the following spring, she felt depleted and tired, a condition that she insisted could only be because of her and Murray's relationship problems and this new dislocation. Returning to London that summer, she fell sick again with an illness she ascribed to *littoral* poisoning: walking with Murray on a towpath beside the Regent's Canal, she dropped her Evian bottle into the river. He scrambled down to retrieve it, and she told herself and her readers and friends over and over again about how she'd contracted a viral infection when the polluted water seeped under the cap. She was reacting to tainted water—he'd given her poison to drink—it wasn't cancer at all!

This assault prompted the last rupture between them. As Murray wrote later, "[T]here was one blowup too many. This time, neither of us made the conciliatory phone call which usually brought us back into each other's arms." Alone, exhausted, and isolated in her Islington flat, she saw no point in staying. Viegener and others thought she should move back to California. In early September she flew to San Francisco via Chicago, where she'd performed for three nights with the Mekons, checked into a hotel, and consulted her healers. She didn't reach out to Viegener or other old friends until mid-October. As Bob Glück recalls,

"She attributed her illness to bad water. She was very constipated, and instructed me to bring a certain enema. I couldn't find it, and so she didn't use the one I brought, because everything was done according to Frank Molinaro, her astrologer, and he had not authorized this one. She called him every hour or less, consulting him on every move. He passed out business cards at her funeral. Isn't that incredible? As though Kathy's fate was an advertisement for him.

"I gave Kathy a back massage. She was very thin. I tried to figure out what to do for her—she was in deeply serious pain, the kind of pain that makes you frantic. It seemed to me she had entered a magic world. She did not really want to associate with people outside it."

When she finally called Viegener, he offered to drive up and bring her back to his house in L.A. to regain her bearings, but when he arrived, he saw that she was clearly too sick to be moved. He, Aline Mare, and Sharon Grace convinced her to go to a hospital, where doctors confirmed that the cancer had spread to most of her body.

I don't understand, she told Viegener. *I have cancer everywhere. My healers told me I had no cancer. When I asked my master healer, the teacher of all the healers, he told me he saw no cancer because I would not let him see cancer; he can only see what I let him see. So teachers are mirrors.*

* * *

Her body was cremated at the Funeraria del Carmen in Tijuana, and somehow Viegener, who was now her executor, transported the ashes across the border in a sealed aluminum tin. The question became, what to do with them? Acker left no instructions about the arrangements, because she did not want to die. She'd been coaxed into writing a will only when Sylvère Lotringer posed the question of what would become of her work was posed as a hypothetical game. A flurry of emails passed between Viegener and Ira Silverberg, Acker's former agent and friend. A mutual friend had offered his garden, but that didn't seem right. "Let X find other fertilizer for his garden. You should do as you please," Silverberg wrote. "I still think a little in San Francisco, London, and NYC would be nice," he proposed, not unreasonably.

A few miles away from the clinic, people continue to visit the gravesite of Juan Soldado, a dubious folk hero whose remains are interred where he was shot by a firing squad in 1938. Candles and stones, bracelets and pennies and figurines. *Thank you, Juan Soldado, for bringing my son . . . Thank you for granting my emigration . . . Thank you with all my heart for the protection you gave me in my hour of anguish,* the small engraved plaques and handwritten notes say.

To remain in one place is either privation or luxury. No one I know who's died in my lifetime, no matter their age, has been interred in a grave. No matter how loved or accomplished or distinguished these friends have been, there are no scholarship funds in their names, no plaques, no memorial benches or arches. The reasons for this, I suppose, have been detailed in such books as Robert Putnam's *Bowling Alone*, but I still find it hard to accept. Where to inter the remains of those who live in a state of perpetual transience? He divides his time between New York and Maine, between Berlin and L.A., between Jakarta and Sydney, the bios all say. Why not the ashes?

In San Francisco, Viegener and other friends found a French *beaux arts* vase in an antique shop that would serve as an urn. A decision was made to hold a memorial wake at Bob Glück and Chris Komater's home on Saturday, December 13. People would speak, and there'd be a ceremony to transfer the ashes from the can to the vase. The dining room table would be used as an altar, and Sheppard Powell, a Buddhist practitioner, diviner, healer, and longtime partner of the poet Diane di Prima, would be asked to preside.

Seventeen people gathered that night at Glück and Komater's house. Powell led the group in a meditation, breathing in fear and confusion and chaos, breathing out calm and peace, and then he recited a Tibetan chant for her spirit's release. There was a publicity headshot on the altar, some lilies and a little stuffed dog. As Kevin Killian recalls, the house "was filled with New Agey type people who had helped Kathy in her last years. Tattooists, bodybuilders, motorcycle girls, S/m practitioners, herbalists, it was almost like an upstairs-downstairs thing . . . Kathy had hired most of these people at one time or another— they were the service people, I thought snobbishly; but very few artists or writers who were her peers . . ."

"The ritual had this creepy otherworldliness to it, this sacredness," Dodie Bellamy would write in her diary the next day. "As if Kathy were behind the scenes directing our movements . . .

And people were shedding real tears—Kathy's chosen truly loved her—nice people." A young Amazonian woman named Juliette who knew Acker from Gold's Gym cut open the can, and then people were asked to approach the altar alone and commune with the ashes by scooping a cup into the vase. Bellamy couldn't do it. Killian dipped three fingers into the jar and licked them off his hand. Ingesting her ashes was a symbolic means of reincarnating some of the dead hero's genius; he'd done it before, with his friend Sam D'Allesandro's cremains. Viegener was horrified, but then he did it too. As he'd later write, "What hit me most was that K would have no choice about whom her ashes inhabited . . . whatever the meaningless relation between ashes and human, some choice was made available again . . . My first decision as literary executor." Although mostly, Aline Mare recalls, it was messy. "It works best," she emailed last week, "with a paper cone."

* * *

Viegener selected the Fort Funston park site because he remembered how much Acker loved walking there. A short drive south of the city, the park has a spectacular view of the open Pacific. Wide paths dotted with wind-dwarfed cypresses and junipers cut over the bluffs. At the park's steepest point, it's a two hundred-foot drop to the waves.

People arrived at the park that afternoon in separate cars. It was a smaller group than at the memorial. Acker's friend, the editor Amy Scholder, had flown in from New York. Aline Mare and Sharon Grace were both there; Bob Glück, Viegener, Sheppard Powell, and the astrologer Frank Molinaro. Mel Freilicher, a longtime friend of Acker's from San Diego, may have been there. As people got out of their cars and assembled, Molinaro passed out business cards. The general plan was to release the ashes into the sea, although Scholder wondered about this because she recalled that Acker feared drowning. But then again, as Viegener recalls, "She was afraid of death, period, in any concrete way, although it runs through all of her work."

The group took a steep sandy path down one of the dunes, and Viegener carried the urn. Aline Mare recalls Sheppard Powell reciting Diane di Prima's poem "Litany (for Kathy Acker)," written in response to Rudolph Giuliani's attempt to shut down the *Sensations* show at the Brooklyn Museum because of Catholic protests against Chris Ofili's painting *The Holy Virgin Mary*, which was spattered with elephant dung—

> *our lady of mandrake*
> *our lady the bayou*
> *our lady of subways*
> *our lady of blind cats*
> *our lady of albino alligators*
> *our lady of desperadoes*
> *our 300 pound lady who sits on stoops*
> *in a house-dress in the summer night*
> *our lady of tenements*

—although in a literal sense this seems unlikely because the exhibition wouldn't open in Brooklyn until October 1999, but in any event, it is a great poem. As the group scrambled down, Viegener and Scholder paused to wait for the others, and Frank Molinaro, the odd one out, the one nobody in this group liked, rushed up and grabbed the vase from Viegener's hands. The astrologer ran toward the sea tossing handfuls of ash and bone while he proclaimed—"You're free, Kathy! You're finally free!"—before Viegener and Scholder wrested it back. It was bitter cold, and no matter how hard they tried, no one could toss the ashes into the waves, because the wind blew them back.

It hardly felt final. Viegener and Scholder waded into the sea with the final cremains. After that, everyone trudged back up the dune and drove to the Beach Chalet bar up the road to talk and have drinks.

POLITICS

(1971–1973)

Between grief and nothing, I will take grief.
—(Jean Seberg quoting William Faulkner's *The Wild
Palms* to Jean-Paul Belmondo in Jean-Luc Godard's *Breathless*)

New York City, 1971:

The bed, rarely made, floats in a room painted orange with big violet stars.

She spends most of her days and nights in the bed, sleeping and writing. Her hair is cut short. Twice, unable to do anything with it, she shaves it all off.

The inside of the closet is violet, matching the stars. The room could be anywhere, really, although in actual fact it's on the sixth floor of a building in Washington Heights, upper Manhattan, straddling the corner of Broadway and 163rd Street. There are gates on the two skinny windows, facing north onto 163rd. Even in 1971, the old prewar building, with its large corniced lobby, has seen better days.

The bedroom is spacious and shabby. When they arrived in New York, they scavenged for furniture in a friend's basement. There's a black, red, and white Navajo rug, a commode and two nightstands, a wood breakfast table and two matching chairs.

Mornings, the sound of the boiler kicking on wakes them up early, and they go back to sleep. Steam heat moves through the pipes, but it never fully warms the room. The apartment is on the top floor. Down the hall, a staircase leads up to the roof, and sometimes she goes there to look at the view. There's a second bedroom in the back of the apartment, with a desk and a typewriter, two sleeping bags, some spare clothes, and a piano that belongs to her boyfriend's estranged wife but still hasn't been moved. That winter, the United States invades Laos, Charles Manson is sentenced to death, and New York is rainy and cold. Two rival factions of the Black Panther Party engage in retaliatory assassinations. Four people are killed. No one will ever know if the shootings were carried out or provoked by FBI infiltrators.

The woman who lives here is twenty-three, soon to turn twenty-four. Kathy Acker, nee Alexander, grew up in New York, but returning after six years away, she feels alone and estranged. Her family's apartment on East Fifty-Seventh Street is just a few miles away, but she never goes home. Her parents still live there, and she does not want to see them. She won't visit her grandmother, who lives in a hotel apartment on West Fifty-Fourth Street, because she's convinced that her grandmother is in collusion with them. When she thinks of her childhood at all, she remembers the green walls and red flowered curtains of her hated bedroom in *the 57th Street prison*.

I'm ugly, I'm not ugly, she writes, *if I dress eccentrically enough. I'm hideous with my short hair and draggy breasts.*

Her boyfriend, Len Neufeld, is twenty-eight, but he seems a lot older, in a seductive way. Sitting up under the covers one night, she records how he *lies beside me reading* The Presentation of Self *waiting for me so he can get some sleep he works tomorrow his hair's pushed back into a ponytail and wrinkles are lining the top of his face.*

His plan, when they moved here together from San Diego the previous May, was to finish his dissertation, but each day the plan moves a little further away. He owes $100 a month in child support to his soon-to-be former wife and another $20 a month to the lawyer. He'd been invited to study linguistics at MIT with Noam Chomsky, but like Acker, he sees himself as a writer. In the bedroom together, they write down their dreams.

On weekdays, Len Neufeld works in midtown at Burt Lasky's editorial agency, but he makes almost as much every Sunday, when he and his girlfriend perform in the "live sex show" at Fun City, a Times Square emporium owned by Marty "King of the Peeps" Hodas. They take the subway to and from work, where they earn $120 a night for performing six shows, twenty or thirty minutes each time.

Bob Wolfe, a hippie porn entrepreneur, got them the gig in December when he was hired by Hodas to manage the club. Arriving back in New York in the early summer, they'd scoured the classified ads in the *Voice* for nude modeling and sex loops, anything really that would buy them some time.

GIRLS WANTED $75–$100
Per shooting Figure Modeling
& Films. No experience necessary.
Call Robert Wolfe Studio 255-2711

Wolfe's Fourteenth Street basement studio would soon become the ground zero of New York's adult film industry, but the audition Polaroids of nude hippies taken in 1971 offer a baffling clue to the mores of that era. Clothed in their nakedness, affectless girls with flat features and long, stringy hair stand in front of Wolfe's camera, presenting themselves matter-of-factly, without guile, without shame. The women are either refusing to sexualize their bodies, or they don't have a clue how to do it. Just one year later, Linda Lovelace's *Deep Throat* would revolutionize the porn industry and take it mainstream, but until then, any white girl with breasts who was more or less height-weight proportionate would do.

Neufeld and Acker had already performed in perhaps a dozen film loops and photo shoots at Bob Wolfe's studio. As an attractive straight couple without drug habits who showed up on time, they found themselves highly employable. When Wolfe offered them the Fun City job, it seemed like a good situation: with the Sunday-night money, Acker could stay home and write without taking a nine-to-five job. The two months she'd spent as a file clerk for Texaco between her freshman and sophomore years at Brandeis convinced her that she wasn't well suited to "robot" employment.

Besides, unlike in the film loops, no one in the sex show had to have actual sex. The performers wore costumes with feathers and jackets and furs: the more clothes they had on, the longer it took to remove them. And the sex show performers were allowed to invent their own semi-improvised scripts. These scripts could veer off in almost any direction, so long as they reached the conclusion their heterosexual male audiences all waited for: full beaver spreads, the display and massaging of breasts, faux masturbation. Acker and Neufeld were more audaciously digressive than most of their colleagues. In one of their favorite routines, she played a patient confessing her sexual Santa Claus fantasies to her aroused psychoanalyst. They worked her shaved head into the act: she's become Joan of Arc, she's completely delusional.

The young woman who writes in these notebooks likes the sex show because it takes her as far as imaginable from her Upper East Side private school childhood; she hates the show because it's degrading. She banters with customers, but then they jerk off under their raincoats. Sometimes she thinks she's reached a dead end in her life. Should she go back to school, become a fashion designer? Neufeld seems to encourage this. He wants her to be self-supporting, which, she assumes, means he doesn't want to be responsible for her. During the four months they work at Fun City, she keeps several notebooks in tandem. One notebook records her actions and thoughts; another her dreams. She writes all the time, willing herself to break down the boundaries between waking and dreaming. *You have to become a criminal or a pervert,* she writes. *I find I can only talk to those people who are loose in the ways they live to the extent of perversity a strange addiction to 42nd Street.* At readings, when people ask what she's doing, she never says writing. Instead, she tells them *the sex show,* and they say wonderful, great. Later, she hates herself for it, but she still loves the attention. There's no escaping the fact that the Fun City room smells of ammonia, piss, semen. Her dreams about childhood are scenes of escape: a river, a park, a small bit of earth in the cold, damp late autumn. Outdoors and alone, she feels strong . . . *the beginning of a great joy,* she writes in her diary.

Often she describes herself, Neufeld, and their friends as "angels." There are good angels, bad angels, angels who live just as spirits. *The angels are making me into a distortion pulling out my eyes destroying my brains.* Meanwhile, *The show is like the lowest way to make the basic bread completely without responsibility except for the twenty minutes after I get onstage.* Backstage between shows, she writes in the notebooks. She writes in the restaurant next door during breaks. She writes sitting in bed under the covers while Neufeld's awake, and she writes in the apartment's back room when he's asleep. The neighbor downstairs complains about typewriter noise. *[O]ur writing is a religious act and has no other uses.*

2 to 4 SENTENCES

EVERY DAY

she writes in her notebook that March, although most days she writes a lot more. Apart from the few hours each week she spends at Fun City, Acker's two jobs in New York are sleeping and writing:

I can sleep 16 hours a day after a while the distinction between waking and sleeping consciousness disappeared a semi-controllable continuum in which animals and men resembled each other, she writes in January.

And two weeks later: *this writing is getting to be like junk I'm going crazy doing it want more I decided to write so much a day have to write so that I keep in touch with my feelings not to over-write.*

Acker isn't alone in these experiments. She reads Brion Gysin and William S. Burroughs, the instructions for reaching simultaneous wraparound consciousness that will eventually be published in *The Third Mind*. She reads Bernadette Mayer, who is already writing durational texts, graphing the process of emotive thinking. As Acker notes in a diary written several months after quitting the sex show, *B. Mayer's work list of daily events facts (whatever "facts" means) collage from Emma Goldmann's [sic] autobiography I feel her work touches reality I distrust my own "USE only words which directly correspond to images" (Burroughs) what the fuck is going on here?*

Still, in a literal way, she feels completely alone. She doesn't know other writers. Neufeld's friends are much older. His mentor and friend Jerome Rothenberg lives with his wife, Diane, in an apartment on the fifth floor. At work with George Quasha on *America a Prophecy*, an enormous anthology of American poetry from pre-Columbian to present times, Rothenberg is then forty years old and at the height of his fame as a great man of world poetry. He knows all the writers: his address book includes entries for Paul Celan, Julio Cortázar, Henri Michaux, LeRoi Jones, Daphne Marlatt, George Oppen, and Paul Blackburn. Acker has a huge crush on Rothenberg—to the extent that she shows him her uncensored diaries, complete with her romantic and sexual fantasies about him—but he leaves for a Visiting Regents' Professorship in San Diego that January. Almost fifty years later, George Quasha recalls Acker's strategic naïveté. Despite the shyness lamented over and over again in her diaries, Quasha insists, "I'd never known KA to act shy, even if maybe she was. She was intentionally sexy, and I felt her coming on. But I didn't bite."

Neufeld recalls gatherings where people argued about the likelihood of totalitarianism within American government. His friends were an uptown crowd, more intellectually serious than the romantic bohemians at the St. Mark's Poetry Project. At home, they discuss D. H. Lawrence: he faults the absence of social theory in the novels; she thinks he lacks empathy. [Reading Lawrence] *I feel like I'm reading my future history I'm finding out who I could be.* At a party with Neufeld in Riverdale, Acker hears the men talking about current affairs in America, the Lieutenant Calley court-martial, the youth revolution, and it doesn't mean anything. When she talks, they accuse her of personalizing. *Kathy you're always wrong . . . the government is made up of thousands of officials not business*, they tell her, and she disagrees: *I say [the real power lies with] the 1% who have 99% of the money . . .* She feels like a freak with these people. It will be another few years before she sees she's ahead of her time, and longer before others agree.

She suffers from pelvic inflammatory disease (PID), made worse by the contraception she uses, an IUD coil, but she does not take the pill because it makes her breasts even more draggy. Exploring their sexuality, she and Len Neufeld stage three-way encounters in the apartment with ex-lovers and casual friends of both sexes. Is she really a lesbian? Is he bi? Often, she wonders if he really loves her. She writes with contempt about *the whole glorious sexual revolution*, but this doesn't mean she doesn't think about sex all the time.

When she and Len Neufeld hear Patti Smith read at the St. Marks Poetry Project in February 1971, she wants to be her. *I have no way of meeting her of course I won't I probably like being shut in myself safe in the 42nd Street half fantasy-half real underground god forbid I should actually talk to someone who also writes.*

On Valentine's Day, *my fucking* (crossed out) *goddam grandmother just sent me a card saying call me I should lick her ass the shits they're so bugged I don't lick their asses any longer . . . let them fuck me acquiesce in all their holy judgments without saying why . . . they are doing their best to destroy me . . . I decide that my grandmother didn't send me anything I'm going to deal with them by not dealing with them there are no more parents no more possessive feelings it works so simply I'll wake up in the morning wanting Lenny to be next to me I'll kiss the kissable cats masturbate shit get some tea and bread*

* * *

Len Neufeld remembers leaving San Diego for New York with Acker in late May, 1970. "We decided quickly. There was a mutual enthusiasm," he recalls. They were still married to other people, and, he remembers, they flew because he was leaving the old, beat-up car that he shared with his wife to her and their three-year-old toddler.

Married, like Acker, to his first serious partner when he was nineteen, it wasn't the first time Neufeld fled. He'd left two years before with a woman named Dolly when he and his wife, Martha Rosler, were spending the summer at the University of Illinois while he attended a workshop at the Linguistics Institute in Champagne-Urbana. Until the late 1960s, even on the East Coast, fornication was a prosecutable offense that offered grounds for eviction. Like many of their contemporaries, he and Rosler got married so their families and landlords would stop harassing them and leave them in peace.

Alone with their baby in the American heartland, Rosler promptly moved back to New York when Dolly entered the scene. At twenty-five, Rosler was already a practicing artist. For a while she supported herself and the baby doing freelance editorial work from a sublet on the Lower East Side. Six months later, Neufeld's romance with Dolly was over. When he was offered a prestigious National Defense Fund fellowship to do doctoral work at UC San Diego, he flew back to New York to ask Rosler if she'd like to get back together and move out there with him.

In New York, Rosler considered her options. "I thought, I can go back to San Diego, because I can't breathe here. I had to work all night and take care of the kid all day, I was dying." She remembers driving back across country with her husband and child; she remembers lying outside their tent in Arizona looking up at the stars and thinking, "Why am I doing this? Oh yeah, because life is a hell of a lot easier in California."

Like Neufeld, Rosler had done her B.A. in linguistics, but for the last several years she'd been making photomontages, and she had every intention of continuing her work as an artist. Eventually her marriage to Neufeld would end, and she'd find that her decision to move to California had been the right thing. After Neufeld and Acker left for New York, she stayed in San Diego and enrolled as a graduate student in UC San Diego's new, famously radical Fine Art Department. Within months, together with Fred Londonier, Alan Sekula, David and Eleanor Antin, and Miriam Schapiro, she became part of a group that devised a new form of political artwork, fusing conceptual art strategies with on-the-ground leftist and trade union activism. A photograph taken in 1980 shows Rosler addressing a home study group, holding a copy of the magazine *Radical Teacher*, #13.

* * *

Kathy Acker lived with her husband, Bob Acker, for more than three years before she met Neufeld. They'd met at Brandeis when she was a sophomore and he was a senior. He was planning to go to graduate school at UC San Diego, and rather than break up and continue depending on family support for her tuition, she left Brandeis and followed him. The wedding took place at her family's Long Island beach house in 1966 on the Sunday of Labor Day weekend. No one expected the marriage to last, and it didn't. Until the marriage, her family still harbored hope that she'd find a rich husband. They were Upper East Side Austrian Jews. Bob Acker's parents were Polish Jews, and he'd grown up in lower-middle-class Queens. Kathy Acker described herself as a German Jew. A hierarchy then still prevailed among New York Jews, descending from German to Austrian to Russian and Lithuanian, all the way down to the lowest-ranked Poles.

Thirty years later, walking around New York City with the media theorist and writer McKenzie Wark, Acker stopped next to the carriages outside the Plaza Hotel and said, *We had our honeymoon at the Plaza Hotel. Jews had theirs at the Plaza, WASPS at the Sherry-Netherland.* Wark was Australian, fourteen years younger than she was, but even so, he sensed that "there was something dreamlike about the New York she was showing me. Like a fable." In fact, she and Bob Acker had left for San Diego right away. A rare family photograph shows her in a white dress and veil, smiling and cutting a cake next to her tall, handsome husband.

They arrived just in time to start the fall quarter and rented a spacious Victorian house on B Street, just south of downtown San Diego. Bob Acker enrolled in the History Department, and she signed up for classes to complete her English B.A.

Acker's accounts of her life, in her books and in interviews, were always selective. She never wrote about or discussed her years with Bob Acker, and Bob Acker himself has little to say about their time together. He graciously replied to my emails, but in our brief exchange he remarked, "I'm surprised there's any interest in the subject. I never see her books in bookstores anymore, and I visit bookstores pretty often." "History," he added, "is hard to do!" A retired attorney, Acker didn't seem eager to play a supporting role in his long-ago former wife's history. I imagine her living quietly during those mid-'60s years in remote San Diego, although doubtless ambivalent about whatever it meant to be a "young wife" during the *Peyton Place* era.

* * *

Before leaving Brandeis, Acker had been one of a handful of classics majors. Years later she'd boast that her undergrad papers were read by the renowned structural linguist Roman Jakobson, although this seems unlikely, since he taught at Harvard. Even if, as she'd elaborate, her Brandeis tutor had studied with Jakobson, it's hard to imagine the tutor sharing an undergrad student's papers with him. But to lie is to try. Like most fabulations, the story contains a kernel of truth, or at least of desire. There's no doubt that Acker wanted to study at Harvard with Roman Jakobson—or rather at Radcliffe, its sister school, because Harvard wouldn't enroll female undergraduate students until 1975.

Brandeis, known at the time as "Jew U," wasn't her first choice of school. By her mid-teens Acker was fiercely precocious, an outstanding student at the Lenox School, a staid and somewhat mediocre Upper East Side private girl's institution that has since merged with Birch Wathen. But until she met the future film scholar P. Adams Sitney, her knowledge of culture didn't extend much beyond the Lenox curriculum. Acker met Sitney at a summer study intensive at Trinity College in the summer of 1963, when she was sixteen, between her sophomore and junior years of high school. Sitney was eighteen. Two and a half years Acker's senior, he was about to begin his first (and, as it turned out, his last) semester at Yale, studying classics. A dazzling polymath, Sitney's poetic passions that summer included Charles Olson, Ezra Pound, Virgil, and Sextus Propertius. Acker had just discovered the Victorian poet Gerard Manley Hopkins. She was already dating another Trinity summer student, but she found Sitney and his poetic enthusiasms deeply intriguing. Sitney remembers the sixteen-year-old Acker as "very intelligent, eager, wonderfully curious and slightly wild in a ragamuffin mode."

That fall, Sitney left Yale to organize the International Exhibition of New America Cinema and moved into a rooming house in New York near Cooper Square. There, he and Acker began an intense three-month affair. Still in school uniform, she'd catch the subway downtown to his place, where they once met Gregory Corso. Sometimes they met at the Film Culture and Film-Makers' Cooperative office on East Twenty-Eighth Street, where Sitney knew everyone. He introduced her to the Gotham Book Mart. They met Jack Smith, Andy Warhol, and Carolee Schneemann and visited Dick Higgin's pre-SoHo loft, where Sitney and Jackson Mac Low were absorbed in typing and editing Stan Brakhage's *Metaphors on Vision*. Her eyes opened wide. They attended performances of Jean Genet's plays and Brakhage's films. On these occasions Sitney's more parentally presentable friend Robert Brumbaugh, who was still a Yale student, posed as a decoy boyfriend to pick Acker up from *the 57th Street prison*. Years later, Acker would write about how *P. Adams made super-8 films of me taking off and then putting on my school uniform. Perhaps this was his version of porn. I loved porn. One day, he asked me to edit his magazine, Film Culture* [*sic*] . . . *I was shocked . . . I did not understand how a grown-up man could think that I knew anything, much less enough to edit one of the finest contemporary film magazines.* In fact, as Sitney recalls, he shot one three-minute film loop of her naked in bed . . . a teenage fascination with nudity. "It had nothing to do with pornography. She never expressed any interest in pornography then." (That would come later.) Nor did she edit *Film Comment*, although she once ran an errand for the magazine. "The truth," Sitney concluded, quoting Stan Brakhage, "is always more interesting."

By the end of that fall, Sitney left New York for Europe. Until she moved to West 163rd Street with Len Neufeld, they would not see each other again.

Given her high grades and the broad range of culture she acquired in her mid-teens, Acker had every expectation of attending an Ivy League school, like Sitney and most of his friends. Radcliffe, with its faculty drawn from the still all-male Harvard, was most elite female school of that time. Cecily Selby, the Lenox School principal, was a Radcliffe alumnus, and she promoted the school among her best students. Acker applied and was stunned when she was rejected. Her high school friend-enemies, the twins Susan and Linda Mueller, applied to Radcliffe and were rejected as well. The Muellers also applied, and were accepted, to Sarah Lawrence, Bryn Mawr, and Wellesley, elite female schools that didn't interest Acker at all. She applied only to Radcliffe and the intellectual, coeducational Brandeis.

Former classmates of Acker's concur that as Lenox School students, the Muellers were bred for success. They were WASPy and smart, well-groomed and pretty popularity seekers. At Lenox, the Mueller twins were Acker's only real peers and academic rivals. If they were young men, or perhaps if they'd been born female thirty years later, the Muellers and Acker might have formed a brilliant alliance: the two "perfect" girls and their daring, intellectually voracious counterpart. But, as it was, they were pitted against each other in a competition that entailed not just brains and imagination, but classic good looks, grace, and poise. It was a fight Acker could never win. And so she loathed them.

No sentimentality here either, Acker wrote, with a nobility worthy of Antigone, on her page of Linda Mueller's Lenox School senior yearbook. *God knows how many fights, dirty or clean, spoken or unspoken, minor or major, we've had—but without you, I would have gone to sleep . . . I don't know what sort of people*

I'll meet at Brandeis but I'm sure that I'll meet no one with as much drive and personal power and magnetism as you have. I can't say that it has been a pleasure to know you, for our relationship has not been in that realm, it has been a challenge . . . I think that if we had met in different circumstances, mutual respect would've overcome out ambition-causing animosities . . . no need for best wishes, your own personality is too magnetic . . . —you must succeed, Kathy

Although Acker never sought them out after their years at Lenox, the Muellers would haunt her for the rest of her life. At West 163rd Street, she dreams that they're in a fire together: *I had failed in some way . . . I had to impress them or learn how to deal with them.* Back in San Diego a year after splitting with Neufeld, she'd write:

> *I hate the Mueller twins because they're the only people who are as intelligent and beautiful as I am; the head of the school encourages the Mueller twins and I to fight so we can raise the intellectual standards of the school.*

In London, when she was forty-two years old, she'd write:

> *R. was thinking of poisoning the Muller twins. The Muller twins were German. They had long straight blond hair and were strong. Since they were the only pupils who were as intelligent as R, they hated R and R hated them because they were equals.*

> *Though R wanted to kill them . . . as yet he had only pissed into both of their camel hair coats.*

Three years later, living in San Francisco, she changed the Mueller's names, but had still not forgotten them. As she'd write in *My Mother, Demonology,* her second-to-last published book:

I thought about the Jones twins all the time, until my thoughts about their evil were forced to pop forth into the open . . . I knew they were evil because they had long, straight real blond hair and were German.

They looked almost exactly alike.

The most disturbing factor was that they were more intelligent than me. We were the three most intelligent girls in the school, if not the most intelligent the school had ever seen; my imagination soared, but I was a slob, whereas the Joneses were clever, neat and precise.

Liz Leventhal, the Birch Wathen Lenox School archivist, allowed my researcher, Julien Raffinot, to copy the Lenox School yearbook for Acker's 1964 class. Tracing the names of the students, Raffinot looked up some of these former classmates. Fifty years later, they remember her vaguely, a mysterious figure from the long-ago past.

Jean Lindenbaum Herskovitz, who appears as the schoolgirl Jean in Acker's 1973–'74 *The Childlike Life of the Black Tarantula*, remarked that, with her "esoteric" mind, Acker would have been academically more suited to Spence or Brearley. On the other hand, Brearley and Spence were famously sparing in their admission of Jews. In the early 1950s the Lenox School was unofficially known as the only "white glove" Upper East Side private girls school that was widely open to Jews, and Jews numbered roughly 70 percent of its students.

A photograph in Acker's class yearbook shows a five- or six-year-old child that might have been the young Kathy, wearing white woolly gloves and a matching wool bonnet. Expectant and smiling, she's stretching her small arm to reach the brass handle of the school's massive front door. In fact, Lenox was open to virtually any white student whose family could pay the tuition. The classes were small, but as Ellen Bilgore, another former classmate, recalls, there was little cohesion within their small class of twenty-four girls. Some were rich, living in ivory towers with all the entitlements. Others came from abroad. Some were jocks, some were bookish, others were into drama. Personalities clashed. Bilgore recalls that Acker was rarely seen not holding a book, a series of totems signaling that *she was smart*. To Bilgore, the message Kathy hoped to project to the class was that she cared more about books than about being part of the group or making close friends—at least *not with them*. She shocked her sophomore-year classmates by announcing that she'd already had sex with three partners. [T]he actual physical pleasure was of course minimal, she'd concede later on in her diary, compared to the pleasure of becoming who I wanted to become. At Lenox, Bilgore recalls, girls were forced into a false, claustrophobic intimacy, a life that revolved around cliques and competition. The students were academically tracked into A and B groups, an injustice Acker would later reprise:

> *I don't see Jean in classes. I'm in section A and she's in section B. They stick the rich kids in section A and the poor ones in B, they want us to learn that poor means stupid. We hate them but what the hell . . . Blow up the school.*

"Don't quote me," another classmate later texted to Raffinot, "Cathy [sic] was always what we used—in the days when one was really innocent—to call a 'slut.'"

> I read the high [sic] School
> book. Wow. She was really
> off the wall. Drugs?
> Insanity??
>
> . . . Why is anybody writing about
> her, except as

a clinical study? . . .
I am riveted that what I
saw when she was little
bubbled up into what she
became. I see a screwed up little
girl.

. . . And an "adult" ravaged by
drugs and real, clinical [sic]
crazy . . .

. . . Poor thing
seems to have been alone,
with no one to lock her
away, and get her better.

. . . It is so odd that this is
being treated seriously

Like the emperor has no
clothes.

I have to say that there is
brilliance there. But it is so
perverted

By the craziness.
What got this started?

We shld talk again when
you can tell me more.

Right now, I have to watch
Wolf hall!

All the former classmates Raffinot spoke to recalled that Acker was known at the school for being intellectually, socially, and sexually precocious, but, at the same time, neglected, unkempt. The school had a half holiday each Friday. Everyone in their class took turns inviting each other home to have lunch and spend the free afternoon together, except for Acker.

Nevertheless, on her yearbook page, Acker appears as Karen Weill Alexander (nickname Cassandra): an averagely pretty young woman with gap teeth, full lips, and a shoulder-length flip.

> *Some people think that Kathy is a beatnik; others claim that she is an existentialist; but Kathy says that she is just plain Kathy,*

the yearbook committee wrote on her page.

> *Whatever she is, she's different. She's more intellectual than many members of her class; she reads more; and she acts more avant-garde. She practices a studied nonchalance, taking things in her stride, letting trivial matters in one ear and out the other. Her close friends complain of her "stupid look." This look is only the facial expression that she uses when she hears the names of baseball players and television actors that she cannot recognize. It is possible that in the next shipment of books to India Kathy might be added to the cargo, for it is noticed that she often has unreasonable arguments with Mrs. Bacon. Despite Kathy's exotic, but sometimes esoteric mind, she might, one day, return to Lenox, as the Poet Laureate.*

Although she never wrote or even thought much about Acker after high school, Linda Mueller Vasu remembers her well. To her, the rivalry between Acker and her and her twin sister, Susan, was more of a friendly, academic competition. She agreed with the other ex-classmates about Lenox: it was a school without strong admission standards that assembled a weird mix of girls.

At school, she believes, Acker wasn't sufficiently recognized, which only increased her defiance. Looking for any opportunity to make herself seen and heard, Acker walked the halls of Lenox with Modern Library editions of Dostoyevski, Gogol, and Turgenev, their covers face-out for all to see. "Kathy," she said, "was a rather unhappy, though intellectual committed member of the Lenox class. It is easy to see the Formation to Mission of Kathy Acker in the tiny crucible that was Lenox in NYC at the time."

After Wellesley, Mueller attended graduate school at Columbia University. She studied semiotics with Sylvère Lotringer, whom Acker would meet several years later at a benefit party downtown for *File* magazine. When Raffinot reached her, Mueller-Rasu was teaching *Oedipus Rex* at the Connecticut girl's school where she now works, and it seemed uncanny to her because, preparing to speak about Acker, she'd done some online research and observed the way her life and career have been treated as mythic. "Kathy," she said, "was a mess. She had the look of a young girl who was neglected. Not just that she didn't care, but that no one cared. Not her mother or anyone else. Her shoes were scuffed, her clothes were ruffled, she smelled bad. Nobody ever went to Kathy's apartment. The only time anyone ever saw her mother was at graduation. She was always in the margins, a shadow." Like Linda and Susan, whose parents were also divorced, "she related strongly to Thomas Hardy, with his elegiac descriptions of disappointment in life and in love, and intractable fate."

Fragments of memories, nightmares, and dreams of the school recur throughout Acker's writing. Lesbian schoolgirls, schoolgirls as Sadean subjects and whores, but most of all, a feeling of deep isolation. Like the images of William S. Burroughs's St. Louis childhood and his cast of underworld characters lifted from boyhood pulp fiction, with such colorful names as Salt Pork Mary and the Sanctimonious Kid, a handful of ghosts and screen memories float across all of Acker's work—the silks in her grandmother's bedroom, Laure the Whorish Schoolgirl, gray cities, the Times Square live sex show. There are snowy Central Park Christmases, a girlish mother, a boorish stepfather, a wealthy but disappeared biological father. There are the lesbian schoolgirls, the despised Mueller twins and Miss Jean St. Pierre, their beloved English teacher. *Miss St. Pierre was the youngest of our two literature teachers, and therefore poor*, she writes in *My Mother, Demonology*. *Though poor, Miss St. Pierre ruled over the library. I ran away to here . . . In this place, Miss St. Pierre, who looked like my mother except that she wasn't beautiful, showed me books to read.* (In 2003, the real Jean St. Pierre, who'd long since moved to the English Department at Phillips Academy, received an award for outstanding teaching.) *In the school that I attended I learned, seemingly by chance, that pain, if anything is a bad smell. And I tried to run away from the pain named childhood the way you would flush a huge shit down the toilet. I've been running ever since.* The masochist O of Pauline Réage's novels who appears in Acker's 1983 *Great Expectations* will become "O," short for "Ostracism": *I knew that I didn't belong in this society of only girls; I was strange; I tried to hide my strangeness . . . The girls couldn't ostracize me because I wasn't one of them . . . All of Us Girls Have Been Dead for So Long*, she writes in *Pussy King of the Pirates*, her last full-length work.

She toughened up when she went to Brandeis. Her friend Mel Freilicher recalls her hanging out with "the very coolest upperclassmen" and shoplifting from Design Research. As her dorm mate Sue Shapiro would later confide to Len Neufeld, she was known for having very loud sex in the dorms. When she made a halfhearted attempt at slitting her wrists, two of her dorm mates slit theirs, and the resident adviser begged her to stop before they all bled to death. Notwithstanding her dramatic, rebellious behavior at Brandeis, Acker read all the time.

Acker finished her B.A. at UC San Diego in May '68 and began earning credits for an M.A. in English, but the classes held little interest for her, and her graduate studies didn't last long. Bob Acker continued his history degree. There was not much in San Diego to do. Even when she was no longer enrolled, she spent most days on the campus, tutoring Greek and attending the Poetry Club. At home she baked bread, designed and sewed her own clothes. Bob Acker was often depressed. Cocooned together against a harsh world, their best times were spent playing cards, chess, and Go. It wasn't until the next fall that Acker's world opened up, and she met the two people who'd become her first important mentors and her lifelong friends.

* * *

David and Eleanor Antin drove out from New York in June '68 with all their belongings crammed into an old Cadillac. David was going to start teaching that fall at UCSD. They were in Phoenix, he later remembered, the day Andy Warhol was shot. Three days later, checking into a desert motel, they heard the radio news that Robert F. Kennedy had just been assassinated. Both Antins had grown up in New York. They'd been deeply involved with the downtown cultural world, but they'd gotten bored by the end of the '60s. The scene had become claustrophobic, anxious, and inbred, and they saw no reason to stay there. "[It was] the last gasp of Minimalism . . . Pop was over. So was the great Judson Theater stuff," Eleanor Antin would later remember. She'd just finished *Blood of a Poet Box*, her first major conceptual work, comprised of a collection of microscope slides filled with blood drawn from one hundred poet and artist friends and acquaintances. She wasn't exhibiting yet, but everyone knew about Antin's project. Giving Eleanor blood had become part of the scene. At house parties, performances, and openings, she'd bring out her Sewing Susan kit packed with cotton, antiseptic, and needles and prick people's fingers. Eleanor Antin was then thirty-five. David was thirty-seven years old, and they had a year-old son.

When David Antin's friend Allan Kaprow declined an offer to teach at UCSD and proposed him instead, they both thought, Why not? The job would entail directing the university gallery and teaching some classes in writing and art. Teaching had never been one of Antin's goals. He'd never taught a class in his life and had no idea what to expect. But as he'd write later on in his poetic essay "california—the nervous camel," his boss, the artist Paul Brach was unfazed. Brach assured him:

> . . .. itll be very good people
> will come to your classes   they wont know what youre talking
> about youll be talking about art itll make them feel better because
> youre talking about it

Neither of the Antins had spent any time in California, but when David flew out to take a look at the job, he was impressed by how provisional everything seemed. A small earthquake hit the same day. Watching the palms shake and water spill out of the pools, he thought, "This is the right place to be." Whatever the future contained was already there. California, it seemed, would either lead the U.S. over a cliff or lead it back to safety. The La Jolla campus, built on a tract of land obtained from the U.S. Department of Defense, struck him as a group of scientists "standing around with an open checkbook under a palm tree." Conceived as a retreat-like research institute, the sprawling campus had opened just eight years earlier. Located at the heart of the U.S. military-industrial complex, the new university was committed to supporting cutting-edge work, not only in the sciences but in the arts and humanities. To the disgust of the larger San Diego community, the Marxist philosopher Herbert

Marcuse found refuge there after losing his tenure at Brandeis over a series of political feuds. The local branch of the American Legion offered to pay Marcuse's salary if he agreed not to teach any classes.

Later, perhaps attempting to position her work within an intellectual history where it rightly belonged, Acker would claim that she'd followed Marcuse from Brandeis to UCSD, or that Bob Acker was Marcuse's assistant and chief acolyte. In fact, neither she nor Bob Acker attended Marcuse's classes or knew him at all. If anything, they and their friends were at odds with him. In his essay "time on my hands," David Antin would later describe the great man as "a kind of middle European intellectual, sort of elderly intellectual, who used to kind of parade down the La Jolla streets with his hands behind his back as if he were walking down the streets in some wonderful German city peering at the bakery windows, looking longingly at whipped cream cupcakes." When a Marcuse acolyte attacked Martha Rosler's work, the whole art department rose to defend her.

Those who accepted invitations to leave the East Coast to teach at UC San Diego found themselves well supported financially but intellectually and culturally marooned in different and similar ways. As Antin would write:

> it was 1968 when I first visited and I was sure that I had been returned to 1952 all the women wore white gloves I hadn't seen anything like this since the fifties and even then living in new york I hadn't seen very much of it and here there were the people who lived in la jolla in rancho santa fe and on point loma theyre pleasant people awfully pleasant as pleasant as wonder bread the men wore dark blue blazers with brass buttons and cream colored pants with check shirts and they all watched the stock market . . .

Shopping for a fridge shortly after arriving, he found the walls of the Solana Beach used-appliance store covered with photographs of Adolf Hitler.

> *I-5 wasn't even completed at the time we moved into solana*
> *beach and south of oceanside it was still a little two lane road then*
> *but eventually a few years after we came they completed it still*
> *there were relatively few cars running on it especially at night at*
> *night it was like watching a kind of eccentrically programmed light*
> *sculpture   after ten pm car lights would show up once every five*
> *minutes or so   and if you went to your front window or stood . . .*

> *. . . on this sloping lawn and looked toward the*
> *highway after ten oclock you could stand there for five or six minutes*
> *before you saw two or three cars go by . . .*

Once he and his family were settled, Antin had to figure out what and how he would teach. He knew that when undergrad students signed up for a poetry class, they assumed they'd be challenged to bare their innermost souls. Reluctant to deal with hundreds of bad student poems, much less the real pain from which they arose, he adopted a quasi-Oulipian rule. "Look," he recalls telling them, "I'm not good at psychology. But do me a favor, let's work this way. You can write about anything in the world you want except . . . somebody else knows more about it than you, and it's already in a book in the library. Go to the library and steal it."

Acker became close to the Antins as soon as they met. She gossiped and talked about art with Eleanor, babysat for their kid, and sat in on all David's seminars. She'd already decided she was a writer, but she didn't know what or how she should write. Teachers and older writers talked to her then (as they talk to young writers still) about the importance of "finding her voice," but it seemed to her that she, like most of her friends, had many shifting identities—or maybe none. Likewise, the idea of inventing a plot and creating relatable characters seemed absurd: a stretch not worth making. Antin's idea that writing could be composed of and around other texts removed that pressure and offered entertainment and freedom. Eventually this technique, which would come to be called "appropriation," became central to Acker's style and intellectual strategy. *This writing is all just fake (copied from other writing) so you should go away and not read any of it*, she'd write in her 1983 "Translations of the Diaries of Laure the Schoolgirl."

"Go to the library," Antin instructed his class, "find someone who's already written about something better than you could possibly do at this moment in your life, and we'll consider the work of putting the pieces together like a film. Within about four or five weeks," he said, they were "producing wonderfully quick, shifting beautiful things, like race drivers shifting gears." Throughout her career Acker would describe how she'd apprenticed herself to David Antin. The idea, he explained, wasn't just to cut and paste things by rote, but to find the connections between disparate realities. "A piece of Aeschylus and a plumbing manual have to be brought together in some sort of way. You could make it be like a car collision on I-5" . . . or then again, "you might want to slip things into each other, as if Aeschylus was being sodomized by the plumbing manual." After a while the students began finding the library too far to walk and began faking it, all the while claiming they were using found sources. Freed from the demand of creating "original" work, they started making things up. Antin, who thought he didn't know how to teach, became one of the most popular teachers at UC San Diego.

* * *

Acker and Len Neufeld met while they were both sitting in on Antin's poetry class in the fall of '69. She was already one of its stars, and Neufeld was hugely impressed by her. On track for an academic career in linguistics, he wrote poems whenever he could. Like her, he wanted to be a writer but wasn't sure yet what that meant. "Kathy was beautiful," Neufeld recalled when we talked at his Brooklyn apartment two and a half years after her death. "Very sexy, very interesting. She dressed sexy, she had curly hair, she wore little round glasses. She was full of energy and ideas. And she was writing poetry, although she hadn't published anything yet."

He looked her up to exchange poems the day after the class, and things between them clicked right away. They got together within weeks, maybe days. "The first time, we were sitting with a friend of hers, Bee, talking and playing footsie—and Bob Acker looked away. She gave me such a look . . . So when we left, we found a little restroom in one of the buildings, went in and locked the doors and used the couch.

"The fact we were both married didn't mean shit. In 1969 I was twenty-six, twenty-seven years old. Kathy was twenty-two, twenty-three. Martha and I were never happy. I was looking for an escape. I felt inadequate in my marriage, but not with Kathy. She demanded very little of me. She needed support and approval and willingness to go along and be with her, and that was easy."

Similarly, from the first months of her marriage to Bob, Kathy felt trapped. She knew she'd been wrong about marrying him, maybe wrong about marrying at all. In New York with Len Neufeld, she considered the end of her marriage with some confusion, but not much regret. Writing in one of her notebooks at West 163rd Street:

Acker came over yesterday and we tried to talk or I tried to find out who he was and he wanted me to become come to me in the prison we had been I was trying to get rid of my parents in my mind and

feelings and to have the calmness to do what I wanted or to find out
what I wanted or why he wanted a permanent Acker cock wor-
shipper who was also intelligent and reasonable looking given
20-year old junkie standards of good-looking so friends and strangers
would think you must be quite a man to have such a wife also some-
one to pick up his clothes after he dropped them on the ground which
his good Jewish mother when she came to San Diego yelled at me for
not doing and to wash the dishes we both needed someone to hang
on to for life because we were scared and made schizoid

Among their group of friends, many of whom had married just
to have sex in their late teens, casual hookups were common.
From the time they got together in San Diego, and later on in
New York, Acker and Neufeld saw other people, often at the
same time. As Martha Rosler recalls, "You went to a party and
you got stoned and you felt like sleeping with someone, you slept
with them. They were a friend . . . And it was all very low-key.
You could sleep with a friend without it becoming something."

But soon Neufeld and Acker's relationship did become something. Acker called Neufeld at home endlessly, asking for help
and complaining about her depressed, angry husband. Could he
help her get Bob out of bed? And each time, he went. Soon he
began bringing her back to his and Rosler's Solana Beach home.
Since their child was still too young for day care, Rosler spent
most days at home making art and taking care of the kid. Soon,
much to Rosler's chagrin, Acker's presence became part of their
domestic routine. "Oh," she thought. "Hi Kathy. That's nice."
She recalls making dinner for them "while they're doing teenage
things, making big posters for poetry readings. I remember one
scene where I'm putting stuff out on the table, and they're sitting
on the floor under the table drawing posters. And I thought, I've
been married to this guy for six, seven years by this point. What's
wrong with this picture?"

Finally, things fell apart when Rosler came home to a locked screen-porch door one afternoon and found them in bed. "I thought: this is a message to me, and I'm getting the message." She told them both to get out. Within days, Len Neufeld moved into the B Street Victorian—"a big wood house painted green—no, it wasn't especially fixed up"—and Bob Acker moved out.

Neither of their exes were thrilled with these new arrangements, but everyone did their best to adapt. Often, the two couples hung out with the Antins and other friends to talk and play chess. As Rosler recalls, "Lenny was madly in love with her. And very happy, very satisfied." At twenty-two, Rosler recalls Acker's look as "sort of beatniky. She was sweet. It was a familiar form—she'd been to Brandeis, she was a Brandeis type, you know? Sleek and clean. Jewish and smart and self-confident, but also vulnerable. Her persona was about being the victim—a kid from the Upper East Side pretending to be a waitress down on her luck." Rosler was already deeply involved in antiwar and other political movements; Acker and Neufeld were not. Rosler wondered why Acker needed to take up with Neufeld just to leave Bob. "She needed to send out these calls for help—rescue me. Which is hard to respect. Kathy was sending up balloons saying *Rescue me, rescue me.* She tried to seem fragile." But then again, Rosler observed, "Kathy's whole persona depended on an endless series of reflecting, fictive personas, like a hall of mirrors." Regarding child care, Rosler and Neufeld arrived at an uneasy détente.

To Len Neufeld, the months he spent with Acker in San Diego were exciting and happy. But they'd decided to be writers, and they both knew that New York was the best place to put out their work and meet other writers. As soon as he finished his coursework, they left for New York.

* * *

Kathy had bad PID. It really upset her. We had to pay for a doctor. Before that she was very aggressive sexually—she was very out there, with different people, doing different things. One of those people who—she never feels alive or like herself unless she has a cock inside her. So PID was devastating.

—Len Neufeld, interview March 8, 2000

In New York, they moved into the huge, empty five-room West 163rd Street apartment Neufeld had once shared with Rosler. For a while, he continued receiving his fellowship checks, but once it was clear that he was no longer enrolled, the payments stopped coming. Within weeks of arriving, Acker had acute pain in her pelvis and abdomen and went to the hospital. There, she was diagnosed with pelvic inflammatory disease (PID), an affliction most common among women aged twenty-one to twenty-five who have—or have sex with people with—multiple partners. As she'd write four years later in *The Childlike Life of the Black Tarantula*:

> *I move to New York because I write and want to meet writers. I have no money, no way of getting money, no friends in New York no parents. Get Pelvic Inflammatory Disease, walk into Columbia Presbyterian clinic: woman vomits blood over floor . . . [T]hree hours later I'm now in shock slightly hallucinating doctor gives me four shots of penicillin in ass . . . gives me endless bottles of synthetic opium and Nembutal to shut me up. A month later I'm even sicker.*

And again, in *I Dreamt I Was a Nymphomaniac: Imagining*:

> *I had come to New York to be an artist: I thought I had to go to New York to be an artist. It was summer. The air became hotter and hotter. People, driven crazy by heat, hit each other over the*

heads and pissed on each other's faces. To relax: they stole cars. I
became extremely sick. I was living with this weasel on a half-
couch and a single mattress in a large empty room. We were lying
in "bed" about two in the morning. Suddenly I knew I was dying
. . . My lover called the cops, came back to me. He told me I
probably wasn't dying. I was screaming too healthily.

The hospital was the worst hell I had ever been in.

Frighteningly ill, she needed doctors and medicine. She asked her
family for help, but they refused her. Grudgingly, they'd accepted
her withdrawal from Brandeis and her marriage to Bob Acker, a
far cry from the future they'd imagined for a girl who'd come out
at a Jewish society ball and attended the Lenox School for twelve
years. And now, still married to Acker, she'd fled once again with
a graduate student with no real profession who was already a
father and married to somebody else. No wonder she'd caught
PID, a chronic condition frequently caused by such STDs as
gonorrhea. When Acker skipped the rehearsal for the Jewish
debutante ball to go out with P. Adams Sitney, her mother had
slapped her in the face and called her a whore; had she been
wrong? *[T]hey pissed on me when I was sick*, she'd write in her
diary, *obviously didn't give a damn if I died then called me up and
told me that I had given my father a heart attack.* She felt truly
poor for the first time, and completely alone.

* * *

Thinking about how to get money, she and Len Neufeld looked
through the *Village Voice* classified ads. The minimum wage in
New York at the time was $1.85, which made Bob Wolfe's ad,
with its promise of $100 per day, deeply appealing. Neither
Acker nor Neufeld had ever done sex work before. Still, the

Fourteenth Street studio, with its roster of casual amateurs, didn't seem like much of a stretch from the ambient sexual encounters they and their friends were already having. Sometimes, as she wrote in her diary, her long-ago avant-garde mentor and boyfriend P. Adams Sitney would stop by the apartment and say, *let's see your tits, let's see your cuntie,* and then for a laugh Neufeld would appear and they'd goad the staid scholar into having a three-way. Was this any worse?   Since getting together, she and Len Neufeld enjoyed an open relationship, although as Neufeld concedes, perhaps he more than she. Nevertheless, at the time, the entrance to Wolfe's Fourteenth Street studio didn't seem like a descent into a fiery pit. More like, *a good gig.* The films were hard-core, but as Neufeld recalls, "Kathy wasn't scared, because it was a safe situation. If she liked the other person, she enjoyed it. Often I took her, even if we were not working as a couple."

Throughout her career, in book after book, Acker would describe the cyclic despair of doing sex work to buy medicine so she could keep on doing sex work, crafting these months of her life into something more allegorical than her actual life on West 163rd Street. In *Algeria* (1984), she'd reprise most of the Santa Claus skit as a comedy.

> Omar: *There are lots of men out here. (Pointing to the audience and looking at them with wide eyes). They're all staring at me and they're waiting for me to take my clothes off.*
>
> Hacene (knows he's got a real loony this time): *Miss Fendermast, this is a private office.*

Her years in New York with Len Neufeld would be retold as a fable; a young woman's descent into an endless vortex of exploitation and poverty.

[She] had such a bad ovarian infection she'd be screeching with pain if either touched or if one bit of the pain-killing synthetic morphine she was shelling out $100 a week for to kill the pain so she could keep working to pay for the pain-killer wore off—if it all wore off . . .

Before she worked the sex show she had earned all the money she needed especially the money for all the medicines by starring . . . in sex films. She had thought of earning her money this way because when she had gone to a top Eastern university a doctor friend had told her her face was ravishingly beautiful. She had gotten these beginning model jobs by looking in the back pages of the Village Voice. Then men had told her she was too nice a girl to be an escort and why didn't she go back to school or they pulled her leotard away from her breasts and told her her breasts were too large or too small. She was very ashamed of her breasts. She hadn't been getting money for a while and more important than money, though that's all-important, she had to keep working to show herself she was surviving whatever she had to do.

—Great Expectations, 1983

Over the years, as she experienced new forms of grief, the tone of these stories and their effect on the narrator would shift. Her picaresque tales about a young woman's economic survival in old-time New York during the era of sexual liberation would be recast as dirges. Engaged, in her early forties, in a disastrous sado-masochistic affair with a married lover, and suffering what seemed like a public professional humiliation when her UK publisher issued an apology on her behalf to the mass-market writer Harold Robbins for her appropriation of a fragment of one of his novels, she'd revisit these early experiences as something more somber and fatal, a meeting of Eros and Thanatos. No longer Moll Flanders, she'd use her recollections of sex work to enter the deathly, delirious space of Nagisa Oshima's *In the Realm of the Senses.*

I started working a sex show to abolish all poverty and change the world, she'd write wryly in *Nymphomaniac*. But in her 1988 novel *Empire of the Senseless*, she recalls *the desperate voyeurs who sought sexual gratification in the masturbatory contemplation of a remote object of fantastic desire . . . the way in which patrons of this seedy burlesque house fell prey to its psychotically disturbed perverts; the degradation of the performers who not only put their flesh and minds on parade in the tradition of the Miss America beauty pageant but also were forced to watch this deterioration . . . In other words, the primal urge of sex had become a revolting phenomenon.*

Two years later, writing under the influence of William Faulkner's *The Wild Palms* in her fifth full-length novel, *In Memoriam to Identity*, the Len Neufeld character—referred to in earlier books as "Lenny" or "L"—would become "my rapist": *Taking my medicine and holding my clothes about me, my arm linked through the rapist's arm, as if we were the figures in a tarot card, I walked into light . . . The rapist and I were linked and I hadn't died. Since I hadn't died, I no longer felt pain or knew any of the problems I had had . . . After her visit to the rich doctor, for weeks she lay in the improvised cot in her boyfriend's and her apartment except when she was working in the sex show to pay for the expensive antibiotics she now had to take . . . When he was off work pimping and he could relax, my boyfriend took acid.* Describing their Santa Claus routine, she writes: *the doctor was beginning to control her. As control always works, through imagination . . . "Are there really men out there who want you and, if so, how do they want you?" As he said this, the doctor's right hand reached under the girl's skirt . . . The audience could see that his hands were beginning to give her pleasure. "Is your body lying?" . . . The doctor was beginning to control. So the girl turned around and kissed him.*

During the months she was writing *Identity*, she was walking outdoors under a bridge with her married lover, and when he told her to strip, she did. He caressed her skin with a knife, and she knew then that he might kill her. At the time, the idea of this death made her feel peaceful and good, which she later found more than disturbing. *It's as if there's a territory*, she writes on the last page of *Identity*. *The roads carved in the territory, the only known, are memories. Carved again and again into ruts like wounds that don't heal when you touch them but grow.* And five years later, in *Pussy, King of the Pirates*: *[T]he sex during the sex show had sent her over the edge, over every edge, over her self, flying until all that was left was sky and endless blackness. During the loss of herself, "she" had become scared. O realized that she wanted this sex, that she needed it, this sexuality that she had known when she was a whore.*

Disinclined toward conventional narrative but determined to write constantly, producing a book at least every two years, Acker worked and reworked her memories until, like the sex she described, they became conduits to something a-personal, until they became myth. This was the strength, and also the weakness, of her writing.

* * *

I want to bring in the total way we experience, she wrote in her 1971 West 163rd Street diary . . . *if I put all this down step by step maybe it'll be obvious how things work . . . I'm wondering if in this stuff I'm not going slow enough . . . which is what fucked up my last series . . . I want to be able to put down on the spot how I experience each event even these words make it seem like there's an inside experiencing mechanism and an outside event because I constantly change lie forget the lie was a lie on top of that I want a record of the way in which I remember . . .*

It was probably February. By now they were working one day a week at Fun City, and there was plenty of time, and enough money, which she liked to spend: a ring for $18; a $75 designer outfit: *I maniacally spend everything presents to keep us me going*

don't think Lenny needs them I never save a cent I then sit and brood
we have no money . . .

More than anything else Len Neufeld recalls of that time, it was Acker's determination to become a writer. "She was very dedicated, almost desperate to find herself as a writer, and I think she did do that. She was struggling hard, she was making progress, but she was frustrated."

Late that March, the other shoe dropped when the vice squad raided Fun City. The couple were performing one of their skits, and the officer claimed that Neufeld had his hand on her genitals. Arrested for public lewdness, they were booked, finger-printed, and interviewed by a young cop who asked them, "Are you on drugs?" Acker used her right to a call to phone P. Adams Sitney, who'd watched them perform at Fun City, but it was Bob Wolfe who bailed them out the next day. The night she spent in jail would inspire "THE WHORES IN JAIL AT NIGHT" section of her 1979 story, *New York City in 1979.*

The charge was eventually dismissed with a fine paid by club owner Marty Hodas, but the case dragged out over several court dates. *We had to be in court at 9:30 the third session for our public lewdness cases the court-room was the big fat stinking stomach of a politician . . . the fucking lawyer kept taking forever 5 million deals with the DA . . . most of the criminals were black may they live forever it's the asshole of the shittiest bureaucracy that will exist,* she'd write in her diary. Or, as she'd recraft the scene in *Great Expecations*: *[t]he hippy male was wearing a Bill Blass suit. The hippy female was wearing a middle-price gray suit with an ascot. They wanted to show the judge they were a cut above his usual defen-dant . . . Then the boss appeared and walked up to the judge . . . "Haven't I paid you enough?" "Not here," the judge loudly replied.*

As Neufeld recalls, they weren't especially scared or upset about being in jail. Still, they'd had enough. Unable to actually quit Fun City, they had a screaming fight with Bob Wolfe and got themselves fired. Acker successfully filed for unemployment, and Neufeld got her an off-the-books job doing part-time secretarial work in Burt Lasky's office.

Poorer, but no longer conflicted about doing the sex show, Acker and Neufeld stepped up their own forms of sexual experimentation and became enmeshed in a maddening quadrangle with the composer Jackson Mac Low and his artist wife, Iris Lezak. Iris loved Lenny more than anyone she'd met for a decade; Lenny liked sex with Iris and encouraged Kathy to try it. Kathy supposed that her boyfriend never felt fully at home in his body, and giving pleasure to women helped ground him. Although, she later wrote in her diary, *I'd like to kick her guts out and tear her flesh apart*. Len Neufeld recalls that at the time, Acker didn't have any female friends. But on the other hand, she was finding that Lenny's desire *to fuck the women we meet . . . separates me from other women and forces me to as usual live in a male society the straight women aid in this collusion . . .* Iris begged Kathy to sleep with her husband in order to keep peace between the two couples, and Kathy tried it, but even though she admired his work, she found Jackson Mac Low a bit weird, and she wasn't attracted. After that, Jackson developed a huge crush on Kathy, which went unrequited. Finally, when his marriage to Iris Lezak ended, Jackson told Kathy he'd never love anyone except Iris for the rest of his life. He missed her terribly. *[T]he political economic and social repercussions of this lunacy are our death the funereal position of this country*, Kathy concluded.

Still, she continued to write, to this kind of lunacy, and through it. She began titling her diaries, as if they were deliberate works, which in a sense they always had been. Even though "Poems 5/71—6/71" contained no actual poetry, she was a poet, in the sense of the word as she and her friends understood it. Eleanor Antin's *Blood of a Poet Box* included plasmatic samples from Carolee Schneemann and Yvonne Rainer because Antin considered them "poets in the real sense, in the sense that all good artists are poets."

* * *

On May 7, 1971, Acker read at the St. Mark's Poetry Project open-mike evening. It was the first time she'd read in New York, and she went home ecstatic. As she'd write in "Poems 5/71— 6/71," *I read this aloud in St. Marks last night warm responses from the women listening made me realize that I was writing for other women so they'd feel connected.* In a letter to Jerome Rothenberg, she reports, *I decided I wasn't a poet unless I read my stuff publicly aloud so Lenny & I went to St. Marks last night the open shit and it was very beautiful I feel all religious all these women were coming up to me afterward and saying your stuff was really great it really moved me so I'm feeling terrific . . .* As she'd affirm in the diary: *to make this poem not only my blood but my work I have to angelicly constantly publicly read this aloud publish it make myself known and heard*

Rothenberg was impressed and touched by her work. He offered to show it to someone he knew at Dial Press, whose authors included Elizabeth Bowen, James Baldwin, and Norman Mailer, but she was wary. *I don't think I want to publish with Dial,* she wrote him. *[I'd] have to stress the 42nd Street shit that's only 1 part and is NOT what my writing's about love love Kathy.*

By the end of the year, her living situation with Neufeld had badly deteriorated. Her handwritten December diary, signed and titled "DIARIES } DIARY OF THE WORLD" recounts fights and slammed doors, brief reconciliations, and misunderstandings. More pertinently, for the first time, she divides the text into sections with a series of intertitles, a technique Acker would use throughout her career in all her published writing. *END OF THE DIARY: DREAMS IN THE NIGHT,* she writes at the top of one of the pages. She writes about genocide, beauty, and plagues, and she wonders, *Does language correspond to reality? Can you get to reality (that's the goal, because there's a reality despite me) by using the language in a certain way? Yes (because I'm a poet). Don't separate from sensual reality (diary). In what way? . . . Magical connection (real magic) between putting-down-word & reality . . . If I think too hard or too programmatically & fast I get away from what's happening.*

And here, the record drops off. In New York until the summer of 1972, she wrote *The Burning Bombing of America*, a short but rambling and self-conscious experimental work that remained unpublished until after her death. Whatever notebooks or diaries she might have kept or letters written between January 1972 and the last months of 1973—when she started writing *The Childlike Life of the Black Tarantula*—have disappeared. Over the years, in New York and London, as her reputation became more established, she sold notebooks and letters to bookshops and dealers to raise extra cash: perhaps these papers exist in private collections. *I gotta go . . . I just feel so lonely with you*, she'd finally tell Lenny Neufeld in August 1972, and for two years after that he was devastated. It's likely, however, that during her last months in New York she formed friendships and acquaintanceships with other peer writers.

There's no doubt that Acker attended Bernadette Mayer's seminal *Memory* exhibition, installed at Holly Solomon's 98 Greene Street loft in February 1972. The show was substantially reviewed in *The Village Voice*, and—like Antin's *Blood of a Poet Box*—everyone knew about it. Two years older than Acker, Mayer was already a key figure in New York's performance, art, and poetry scene. Between 1967 and 1969 she'd edited the influential *0 to 9* magazine with Vito Acconci. Like Acker, Mayer was a student of classics. Born into a working-class family in Queens, orphaned in her early teens, Mayer's training took place in Catholic schools, and she received her B.A. from The New School.

Consisting of 1,116 photographs taken over thirty-one days in July, the exhibition was accompanied by a series of audiotapes of Mayer reading from her journals and notes recounting each day. Even more rigorously systematic than Acker's writing experiments, *Memory* parsed the author-as-subject's perception to a point of near schizophrenia. As the scholar Liz Kotz has written, "Whereas the very intensity of surface detail in Mayer's *Memory* paradoxically atomizes personal experience into an endless flow of pictures and recited recollections; its authorship is distributed among various functions that don't necessarily cohere into a single self."

"After I finished doing it," Mayer recalled in a 2007 conversation with Charles Bernstein, "I totally went insane." Mayer entered intensive psychoanalysis and persevered with a follow-up, textual project, *Studying Hunger*. The book begins:

Listen

I began all this in April, 1972. I wanted to try to record, like a diary, in writing states of consciousness, my states of consciousness, as fully as I could, every day, for one month. A month always seems like a likely timespan, if there is one, for an experiment. A month gives you enough time to feel free to skip a day, but not so much time that you wind up fucking off completely.

I had an idea before this that if a human, a writer, could come up with a workable code, or shorthand, for the transcription of every event, every motion, every transition of his or her own mind, & could perform this process of translation on himself, using the code, for a 24-hour period, he or we or someone could come up with a great piece of language/information.

Anyway

when I began to attempt the month-long experiment with states of consciousness, i wrote down a list of intentions. It went like this:
First, to record special states of consciousness. Special: change, sudden change, high, low, food, levels of attention
And, how intentions change.
And, to do this as an emotional science, as though: I have taken a month-drug, I work as observer of self in process.
And, to do the opposite of "accumulate data," oppose MEMORIES, DIARIES, *find structures*
And, a language should be used that stays on the observation/ notes/leaps side of language border which seems to separate, just barely, observation & analysis. But if the language must resort to analysis to "keep going," then let it be closer to that than too "accumulate data." Keep going *is a pose;* accumulate data *is a pose.*
Also, to use this to find a structure for MEMORY & *you, you will find out what memory is, you already know what moving is*
And, to do this without remembering

Bernadette Mayer would become an important, though never acknowledged influence on Acker's subsequent work through the mid-1970s. She made a great deal of effort to strike up a casual friendship with the more established and accomplished writer. After leaving New York, she wrote postcards and letters to Bernadette Mayer and other writers she'd met at the St. Marks Poetry Project: Barbara Baracks, Harris Schiff, and Jim Brodey, but her most continuous and apparently one-sided correspondence was with Mayer.

In July and August 1972, Acker paid an extended visit to San Diego with Mel Freilicher, David and Eleanor Antin, and other old friends. Neither she nor Len Neufeld knew it then, but this summer trip would precipitate the final ending of them as a couple. She gave a few readings in San Diego, and while she was there, she combed through the notebooks she'd kept in New York. Typing and retyping these fragments, she composed a single text. Was it a poem or a story? The distinction would not matter much yet. In any event, she created a disjointed but emotional narrative, changing some of the original lines in the diary to make them sharper and stronger. *I'm sick of fucking and not knowing who I am*, buried in one of the earlier handwritten diaries, would appear as the final line of the text as a more strident, declarative statement, a manifesto of what it's like to be twenty-three: *I'm sick of fucking not knowing who I am*. Most of the excerpts she used were accounts of the shows at Fun City. She describes the look and smell of the club and the people she met: pimps, junkies, whores, and gay party boys, with their stories about busts, bail, and prison.

Years later, in an interview with Sylvère Lotringer, she would recall: *I was working in a sex show in Forty-Second Street and I had two lives, the poetry and the sex show . . . It pretty radically changed my view of the world . . . You see people from the bottom up, and sexual behavior, especially sex minus relationship—which is what happens in 42nd Street—is definitely bottom. Then you see it in a different way, especially power relationships in society . . . And I think that never left me.*

She typed up the text, double-spaced, adding the colophon *Papyrus Press, San Diego 1972*, and brought it to an offset printer. She was twenty-five years old. It was her first, self-published work. She knew then that the rhetoric of the New Left didn't begin to describe the existential situation in the United States as aptly as the dynamics of sex work. Her collaged text described her brief and partly self-willed season in hell in long, run-on sentences. She offered no explicit analysis of this situation. There were no explanations, confessions, apologies. She called the work *Politics*.

THE CHILDLIKE LIFE OF
THE BLACK TARANTULA

(1971–1974)

you have abnormal childhood   you will have to live childhood over again.
—Kathy Acker, "Journal Black Cats Black Jewels" (1972)

Solana Beach in 1972 was a sleepy, shabby Southern California beach town within reasonable distance to cities but surrounded by the natural world, where one could live fairly cheaply. Rents were low, and there wasn't much there to buy. Twenty-four miles north of San Diego, about two hours by car or train from L.A., it was popular with surfers and retirees. Originally developed in the 1920s as a housing tract for migrant citrus workers, its main street was set back from the beach by three blocks. The town had a public library and a movie theater, several bars, a massage parlor, a new Vons supermarket, and a cluster of mom-and-pop stores. Not everyone had cars. UC San Diego students hitch-hiked along Torrey Pines Road to the La Jolla campus fourteen miles south. Often, drivers rolled down their windows to ask their pedestrian neighbors if they needed a ride.

By the spring of 1972, Acker's relationship with Len Neufeld in the apartment at West 163rd Street was in limbo. They hadn't yet broken up, but most nights they slept in separate rooms. She was afraid to break up, as breaking up would mean moving out of the apartment, and she wasn't totally committed to her life in New York. Since the first open-mike reading she did at St. Marks one year earlier, she'd become better known, but she was still somewhat intimidated by her peers: *those uptight-about-fame condescending creeps in NY*, as she'd describe them in a letter several months later to Jackson Mac Low. Of course she wanted fame too, but at the moment it seemed out of reach. And so she fled. She had a little money saved from working off the books for Burt Lasky while collecting unemployment from the Fun City job. Instead of using her savings to rent an apartment and suffer through another summer in New York, she decided to go back and stay with her old San Diego friends while she figured out her next move. Mel Freilicher and other Brandeis friends were still there, and David Antin, who wholeheartedly believed in her and her work, remained an important influence.

During the two years she'd been in New York with Neufeld, the Antins had left their small Solana Beach bungalow, hidden behind a wall of oleander trees, for a much grander, shambling stucco house with a big terrace, perched on a bluff overlooking the beach. Len Neufeld and Martha Rosler's house in Solana Beach was where Acker had found refuge from her marriage before things blew up and she and Neufeld left for New York. As she was still reeling from *the shock of going from a really protective environment to a totally frightening environment*, arriving back at Solana Beach early that summer must have felt like a return to the womb. The town hadn't changed much. Shady eucalyptus trees lined the thoroughfare that passed through the Torrey Pines State Natural Reserve. Tall bluffs guarded a wide sandy beach. The town itself was anchored by a big, half-empty parking lot. A photograph from Eleanor Antin's *The King of Solana Beach* series produced in 1974 shows the artist dressed as Charles I, addressing four of her "subjects"—skinny long-haired surf kids drinking beers—from a park bench on the bluff above the town parking lot.

It's probable that David Antin helped Acker arrange the offset printing of her pamphlet *Politics* at what appears on the colophon as "The Community Press," but beyond this, there isn't much documentation of what she did during those West Coast weeks. Mel Freilicher was separating from his girlfriend, finally coming out as gay, and it's likely that Acker moved between the Antins' at Solana Beach, the UCSD campus, and Mel Freilicher's Del Mar apartment, just one town away. Her prose poem "Journal Black Cats Black Jewels" is dated Summer 1972. In it, she writes: *roam over San Diego without purple head father pick up grains watercress onions goats mumble are ecstatic descriptions I am I . . .* In "The Revolution and After," another prose poem written around the same time, she writes: *even among freaks am freak . . . go moving San Diego Santa Cruz San Francisco Bolinas Seattle no where to move into all rooms too expensive $60. Maintain life indefinitely I'm running out of money $ doesn't exist . . .* and: *your stuff isn't personal enough you don't think program through thoroughly you'll never write (survive) you don't deserve notice consideration longing cook sweep clean all two-year-past work is O.K.*

By early August she was looking for a ride back to New York.

Peter Gordon had just finished his music composition B.A. at UC San Diego. He graduated a year early because so many of the school's classes were of interest to him. He and a roommate were sharing an upstairs two-bedroom apartment at 136 ½ Sierra Avenue in Solana Beach. Gordon had turned twenty-one that June, and he celebrated his birthday by taking his first acid trip. He was still somewhat involved in an on-again, off-again romance with a graduate student, Winifred Mastro, who was one of Acker's and Freilicher's old Brandeis friends. By August their romance was mostly off, as she'd started sleeping with one of Gordon's professors.

Peter Gordon's plan was to take a road trip to New York with his friend JW before returning to Solana Beach and beginning a UCSD graduate degree in the early fall. JW, who'd already come out as gay, was another Brandeis émigré. Gordon and JW applied as drivers at a drive-away car service in San Diego and were given a late-model Pontiac sedan. When Acker found out about their trip, she offered to come along for the ride. Gordon wasn't uncomfortable about traveling with JW—the scene there was very relaxed about sexual orientation—but he thought having a girl along for the ride would be fun. Suddenly the trip seemed more interesting to him.

They left San Diego in the late afternoon and drove all night, gossiping about mutual friends and discussing books, music, cooking, food, aesthetics, and philosophy. Gordon explained how he found himself in a quandary, not sure how to reconcile his cooly formal, compositional ideas with his love for playing rock and roll. To Acker, the answers all lay in form. The disjunctive poetry she wrote was a way of capturing the fragmentation of her life in the Times Square sex show and everywhere else. Approaching Flagstaff, Arizona, around dawn, they got off the interstate on Four Mile Road to stretch their legs and piss. Acker scrambled up a desert boulder, peeled off her Indian hippie shirt, and lay out to soak up the early-morning sun. They'd been talking nonstop all night. Catching sight of this topless woman on a rock, Gordon walked up and remarked, nonchalantly he hoped, "Tits." She looked at him and even more nonchalantly replied *Do you want to fuck?* He said, "Why not?" It was a scene straight out of Antonioni's *Zabriskie Point.* He climbed up on the rock. She was twenty-six, five years older than he was, and she knew just what to do. They lay out on the boulder fucking while JW stood beside the car and watched. In Albuquerque that night, they ate bad Chinese and checked into a motel. JW slipped out discreetly so they could fuck more. By the time they got to Kansas City, they were romantically involved.

On August 23 in Liberal, Kansas, Acker sent a postcard to Bernadette Mayer in New York:

Coming in crazy. Becoming Kerouac, then too many men. Secret messages for you. No $. Working my way ha-ha am seeing the country—no more paranoia. Love love Kathy

Acker and Gordon were still together when they reached New York. He ditched other plans, deciding to stay with Acker and Len Neufeld at the apartment on West 163rd.

As Gordon recalls, "This was the early '70s, things were still quite fluid sexually, so for Kathy and Lenny to have some sort of arrangement didn't seem weird. I stayed in Kathy's workroom, which had a bed. For as long as I knew Kathy, she always wrote in bed. I pretty much stayed in Kathy's room and didn't really cross paths with Lenny. I had various stuff to do and was out in the evenings when Lenny was around. He had a job, so he was gone during the day and was in bed by the time I came back. He did show up while we were in bed once, pretty upset when he got the idea I was around for more than a night or two. But aside from that, I was spared whatever drama was entailed."

Ten days later Gordon flew back to L.A. to stay at his family's home in Tarzana as he'd originally planned. A rush of correspondence followed him from New York: "I was staying at my parent's house," he says. "And letters would arrive with the envelopes inscribed around the edges with slogans like WHY NOT FUCK NOW? WHY NOT COME NOW! DEATH TO THE FAMILY! THE FAMILY IS THE ROOT OF ALL EVIL! in red and blue marker ink." But Gordon's parents, a writer and a psychotherapist, were more amused than shocked.

Preparing to start the fall quarter, Gordon returned to San Diego alone. "For me," he recalls, "it was all very fast and intense. We had this hot little affair, and then . . . three weeks later, in late August, Kathy shows up at my doorstep in Solana Beach with two bins of clothes, dozens of cartons of books and three cats." Acker moved in, and his roommate moved out. Here was the solution she'd been looking for. She had to separate from Neufeld, but without the pretext of a job or graduate school, she could never have moved back to San Diego on her own. She'd tell Barry Alpert in a March 1976 interview, *I had to get out of New York for personal reasons.* Already she was discovering the power of truncation when creating an artistic biography.

Acker and Gordon would stay together for the next six years, supporting each other's artistic work intellectually and emotionally, collaborating on performances and radio shows, eventually leaving San Diego for San Francisco, and San Francisco for New York. They married in the throes of her first cancer scare in February 1978, although they were no longer close, and separated later that year. Eventually they would both come to find their mostly asexual relationship too confining, but the first years Acker spent with Peter Gordon were the most peaceful and among the most productive of her life.

* * *

It sure is nice to wake up and walk out of the door in a bathrobe see the sky no one wants to rape me, she wrote to Jerry and Diane Rothenberg soon after she arrived back in Solana Beach, making sure—as she almost always did—to add a dash of sexual frisson to the letters she sent to her mentor and his wife. *I've got a wife named Peter.* After two dark years of being sick with PID and hovering around the edges of a literary competition that she knew she couldn't win, Solana Beach was a reprieve from her old life in New York. This time the age gap between Acker and her partners was reversed. Gordon, five years younger, was unequivocally her best friend. Soon she'd begin referring to him as her brother. The two settled into a domestic life that allowed them both room for relationships and sexual adventures with acquaintances, strangers, and friends. Their Sierra Road apartment was just a block away from the new Antin house, and the two couples became close, constant friends. A shared dog moved between the two domiciles. Often Acker babysat for the Antins. She and Gordon made money by modeling for Eleanor Antin's life drawing class. When Eleanor was mailing out her *100 Boots* postcards, she trusted Acker and Gordon to meticulously handwrite the six hundred addresses on her list.

Almost immediately Acker began a new round of writing experiments. Her long poem *Homage to LeRoi Jones* samples from, and responds to, Jones/Baraka's short novel *The System of Dante's Hell*. Published in 1965, *System* powerfully signaled Jones's break from his Beat contemporaries. It was, as critic Robert Elliot Fox writes, a fugitive narrative that described "the harried flight of an intensely self-conscious Afro-American artist/intellectual from the neo-slavery of blinding, neutralizing whiteness, where the area of struggle is basically within the mind." Another long Acker poem, "Excerpts From: Entrance into Dwelling in Paradise" is a mash-up of, presumably, John Milton's *Paradise Lost* and her own notes:

> *the gate was arched like a great hall and over walls and*
> *roof ramped vines with grapes of many colors; the red*
> *like rubies and the black like ebonies; . . .*

> *. . . and into wine quench in me anguish what really*
> *reality is what paradise is Nixon wins Biggest Land-*
> *slide in History what paradise is One Million People Die . . .*

. . . I don't talk about my self (feelings) I don't
know how to begin wrapping around a I see few people but
Peter find other people make me tense set frenzy in a way I don't
like myself to act I dislike Peter when he's my only company . . .

To Eleanor Antin, Acker's first round of Solana Beach experiments seemed a bit self-indulgent, even forced: "It was the usual free-form confessional stuff." Four years later, Acker herself would dismiss these attempts as *Prose poems, lyrical images . . . Jerry Rothenberg was a huge influence. Pretty, very pretty sort of things. I don't remember much; they're awful.* But her discipline in conducting these experiments was unwavering. She was still searching for the right compositional strategy to use in her work, what others might have described as "her voice." She and Mel Freilicher talked about starting a new magazine, *Before 30 Except George*, but the project never got off the ground.

After finishing *Homage*, she wrote to Bernadette Mayer and her then partner, the filmmaker Ed Bowes:

dear Bernadette! dear Ed! This typewriter doesn't work and neither does my spelling or typing! Enclosed find poem/writeout of beginning of story by L.J. MY POEM [Homage to LeRoi Jones, 1972] I'm doing the same thing process of cut up to all writing I'm doing it it feels terrific! There are no poets here besides David so I'm going crazy . . . All I do is write have sex talk about my sex and other peoples! I don't have any money owe $400 to friends looking madly not too madly for job. I really love doing cut up like destroying everything and making music out of it I especially like writing absolutely anything I want because I know it's going to be destroyed . . . this place is paradise if I can survive absence of poets and BOOKS. Send books will pay commission anything I'll send POEMS BACK LOTS OF POEMS ENDLESS NUMBER OF CUT UPS NEED POET TALK LOVE Kathy

Over the next three years Acker would write to Mayer at least a dozen times.

Reading beyond Acker's exuberance—whether spontaneous or forced—it's clear she was asking the older writer to read her in-progress work and trade her unpublished poems for free books. Except for two brief postcard notes about the logistics of a reading at the St. Marks Poetry Project that she arranged for Acker early in 1975, Mayer's replies, if they exist, have not been preserved.

Acker's letters are an anomaly within the Mayer/United Artists magazine archive where they are preserved. With painful and almost tone-deaf eagerness, Acker chatters on about her own writing, her finances and debts, her crushes and sexual flings. *Dear Burning Dot*, she writes in 1974 from Albuquerque, *Spring is here sex sex. Slept w/ 2 wonderful men in Albuquerque & feel wonderful; left Albuquerque & feel miserable, sad.* From Solana Beach, spring 1973: *By the way . . . could you give me info about a guy I think you know Dan Graham. This is scene: I met him at Davd's (Antin) for various reasons known & unknown developed super crush on him, called him up, "will you sleep w/ me?" "yes" slept w/ him one night. That morning he says "call me Friday," like he really wants to see me I call him no answer 2 days later get hold of him, he acts like I'm the biggest creep possible . . . I'm hurt mainly 'cause I'm confused . . . if you have any info, pertaining to subject, please reply, any info is of interest.* From San Francisco, 1974: *I'm just broke like crazy so I'm bugging anyone to send me free books in my Jew mood you don't need to fucking yell at me . . . I'm just fuckin freaked like I haven't yet used anything to kill pain for all those abortions but goddam aint going to fuck no one without vasectomy unless he/she got NO cock at least no sperm the cats are having a great time . . .* A few months later: *I gave a friend of mine a blow-job in the bathroom and I met Ed Dorn so I felt totally fantastic . . .*

The poets Susan Howe and Alice Notley were among Mayer's other correspondents at that time. Exemplary of literary friendships, their thoughtful, neatly typed letters convey their responses to books (Laura Riding, Geoffrey Chaucer, Simone Weil, and Virginia Woolf), their pregnancies, their families and mutual friends in prose that is circumspectly sparing of the word *I*. Like Mayer, Notley grew up working class without independent means. Although they both lived close to the bone and were often broke, their letters rarely mention finances. Instead: "I found my old notebook from when I was reading [Laura Riding's] *The Telling* but it didn't bring back enough for me to remember why I thought it great. It is based on the following peculiar notion (I think): that everyone has access to memory of a time before they were born, 'when Being was not number,' and the terrible division into men and woman hadn't taken place . . ."

When Mayer, while working at the St. Marks Poetry Project, scheduled a reading Acker had been asking her for months to arrange, Acker changed her dates three times and then asked the other writer to fund her plane fare by applying for a New York State emergency artist loan. *money*, she wrote, *is a problem. No more phone here, to get money for my books Peter & I are borrowing begging & not eating cause Peter's father don't have no more money.* In a postscript Acker adds: *I figured out my male stars are David Antin, L. Wiener, Ashley, Peter. Dan Graham on outs. You & E. Antin my female stars.*

Handling these letters with archival gloves in the sanctum of the Mandeville Special Collections Library at UC San Diego, one is tempted to give them an evidential weight they couldn't possibly have had when they were written and read. Throughout the 1970s postcards and letters were used for all kinds of loose talk. An off-peak three-minute long-distance call cost $1.00, about two-thirds the hourly minimum wage, while a stamp could be bought for 11 cents. Like all correspondence, the content and tone of Acker's letters varies according to whom she is speaking and what she hopes to achieve. She was always extremely focused. Still, immersed in the Poetry Project's anti-celebrity ethos and self-supporting since her mid-teens, Mayer must have found Acker's entreaties somewhat nervy and strange.

Years later Acker would avenge her own awkwardness: *[Performing in the Times Square sex show in the 1970s] put me in such a different class as anybody else*, she'd tell Larry McCaffery in a 1990 interview. *Being in that kind of world made me see things so differently. For instance, I could see that politics were what was involved in separating me from the St. Mark's crowd class—because they were basically upper-middle class, while Forty-Second Street wasn't.* (The New York and post–New York School scenes that coalesced at St. Marks were notable for the emergence of such high-literary writers as Ted Berrigan and Ron Padgett, who'd attended state schools thanks to the GI Bill.)

Though Acker and Mayer were born just two years apart, the differences between the letters from Mayer's other correspondents signal a deep generational divide.

* * *

One block away from the beach, Peter Gordon's apartment on North Sierra Avenue occupied the top half of a two-story bungalow. The entrance was in the rear. Perhaps shaking the sand off your feet, you entered it on a makeshift wood staircase, built when the landlord converted his house to a duplex. The front room, used as a bedroom, faced west toward a sliver of ocean beyond the bluff. While Gordon attended his classes, Acker liked to sit up in bed writing notebooks in fat, cursive script. Later she'd go into the workroom to type up her finished pieces. San Diego was paradise, but she had to be careful not to be lulled into inertia. She wrote every day.

Gordon lived on a stipend from UC San Diego and some modest parental support, but as they were more or less splitting expenses, Acker needed to find some kind of job that wouldn't impinge on her writing and the morning dream-drift she channeled into her work. Their friends among the ex-student crowd in San Diego were editing textbooks for a local publisher or working as room-service waiters, complaining about shit jobs that ate up their time. But there were a handful of strip clubs around the county that catered to sailors and workers. Most of the women who worked there were hippies, dancing one or two shifts a week to get by. They chose their own songs off the juke-box and improvised costumes from thrift stores. It didn't take Acker long to decide that stripping would be a lot better than full-time "robot" employment. She called herself "Target" and "Kathy Kat" and worked for a small local mafia that rotated the girls from club to club between sets in a pink van, keeping the flesh fresh at every establishment they ran.

While the Fun City job in Times Square was a descent into hell she'd attempt to unravel in writing for the rest of her life, stripping in San Diego felt benign, almost light. As Mel Freilicher would write five years after her death, "In San Diego, she rather happily worked as a stripper . . . Kathy, aka 'Target,' would do an interpretive strip to 'Che' by Ornette Coleman, after carefully explaining to the audience of mostly sailors who Che was and why he was so venerable." As she told Barry Alpert, *[San Diego was] a nice place to work as a stripper. I worked in a nice place. You didn't get much money, but sailors turn out to be very nice people. But there was nothing to do.* Waiting backstage for the van, she listened to her coworkers talking about bad boyfriends and drug busts and reprised their stories in a text she'd title "Stripper Disintegration."

She danced for a while and then quit and tried tutoring Latin. But there wasn't much work, and tutoring paid only $5 an hour. Eventually she took a job at the massage parlor in Solana Beach. The Antins' veterinarian, who was a regular, became an admirer and offered to help her, convinced that she could *do better* in a higher-end brothel a few towns away. They all had a good laugh over this. From there, Acker drifted back into working the clubs, but it was really no joke. She was about to turn twenty-six; she had to come up with a more sustainable way of supporting herself. She and Gordon were already planning their move to San Francisco. He wanted to finish his M.A. at Mills College with the operatic composer and ambient music pioneer Robert Ashley, and they both thought they'd be happier in a real city. But they couldn't leave until he finished the spring quarter in June.

Finally, that spring, she came up with what seemed like a genius idea. She was a writer supporting herself in the sex industry: why not *write* about sex and stop stripping? But to do this, she'd need an advance. The story she'd tell Jackson Mac Low, and many others, was that she and Peter Gordon asked his father if he could help out by being her patron while she wrote the first book, which she'd call *Rip-Off Red, Girl Detective*.

When I fact-checked this story with Gordon last year, he replied, "I can envision my dear late father reading about his patronage of Kathy: looking at me with an arched eyebrow and a slight suggestions of a wry smile." Gordon's father was no Maurice Girodias. Far from being a patron, he was a writer himself, supporting his family by working for Voice of America and writing scripts. Nevertheless, Acker seems to have been determined to cast her boyfriend's dad as a patron and, by extension—even more gratifyingly—as a substitute father. Since cutting ties with her own family three years before in New York, she'd had friends and mentors, but no one who offered real financial support. As she'd write to Jackson Mac Low that summer, *I live with Peter, my brother, friend, lover, who's the first decent wonderful blah blah his parents understand I'm their daughter &*

they've accepted my fantasy of a real brother-sister relation & his father's supported me for the last 4 months (minimal, but support!) so I could write Rip Off Red, *which is the most wonderful help I could get from anyone & for the first time in my life I feel free & open enough to try to risk myself in order to deal with myself & find out about stuff.* Still, her real patron was Peter Gordon himself: "I shared whatever I had with her, and we scraped and struggled for money."

Among the "stuff" Acker was finding out during those months was the difficulty of maintaining sexual relationships with women: she didn't have sex with the women she loved, and she didn't love the ones she had sex with. This was a conundrum Acker would continue pursuing for most of her life. But the myth she devised of the Gordon family's financial support during those months gave her the confidence boost that helped her to finish the book. *I'd love to fuck the whole family*, she wrote.

Written in the first person and hung on the slenderest narrative thread, *Rip-Off Red* follows Rip-Off Red, Girl Detective and her boyfriend, Peter Peter, as they investigate the abrupt murder of Spitz, a glamorous young woman who sat next to them on a plane ride from the West Coast to New York. Slightly drunk, Red masturbates under her coat to a montage of fantasies that become true when Spitz suddenly kisses her. She and Spitz slip out to the bathroom to have sex. The narrative giddily, often hilariously, swerves from pulp fiction's terse present tense—*I have to find out how Spitz was murdered*—and tough-talking wisecracks to lyrical flights of pornography. There were plenty of precedents for paperback porn published by highly literary writers—from Alexander Trocchi's string of "erotic novels" written in the mid-1950s for Olympia Press, to Diane di Prima's 1968 *Memoirs of a Beatnik*, to Fanny Howe's 1966 *Vietnam Nurse*, an antiwar story told as an erotic romance for Avon Books's popular "Nurse" series. Still, with such passages as

I have to disintegrate my mind to the point my mind is insepara-
ble from the common mind or my "unconscious." By thinking:
dreaming, following sexual and other desires, and by inflaming
you with sensuous images, we can get rid of the universities, the
crowded towns, the bureaucracies. I call up images of myself, or
just images . . .

it's hard to imagine that Acker ever believed *Rip-Off Red* could be sold as commercial porn. But that's not the point. More important, while writing *Rip-Off Red*, Acker turned away from the "pretty, very pretty" lyrical prose poems she'd been laboring at since arriving in San Diego and found a sustainable method of working. She was now writing books.

That May, while she was still writing *Rip-Off Red*, Acker composed *Some Lives of Murderesses*, a delirious, blunt, and fragmented first-person text that would become the first part of *The Childlike Life of the Black Tarantula*, a six-pamphlet serial. In *Some Lives*, she transposes fragments of such obscure mass-market biographies as *Rogues and Adventuresses* into the first person and intercuts them with her entries from her own diaries. Cut and paste, snatch and grab. Five years after attending David Antin's poetry seminars, she'd discovered a way to use his compositional mandate—*go to the library, steal!*—for her own purposes.

The six installments of *The Black Tarantula* would establish Acker's reputation in the art and avant-garde literary worlds. The goal she states toward the end of the final installment—*I was interested in "fame" as one end: (1) people whose work I want to find out about would talk to me, (2) I would somehow be able to pay for food rent etc. doing something connected, (3) artists I fall in love with would fuck me*—would soon be at least partly realized. Throughout her career she'd be asked over and over about how she started her work as a "plagiarist" or "appropriationist" when she wrote *Black Tarantula*, but when she talked to Barry Alpert in 1976, her account hadn't yet crystallized into an origin myth. As she explained to the critic over lunch at an Indian restaurant, she was bummed about an unrequited crush [on artist Dan Graham] and *thinking about changing* herself. And at the time

> *There were other women . . . art world women like Adrian Piper, who were doing pieces about changing themselves, changing parts of themselves . . . Martha Wilson, for instance. I simply didn't know it. That's interesting to me that people get interested in the same problem at the same time without directly influencing each other.*

> *. . . I was very interested in the use of the "I." So I went to the UCSD library . . . and took out whatever books about murderesses I could get. I figured, of all the people I could figure out I'm not, I know I've never murdered anybody. At least directly. I picked out books that were anything as long as it wasn't psychological. Crappy novels like* Blood on the Carpet *I remember was one I picked up . . . I didn't deal with any fiction in* TBT [The Black Tarantula]. *It was reporting . . . I didn't even want to deal with the problem of fiction. I took these books home . . . and then I sat down and wrote out . . . I tightened up the language and played games with it. Basically I just copied . . . only I changed the third person to the first person, so they'd seem to be about myself. And then I set up sections within parentheses what were just diary sections . . . about who I was, what I was doing . . . train of thought stuff . . .*

> *So there were two I's in the book, the I without the parentheses and the I within the parentheses . . .*

> *Gradually what happened was the two I's started playing games with each other, becoming one. It was set up as a cold-blooded experiment about what would happen.*

Written in the historical present—the tense most often used in Latin histories—*Some Lives of Murderesses* uses the same form of tersely declarative direct address she'd adopted as *Rip-Off Red*, minus the Chandleresque hard-boiled detective affect. She worked on it quickly and didn't go back to revise. *I become a murderess*, she begins. *I'm born in the late autumn or winter of 1827.* And: *I'm born poor St. Helen's Isle of Wight. 1790. As a child I have hardly any food to eat.* Tonally, there's a comic resonance with the arresting "I Dreamed" Maidenform underwear ads, ubiquitous during the 1950s and '60s: *I Dreamed I Was Wanted . . . Took the Cue . . . Was a Toreador in My Maidenform Bra.* Meanwhile, the "I" within parentheses agonizes: *I call up D in Los Angeles do you want to sleep with me when and where . . . No call three days later I have to see D I don't know him hello I've got a ride to Los Angeles lie . . . We don't touch talk about anything personal until we get to motel never talk about anything personal spend night together . . .*

The experiment works. It's a lighthearted act of Artaudian cruelty. Almost magically, the diary writings Acker had been trying so hard to lift into poetry are transformed into literary *materiel.*

She showed her new work to the Antins, and they were impressed. Eleanor insisted on sending the piece to her friend Carol Bergé, who edited the popular literary magazine *Center.* When Bergé wrote back that the work had no merit and its author was most likely schizophrenic, they devised a new plan. Before Eleanor Antin found gallery representation, she mailed postcards of frames from her ongoing photographic series *100 Boots* to a list of six hundred friends and acquaintances. She mailed the cards out once a month. It didn't cost much, and it gave her a deadline. People began looking forward to them. Where would these boots go next? To a church or farm, to a strip club or government building? Although Antin's DIY strategy has come to be seen by art history as "incorporating a method of exhibitioning into her work which navigated its own way through the art world and around traditional gallery shows," at the time it was the only means Antin had of showing her work. As David Antin would later explain mail art, "It was poor people's art . . . Anybody could do it if they had the intelligence and the energy. And Kathy had both intelligence and energy. And she had desire." He gave Acker the *100 Boots* mailing list, and she decided to repeat Eleanor's strategy. Instead of sending out *Lives of Murderesses* as a one-off pamphlet, she'd expand it into a serial aimed at the insider audience the Antins had already amassed. Calling herself the Black Tarantula, she'd write and print one installment a month, mail each one out to the list, and see what happened next. She'd call the series *The Childlike Life of the Black Tarantula*. Eventually the six installments would be gathered and presented together in Acker's first non–self-published book. Until then she was content to remain anonymous, her real identity known only by hearsay. The art world hadn't changed that much since Eleanor Antin produced *Blood of a Poet Box* in 1968. Everyone who mattered then *knew* that the Black Tarantula was a young woman named Kathy Acker. Then, just as now, rumor and hearsay were far more effective tools for advancing a nascent reputation than plastering one's unwanted name all over the place.

Almost immediately Acker talked the Solana Beach newspaper into letting her print the pamphlets for free on their press. By now it was June. She and Peter Gordon were leaving for San Francisco the following month, and she still had to finish up *Red*, print and mail out the *Murderess* pamphlets, and begin a second installment. She pushed herself hard and developed an ulcer.

The next pamphlet, dated June 1973, was called *A Point-to-Point Comparison Between My Life and the Life of Moll Cutpurse, the Queen-Regent of Misrule, the Roaring Girl, the Benevolent Tyrant of City Thieves and City Murderers, the Bear Lady*, and it begins: *I'm born crazy in Barbican, four years after the defeat of the terrible Armada.* Soon she switches to the parenthetical "I": *(I leave my parents, then my husband, my career, I'm very good at making money. I have two main problems: (1) how to earn $200 to $300 per month to eat, pay rent, without becoming a robot and with my clothes on (2) do what I want which is real, approaches reality. End of my life.)* Immersed in her readings of eighteenth-century novels, she adopts the declarative voice of the picaresque narrator and states the history and hopes of Every Female Late-Twentieth-Century Artist to startling and comic effect. Already, Acker's parenthetical "I" is becoming more strident.

[T]he Black Tarantula series, she writes to Jackson Mac Low, *coming out once a month is basically my way of making myself schizophrenic w/out the censor . . . I'm doing this after reading a book by Mary Barnes & Joe Berke . . . also many accounts by schizo-phrenics, Laing, books on Tibetan Buddhism, the whole Kinglsey Hall crew etc with the idea that if I do this slowly & don't scare myself by sudden shocks I'll be able to deal w/ other people more honestly & directly, evolve new ways of being w/ people . . . crack up the old identity god. So I copy texts (get rid of style, expressionism in writing) and become the people of he texts: Black Tarantula #1 . . . was trying to crack myself by making myself incorporate obviously foreign identities . . . Black Tarantula #2 was another crack, I iden-tified strongly w/ Moll Cutpurse, so I took cracks at my feelings of identification. All right for this shit, now I'm crazy as a bedbug. No, but very real openings in the mind have been reached, so something's happening. I'm not sure of all the implications of what I'm doing . . .*

"Dear Kathy Aker [*sic*]," the Black Mountain poet Fielding Dawson wrote that July on the back of a card from the Russian Tea Room, "I received your long story, and read it last night. It is very very good, your voice is fresh and so new as to be a bright influence on anyone seriously involved in writing. Keep up the good work, and if I can be of any help, let me know. Your style . . .

is utterly refreshing, as is your humor and your divided self; the fantasy projections are in anger and emotional foundation: completely articulate, as is the suspense, and hysteria at the end. You make it work. You are the original . . . and strong. Bless you. PS: I've been after a verbal tone & surface lucidity for years. You achieve it as something natural."

* * *

In San Francisco, Acker and Gordon moved into an upstairs apartment at 46 Belvedere Street, three blocks east of Golden Gate Park, in the heart of the Haight-Ashbury district. Still sick with the ulcer, she writes to Jackson Mac Low: *I couldn't bear leaving SD but had to, couldn't make $ in SD except by stripping & couldn't stand doing that any longer, needed more input than my 5 friends . . . I thought SF would be a good alternative to NY . . . Peter wanted to get to a city, I could lead more of my double sexual life in SF etc. Even though I still haven't gotten over the jolt of entering another new environment . . . I feel I can live here: I live near the park & the beach, I can find part-time work, more stars, artists are so open here, like already these two people just offered, they hardly knew me, to illustrate my pornography, & everyone wants to hear about what I'm doing.*

Instinctively, she avoided the local poetry scene with its stars and acolytes and began writing Part 3: *I Move to San Francisco. I Begin to Copy My Favorite Pornography Books and Become the Main Person in Each of Them.* Her readings on schizophrenia, which may have been prompted by Carol Bergé's off-base response to her work conjoined with her own efforts to "crack herself up," begin leading her back to the mindscape of childhood: a cosmos of wonder, sensation, and fear that will become a basis for all her future writing. Channeling Violette Leduc's lesbian schoolgirl novel *Thérèse and Isabelle*, she recalls her early years at the Lenox School and the dangerous thrill of intimate female friendships: *"I think Miss St. Pierre's a lesbian"* Jean whispers. *I can't tell Jean about everything, who I like and hate, she'd reach too far inside me rub against the open veins . . .* "Do you like being in school?" I ask Jean. "No, I want to do whatever I want to do fuck everyone . . . I want to blow my identity outwards, away, until I'm always running in a black ocean under a black sky and I can control my emotions" . . . Blow up the school.

Almost immediately she begins writing Part 4: *I Become Helen Seferis, and Then Alexander Trocchi*. The pamphlet begins with the epigraph *I've always feared most that someone will destroy my mind*. In it, she collages descriptions of sexual frenzies lifted from published pornography with excerpts from her own diaries. *As the man's cock enters me, every muscle of me begins to shake, every nerve begins to burn and quiver. I'm both liquid and solid. I'm completely pleasure.* By now, she's writing her diaries to use as material in this new work. *I'm no longer interested in my memories*, she writes, *only in my continuing escalating feelings*. She describes herself approaching the point of complete dissolution she'd looked for in childhood, *a black ocean under a black sky*. She finds that sex is the best way to get there. *I'm speaking to you directly. Complete disorder exists.* She'd never cared much for recreational drugs, but *I use psilocybin, mescaline, pure acid; occasionally hash as an aphrodisiac*. Around the same time, she begins drawing dense, intricate maps of her dreams in fountain-pen ink on large sheets of paper. Flight patterns of birds move across regions with names like *The Plains*, *The Village*, and *The Childhood Land* and line drawings of lions and wolves, trees, huts, and streets. A spiraling path leads past a lighthouse; then, at *the magic place*, the path dissolves into a cluster of circles. Small hand-printed captions describe the journey:

I have to
stop at the
right huts to
buy the right things

We walk up and around through the sand

birds sit on top
of each branch

A tree which is
the world which is
my back. Its branches
are moving. Making
sound.

Her maps look like Australian Aboriginal maps of the Dreamtime; they look like the map of the Hundred Acre Woods on the endpapers of *Winnie the Pooh*. They're completely original.

In September, Gordon began classes at Mills, working mostly with Robert Ashley. Ashley—who'd taught at Brandeis in the mid-'60s when Acker was a student there—soon became a powerful influence and a friend to both Gordon and Acker. As a musician, Ashley was exploring some of the same terrain Acker sought to access through her writing. Control, loss of control, the circumvention of rational thought to receive new information from the individual or universal unconscious. While at Mills, Ashley was beginning to work on *Automatic Writing*, which would become one of his signature pieces. Afflicted with a mild case of Tourette's, he'd become fascinated with the eruption of "involuntary speech," the vocal tic that characterizes the syndrome. He wondered if the sound-making urge that overcame him during these episodes was linked to his work as a composer. Wasn't "involuntary speech" a primitive form of composition, erupting from the unconscious? As he'd write later, "[D]uring the time of composing *Automatic Writing* I was in a deep depression, because, among other things to be depressed about, the world was not interested in the kind of music that I was interested in. I was out of work, so I decided to 'perform' involuntary speech. The performances were more or less failures because the difference between involuntary speech and any other kind of allowed behavior is too big to be overcome willfully, so the performances were largely imitations of involuntary speech, with only a few moments here and there of 'loss of control.' These moments, triumphs for me, are documented elsewhere."

At Mills, Gordon and Acker become friends with the composer Jill Kroesen. A student and later collaborator of Robert Ashley's, Kroesen was finishing her M.A. in music composition that year. Kroesen and Gordon briefly became a couple, but then changed their minds. The three friends hung out together at 46 Belvedere and gave themselves pseudonyms. Acker was alternately the Black Tarantula, Rip-Off Red, Gold Lamé and Silver Lamé. Kroesen was Fay Schism ("Fay Schism begins in the Home"), and Gordon called himself Art Povera. They put their utility bills in Art's name and deployed a system for receiving free long-distance calls that worked for a while, until it didn't. Acker and Gordon hosted a Sunday-afternoon radio show on KPOO 86.5 FM, *Poor People's Radio*. Friends such as Robert Ashley and Terry Riley stopped by to perform and do interviews; Acker read from the Marquis de Sade while Gordon played records by the Les Six composer Arthur Honegger. Their place at 46 Belvedere was an ordinary hippie apartment, as Kroesen recalls: a couch in the front, not much other stuff, but printed cloth everywhere.

In the fifth installment of *The Black Tarantula—I Explore My Miserable Childhood. I Become William Butler Yeats*—written in San Francisco that September, Acker intercuts the autobiographical writings of William Butler Yeats with chronologized scenes from her childhood, presented as "evidence." *Age 16: My mother tells me while my father and sister are listening that my father's cock is too wide and short for her, he doesn't fuck her enough. I show I understand what she means.* That fall, the Chilean president Salvador Allende commits suicide when his government is deposed by a CIA-backed coup; General Pinochet's troops round up five thousand alleged dissidents in the National Stadium. In Chile, thousands are tortured and killed. At home, the Watergate trials drag on ad infinitum. Philip K. Dick writes *A Scanner Darkly*, Erica Jong publishes *Fear of Flying*, and *Jonathan Livingston Seagull* stays at the top of the best-seller list for thirty-eight weeks. The Black Tarantula writes,

> NIXON MURDERS CHILE
> AGNEW MURDERS NIXON
> THE POOR STARVE, EAT THEIR
> CHILDREN

while reaching back through the past to recover the texture of childhood. Sensations drift into the text, and she records them. *Everything is incredibly beautiful*, she writes, and *My childhood dream: (narrow down to process)*. Images of her estranged mother haunt her.

"A cold dry windy day clouds blowing through the sky sunshine and shadow. A dead leaf brushes my face. The streets remind me of St Louis . . . red brick houses, trees, vacant lots. Bright and windy back in a cab through empty streets . . . 'I hope you find your way . . . red brick houses, trees . . . the address in empty streets,'" William S. Burroughs writes in *Exterminator*, published that year. In *The Black Tarantula*, Acker recalls a scene from her early childhood before her half sister was born. The passage will flicker through much of her writing in the coming decades like a Super-8 film loop:

My mother puts on black fur-lined boots with two-inch-pointed heels over her tan stockings, an orange-brown tight sweater over a white bra, she has large soft full breasts, a straight orange-brown skirt brown and blue triangles running down her thighs. Bright red lipstick and pink powder. Over this, her black seal coat. She looks young and pretty. We go out of the apartment together, down to the street where it's snowing, three blocks away to my favorite park. Pure white covers over the lower level: the basketball court, skating rink and adult swings, completely; the upper level where seesaws, jungle gyms, and sandboxes used to be, looks like a magic woods. My mother and I play together; she tells me she's my sister. We go to a drugstore to get ice-cream sodas; a man asks her if we're sisters.

My mother tells me my "father" isn't my real father: my real father left her when she was three months pregnant and wanted nothing to do with me, ever.

Beyond the Black Tarantula's brash, trash-talking persona, what's remarkable about this early work is the intensity Acker arrives at: accessing fleshy, emotive fragments of female experience within a framework of formalist rigor.

* * *

"Your phenomenology is phenomenal," Jackson Mac Low writes her in January after receiving a full set of *The Childlike Life of the Black Tarantula*, Parts 1–6. "I dig it the most. I don't get this stuff about people being <u>bored</u> by it . . . <u>I</u> don't believe it & I don't think <u>you</u> do."

Mac Low offers to fund her next series with an inheritance he expects to receive from his mother's estate. Reading her work triggers an extraordinary eight-page addendum to his brief letter, in which he dissects his recent sex and relationship problems with his estranged wife, Iris Lezak. "O Kathy, I'm so lonely when she wasn't here. I was crying for a couple hours this morning, even though we're going to meet for a concert (Joan Jonas) tonight," he writes. It's as if reading her work has suddenly given the fifty-two-year-old poet/composer permission to talk about his most intimate feelings.

Acker completed the final installment of The Black Tarantula by mid-September. She approached three print shops—all of which declined to produce the text-only pamphlet because "it offended their morals"—before she found someone willing to accept the work. Depressed by what she perceived as a lack of response to the later parts of the series, she collapsed with exhaustion in November. She was still dependent on Peter Gordon for financial support, although they were hardly a sexual couple any longer. One or two nights a week she slept with their mutual friend Rich Gold, an arrangement that semi-pleased everyone. *[I] decided this whole country world me is totally not totally but SO MUCH controlled by money interests the best thing I can do is find out how those money-powers work on me*, she wrote to Mac Low. *I sort of tried to commit suicide it was really awful and I hope I never return there again.* In an unpublished text titled "Diary II," she describes two attempts: *I slice open the skin of my left wrist and face with a razor blade I had taken a week before from Gil's house, the razor was too dull; the next day I knotted a black scarf around a light fixture, Peter walked in . . . I now want to find out who's controlling me economically and why.* She thought about turning the text into a new *Black Tarantula*, but then didn't: *it would bore the shit out of everyone.*

Throughout the decade Acker's letters contain many accounts of illness, abortions, fatigue, and suicidal depression, problems that continued to plague her well throughout her forties, but "all of these things," as her friend Roz Kaveney later recalled, "were completely compartmentalized."

During the weeks she was deeply depressed, Acker learned of some stocks and a small trust set up in her name by her biological father a number of years before. It was as if, by writing about her disappeared father as the Black Tarantula, she'd conjured him. Together, the funds amounted to about $350 ($1,950 in today's money), but they'd been withheld from her for years by her parents. When she threatened to sue them, they agreed to release the funds and, "under certain conditions," pay for a trip to New York. Her mother's husband, Bud Alexander, was present at Acker's birth, and he was named as her father on her birth certificate. Acker always knew that her *real* father had abandoned her mother when she was just three months pregnant, but during this contretemps, Acker learned her biological father's name and occupation for the first time. Her mother's long-ago disappeared lover Donald Lehmann was the CEO of Wildroot Cream Oil, a Buffalo-based family business that had been acquired by Colgate-Palmolive in 1959.

Acker never contacted Donald Lehmann, but she continued to think and write about his abandonment throughout her life.

As she was going to read with some friends at the Poetry Project on February 18, she accepted her parent's offer. Early that month, she flew to New York. It was during this trip that she met the artist Alan Sondheim, with whom she'd make *Blue Tape*: an intimate, antagonistic video work that haunts him to this day.

BREAKING THROUGH MEMORIES

INTO DESIRE

(1974–1975)

How can days and happenings and moments so good become
so quickly ugly, and for no reason, for no real reason? Just—
change. With nothing causing it.

—Philip K. Dick, *A Scanner Darkly*

It's doubtful that Acker stayed at her parents' apartment for very long that February, if she stayed there at all. She and Len Neufeld were no longer speaking, and—perhaps because she found his artistic crush on her awkward—she avoided seeing Jackson Mac Low. Bernadette Mayer and her boyfriend, the filmmaker Ed Bowes, were Acker's closest ties to the poetry scene and the art world, so it's likely that she stayed at their place. On February 18, 1974, she and Mel Freilicher read at the St. Mark's Poetry Project with Ed Bowes and two other friends in the "younger poet" Monday-night reading slot.

The previous year, Mayer and Bowes had made two video-tapes, *Sexless* and *matter*, with Bowes's unwieldy video camera. They lived in his loft at 74 Grand Street, one block south of Canal. To Mayer, the loft was depressing. The long, static exterior shots of lower Manhattan in Chantal Akerman's 1977 film *News from Home* record how the neighborhood looked at that time:

the camera holds on a wide, empty cobblestone street lined by vacant industrial buildings, debris blown to the curb. Mayer and Bowes were in the process of separating. Soon Mayer would move to a friend's St. Marks Place apartment, and it's possible that Acker stayed with her there.

In any event, there's no doubt that Acker met Alan Sondheim through Mayer and Bowes sometime during those weeks early in 1974. The New York art world was still small: a series of Venn diagrams in which everyone was related, if not by marriage or blood, then by friendship and sex. Everyone knew everyone then. As Acker described it that year in a postcard to the poet Ron Silliman, *Endless meshes incest*. Sondheim, then thirty-one, was a poet/musician who'd studied at Brown and worked with the poets Keith and Rosemarie Waldrop. Teaching at Rhode Island School of Design after completing his M.A at Brown, Sondheim immersed himself in studies of phenomenology and quantum physics and soon established himself in New York as a promising conceptual artist. Three of his pieces—including a faux documentation of the assassination of Richard Nixon and a diagrammatic display outlining "the general structure of the world"—were shown in the 1973 Paris Biennale. Sondheim knew Mayer and Bowes through his friendship with Vito Acconci, who'd been married to Bernadette's sister, the artist Rosemary Mayer, and in the late 1960s Acconci and Bernadette Mayer produced the seminal *0 to 9* magazine.

Early in 1974 Sondheim and his wife, Beth Cannon, were living in a loft near Fourteenth Street owned by Ed Bowes's brother, Tom. Sondheim and Cannon were soon to divorce. When Bernadette Mayer moved out of 74 Grand Street, Cannon moved in with Ed Bowes. Around the same time, Rosemary Mayer and Sondheim became an on-again, off-again couple as well. Chronology here remains vague. As Sondheim writes in his remarkable, ongoing *autobiog.txt*, an intuitive account of recalled events that begins with the year of his birth: "[I]nformation as true as I can make it. Please back-channel any and all corrections. Certainly my memory may be faulty; there are spelling errors, errors of omission, distortions, repressions, sublimations; there are errors of remorse, errors of hallucination, of dream- or virtual worlds. No errors are intentional, none designed to be hurtful, vengeful, 'setting the record straight.' (there are no records to set straight there are recordings, they set nothing. There are no clues, no cues.)"

Sondheim heard Acker read that night at St. Marks. He invited her over for dinner a day or two later, and they stayed up most of the night and talked. Like Len Neufeld, Sondheim was five years older than she was. Unlike Len Neufeld, he was confident in his work and enjoying some local—in New York, local was all that mattered—acclaim. "At this point I thought myself well on the way to some sort of fame," Sondheim writes in his *autobiog.txt*. "I felt stable artistically, although I was teetering in fact." They didn't fuck then, or maybe they did, but the next day, Acker flew back to San Francisco and thought and wrote about him on the plane. Peter Gordon was her friend, collaborator, brother, but a relationship with Alan Sondheim—or the idea of a relationship with Alan Sondheim—represented something she craved: the kind of deeply challenging sexual, intellectual, psychological exchange she'd glimpsed through her perfunctory encounter with Dan Graham but then failed to attain. Sex was a channel, but sex alone didn't always go very far.

Writing to Sondheim the next day from San Francisco, she suggested that they do a project together. It would be at once intimate and conceptual, a game played between equals. *How close can we get to each other?* she asked. *Will we become each other? Concerning my friendship with Alan Sondheim . . . The last statement of course being dependent on your agreeing to want to work with me: I thought we could send each other as much information about ourselves as possible, not only then via tape, written, video but also overwriting, redoing (as in the* TARANTULAS) *etc. establishing complicated feedback relations.* She went on to argue her case for this still-vague collaboration in a five-point argument that was, by turns, girlishly goofy and incisive about recent art history and its limited stakes. For example, point (2): *I like (don't know what word to use here but I'm sure it's completely understandable) you; this gives me an opportunity to be with you.* Point (4) continues, *I've never seen the intimacy Vito [Acconci] explores in his work explored in a real way as an occurrence between two people . . . and this fascinates me.* And she was right: the "transgressions" of contemporary art at that time were almost entirely confined to the realm of the body. In *Fuses* (1964–67), Carolee Schneemann filmed herself having sex with her then partner James Tenney; in Vito Acconci's 1972 *Seedbed*, the artist masturbated while gallery viewers walked over a platform bridge that concealed his body from them. But neither of these works, or others like it, began to describe the transactional nature of human relationships. Earlier popular movies and books such as Nicholas Roeg's 1970 film *Performance*, John Fowles's novel *The Magus*, and Eric Berne's 1964 pop-psychology classic *Games People Play* described cruelties and psychodynamics that conceptual art failed to address.

Sondheim replied by sending a package of his work to Acker. She wrote him back right away. The potential collaboration with Alan Sondheim was the first artistic work to fully engage her since she'd finished the last *Black Tarantula* almost six months before. Consequently, her next letter to him, written in real time over three days, expands to include almost everything that happens while it's being composed. Memories and events dovetail and cascade with increasing intensity. Phone calls about out-of-state readings and a never-made quasi-porn adaptation of *The Black Tarantula* that was to be called *Deep Tarantula* interrupt and increase her excitement about her connection with Sondheim and their prospective work. *I can't separate this insane project*

I'm doing with you and all my other desires, I mean (. . . all events are so connected help) would you like to sleep with me . . .

By the end of the letter she'd already begun making notes toward their collaboration, which would become an integral part of the final (and, finally, contentious) piece. As she explained in her letter to Sondheim, she composed this questionnaire after listening to a tape of Acconci's *Sleep*:

> *What do I feel about Alan?*
> *What do I feel for Alan?*
> *What do I think are Alan's main characteristics?*
> *What do I think Alan's doing in this work?*
> *How do I feel Alan's work is changing me?*
> *How do I feel this work (concerned with Alan) is changing me?*
> *Do I love Alan (totally stupid ridiculous question but I refuse to*
>   *take it out)?*

And as she writes, he calls her: *I couldn't think what to say because you seemed to be speaking my words. I mean whatever the obvious dissimilarities . . . the similarities are strong & strange.*

The next day, February 28, the day Tony Shafrazi spray-painted "KILL LIES ALL" on Picasso's *Guernica* after Lieutenant William Calley, the perpetrator of the civilian massacre at My Lai, was released on bail, she received the news (*god Phil just called up the Guernica's been defaced how wonderful I'll be back*) and continued writing to Sondheim about her life history to date. She'd gotten up to the part about her high school romance with P. Adams Sitney.

She realized that this outpouring might seem a bit strange, but she couldn't stop. *I don't know what to say. I now feel completely scared . . . UNDERSTAND I CAN'T TELL ANYMORE WHAT HAS TO DO WITH WHAT WHERE THE SO UNDERSTOOD STABLE BOUNDARIES ARE . . .* Sondheim's interest in her—which seemed simple to him at the time, a matter of basic attraction—made Acker feel that she could, and she must, tell him everything about her past/present life. She told him about her father's disappearance, which she linked to her sexual adventures at a young age (*it was a way of getting some love*); her days at the Lenox School and Brandeis University; her relationships with Bob Acker and Len Neufeld; her alliance with Peter Gordon. Perhaps most urgently, she wrote extensively about her distrust of monogamy—*my feelings are . . . always too complex and I can't stand breaking up with people*—laying the ground for a possible relationship even though they were both still attached. Like most human communication, Acker's account of her life fluctuates between rigorous honesty and self-serving white lies. Traumatized by working in the sex show, she said, *I couldn't hardly relate to men at all, didn't sleep with any men besides Lenny . . . when at the end of the summer I said to him I didn't want to sleep with him anymore . . . That was tantamount to my having to move out of the house and, because I couldn't afford to pay fixtures etc. for a new place plus was scared, away from New York.* She leaves out the part about returning to Neufeld's apartment with her new love, Peter Gordon. She wrote almost six thousand words. *I mean in a way this is crazy and totally depending on our seeing each other for 12 hours, then nothing, so fantasies explode, but I'm more interested in my and yours desire to open completely get rid of privacy explore that.*

Meanwhile, the tepid reception to the later *Tarantulas* that she'd complained of to Jackson Mac Low started to shift. In a brief, formal reply to Ron Silliman's request for a set of *The Black Tarantulas* (written at the same time she was composing her letter to Sondheim) she reports that she has no more copies—*there's been an incredible run on them, but will send you Xeroxed copies in, whatever, two days at most when I can get to Berkeley to get cheap Xerox and stapler machine.*

Back to her letter to Sondheim:

I mean why should Peter be a problem to, straightly my loving you (I'm not saying hippie-wise O we all love one another wow) I am saying that I refuse to let structures of a society I didn't pick to be born into determine how I relate to people, just because I love Peter and live with him is no reason that you and Peter can't whatever anything, I don't know, nothing's happened yet . . . o god do you understand at all I feel really close to you that's why I'm fighting, she concludes. With it, she sends dozens of pages of old and new work.

The new writing, dated March 1 and titled "BREAKING THROUGH MEMORIES INTO DESIRE," is captioned "Part III of long work." Parts I and II are almost certainly the same text as the unpublished seventh installment of *The Black Tarantula* that she'd described in her January letter to Jackson Mac Low: a *pretty straight account of my life in November and December* that would *bore the shit out of anyone.* Her meeting with Sondheim has suddenly energized this old work, and Part III begins, *How close can I get to someone? Will we become each other concerning my friendship with Alan Sondheim.*

Audaciously, she continues: *I know who Alan is: Alan is my father. He'd better be my perfect father: take care of me but not restrain me doing anything I want touch me softly with his hands and voice like everything I do. If Alan isn't my perfect Father, I'll turn away from him, unless he touches me again. I'll attack him really hard tear him. I'll make him shrivel into nothing. I have to think about myself . . .*

Reading this text in New York, Sondheim was taken aback, if not offended. Still, he was captivated. As he'd recall wryly three decades later, "[Kathy] placed me in the position of her father; I thought she was my soul mate." He suggested that they make a video together in which they'd "explore sexuality." Eventually they would call it *The Blue Tape.* Within days, he arranged advance bookings for the still-hypothetical work and raised money among friends to buy her ticket back to New York.

* * *

The London-based artist Anna Maria Pinaka has recently written about a still-contentious genre of installation and video that she describes as "porno-graphing." Marked by a "dirtiness" that transcends mere depictions of sex, "porno-graphing" imports "real-life" sexual and romantic situations into public, exhibited work. *The Blue Tape* would "explore sexuality" in highly charged, confrontational ways. The fact that this video has been exhibited more frequently in the past half decade than in the thirty years since it was made suggests that these questions of "dirtiness" have not been resolved.

Still, it's useful to read *The Blue Tape* in the context of the artistic and media mores that prevailed in its time. As Jerry Saltz wrote about Vito Acconci's *Seedbed* (1972), "Acconci . . . masturbated eight hours a day while murmuring things like, 'You're pushing your cunt down on my mouth,' or 'You're ramming your cock down my ass.' In *Seedbed*, Acconci is the producer and receiver of the work's pleasure. He is simultaneously public and private, making marks yet leaving little behind, and demonstrating ultra-awareness of his viewer while being in a semi-trance state."

Chris Burden's 1971 *Shoot* performance famously consisted of the artist being shot in the arm at close range by an assistant. In *TV Hijack* (1972), he appeared on Phyllis Lutjeans's cable TV interview show and surprised her by holding a knife to her throat. Lutjeans refused to press charges. Later, she'd explain how his assault "taught her a lesson": her desire to anchor a show was driven by her own "ego and pride."

It was an era when people seemed eager for "lessons." A deluge of feature articles, photos, and first-person accounts of EST seminars, Synanon "games," sensitivity training, and encounter groups were used to describe—or create the revisionist-hippie, post-political zeitgeist on TV and in mass-market lifestyle and news magazines.

Over the course of a decade between the late 1960s and '70s, the Synanon organization staged seventy-two-hour marathon therapy "trips" at their Marin County and Oakland facilities, which peaked when exhausted trippers broke down. "You will learn more about yourself, your fellow man, the world, the nature of reality than you would in four years. Let your ego go . . . let things happen to you," preached the leader, Charles Dederich. "The game," one survivor reported, "took on each Unbroken's dirty rotten story with great brutality. The broken joined the attack. Some began to hallucinate." Embraced by celebrities and widely accepted within the addiction and thera-peutic communities, Synanon's confrontational treatment became so mainstream that it was often state mandated for youthful offenders in juvenile court. "If you keep people up long enough," Dederich would later admit in a deposition, "you can make them believe anything."

Acker's disclosures to Sondheim seem shockingly brutal when compared with contemporaneous works of visual art. But seen in the context of the massively publicized "human potential" movement, they seem almost benign.

* * *

A couple of weeks later, Acker arrived at Sondheim's New York apartment just after—or perhaps just before—Beth Cannon left. As Sondheim recalls, "[T]he next day and next few days were terrible; we made the tapes—there were more than one—in the midst of the terror. Emily, who had been my student at RISD, filmed the materials on a EIAJ black-and-white Sony deck . . . We pushed things as far as we could. I felt needy. I hated myself. I remember Kathy being suicidal, accidentally locked out of the flat when Emily and I took a break; she'd wanted to be alone. Neither of us were in great shape . . ."

In the first scene of the fifty-four-minute *Blue Tape*, Acker sits on the floor, her back against a white-painted brick wall. Facing the camera, she speaks to the viewer with calm gravitas. Her deposition seems far more contained than the recent events it describes:

> *I met Alan Sondheim when I was in New York about two or three weeks ago. I had dinner at his and Beth's apartment the last night I was in New York and I ended up talking to Alan for about twelve hours. We talked mainly about certain gestural and mental similarities we had both noticed that existed between us. And at the end decided to do a piece together.*

At twenty-six, she looks like a young Emma Goldman. Her brown hair is shaved into a buzz cut. She wears round rimless glasses, a sleeveless wife-beater T-shirt, and a loose button-down shirt. Her neck is wrapped tight in a thick cotton Indian scarf, the kind of scarf they still sold in the head shops that remained on Haight Street.

> *The next day I went back to California. And immediately decided to do a memory experiment. At that point my work was into doing various rather strange memory experiments. And I called this one* Breaking Through Memory Into Desire. *I was trying to find out what the structures or structure of intentions were behind my remembering. . . . And I ended up with a very strong emotional passage which I sent to Alan. Oh, let me also add that I don't know who my father is. He left my mother when she was three or four months pregnant, according to her story. And that in my life whenever a man has tried to act fatherly to me, I've totally rejected him.*

Forgotten for more than two decades, *The Blue Tape* resurfaced in 2000. The filmmaker Tony Conrad, a friend and colleague of

Sondheim's who'd since moved to Buffalo, New York, had kept and restored it. As well as providing an early example of what Pinaka calls "porno-graphing," *The Blue Tape* stands as a record of how Acker looked and conducted herself before she became, as Carolee Schneemann once put it, "her own configurated Kathy Acker."

The camera zooms closer in on her face as Sondheim, off-screen, reads aloud from her text, which has now become evidentiary, the source of a conflict to be played out between them during the next fifty minutes:

> *And I received a work dated March 1st. Section from Part III of long work, Breaking Through Memory Into Desire. "How close can I get to someone where we become each other, concerning my friendship with Alan Sondheim. Being human is too boring and difficult. Who wants to be human all the time. I'm sick of being rational and doing things right I'm becoming a cat. I sit in the bathtub, first Rich comes over afternoon, 1:30, wakes me up. We fuck two, two and a half times. He doesn't come the third time because Peter calls. He's coming home. We don't have time . . ."*

The camera zooms closer in on her face when he reaches the part where she identifies him as her father and threatens to make him *shrivel into nothing* if he fails in this role. Blinking intermittently, she sits very still with a determined, implacable gaze. He continues:

> *How can anyone go from outside in, understand what is outside, except through him, herself . . . But I am nothing. The universe is everything. I have to figure out how the universe works. TBT . . . Alan, I don't understand a lot of what you write. You understand everything I write. I understand you when you talk to me and I feel wonderful . . . I don't have to be a mother to you as I have to be to most people I know. I don't want that, not now . . . I don't want anything but Alan's hand on me. I want to know what's happening.*

When he finishes reading, still on camera, she presents her defense:

At that point what I was trying to do was I had begun using Alan as I would use an analyst to get to memories which were too painful for me to get to any other way. And I think what the issue is, and I think what we've decided, is that I agree with Alan that I was wrong to send him that material. In that way I was ripping him off because I was using him as, say, an analyst.

However what the problem is here and what we're trying to explore is whether I was right to use him at all. That is I feel that when I write I can do anything as long as I'm not viciously saying something about someone they don't want said about them, for my purposes of exploration. However Alan feels that I was ripping him off because I was using him. And he felt that he was able to feel feelings for me. I gave him that opportunity as if I was truly feeling those feelings.

From there, decorum breaks down and the sequence turns into a therapeutic bickering match. Still off camera, Sondheim struggles to process exactly what she's asking of him: "I almost feel that what I should do since you have your father's last name and at least his place of employment, is . . . go and find him. And come back to you a complete mimic . . . And that I would then be able to say to you everything is okay . . ." *But that's not what I want now.* "But then what do you want now? Because I think the change would be so deep in you. At least your crying on the phone . . . was almost as if something was forcing itself out, something you didn't want to come to the surface at all." She tells him she's over it; he wonders if she can reverse her desires so fast, but she protests: *You're telling me you know more about myself than I do . . . It's a question of authority.*

Flummoxed by this, Sondheim protests: "You put things in a control situation so much of the time, I almost feel that I'm afraid of ordinary discourse." He senses, correctly, that she's winning the game: a game that, till now, he did not understand. A philosopher/mathematician, Sondheim assumed he was there to "explore sexuality" with an interesting, forthcoming young woman. Thirty years later he'd simply conclude, "I was more attracted to her than she was to me." But in *Blue Tape*, he protests: "You . . . put me in a position of feeling—of saying that I'm controlling you, when in fact I'm doing nothing of the sort . . . And so what happens is that you somehow gain the power that you're saying you don't have." *Do you want to play my father now?* she asks provocatively.

"Alan is not capable perhaps. Alan is a thirty-one-year-old artist. Alan is not in a position simply to control or manipulate lives."

That's your decision about yourself.

"It's very hard to know what are decisions about myself or what have been decided for me."

When you say a statement like that, what I feel is that it puts me in a guilt situation.

"I did not say that to put you in a guilt situation! I had no inkling that that's going to put you in a guilt situation. I'm not trying to attack you. I'm simply saying as your father, I would feel very safe. Because it would be my choice in the first place to leave you. And you're a very powerful person at this point. And God knows, if you're powerful now, what you're gonna be like in a couple of years. There's gonna be hell to pay for anybody who gets in touch with you. You're gonna burn people. You're gonna kill people, baby, you really are."

Her face lights up for the first time since the tape began. She nods and smiles.

In the next scene, the camera holds on her bare chest. She's fondling her breasts as Sondheim softly reads excerpts and comments on his *General Structure of the World,* a three-hundred-page philosophical work:

I want you to look to the left of the monitor and listen to me talk about the world. I want to talk about the world and I want to have you follow me. I want you to think that I'm a great artist . . .

One of the characteristics of the world is the grounding of its phenomenology in history. What does that mean? Can you follow what I mean? . . . Can you understand how long it took to write that sentence? Do you understand what intensity necessitates? . . .

I am saying this, reading it from a page. I am concentrating on the page. I am paying no attention to the image on the screen . . . Don't look at the screen. Pay no attention to it. Listen to my voice. She's drawing power away from me. I've got to take it back. I've got to convince you that the important thing is to pay attention to the world, to pay attention to the external world . . .

Cut to: Extreme close-up, his fingers massaging her vulva and clit, her voice offscreen:

No, lower. Yeah. No, that's too hard. Higher. No, no, no. There. Yeah, that's okay . . . That's better. Oh that's good . . . No, no, no, keep going. Ow. Shit. Get closer to my clit. No, no, no, not there. Yeah, there. Oh that's good.

Cut back to: Acker, fully dressed as in the first scene, sitting against the brick wall and analyzing the power dynamics of their relationship:

What is interesting to me [about the last section] is how that relates to my and Alan's sexuality to the way we've been having sex the last two days. Because there's a lot of discrepancy between the amount of pleasure we give each other. I'm able to give Alan a lot more pleasure than he's able to give me . . . And this enables me . . . to have more power over Alan . . . I mean, one way in which

> *I feel I have power in a relationship is that I can give Alan a great deal of sexual pleasure. And I often feel that men get their power over me by pleasing me a great deal, so I feel there's a discrepancy there in our power.*

And then it's his turn to speak in this Houellebecqian fugue of unhappiness. Appearing onscreen for the first time, running his hands through his halolike Jewfro, he protests:

> I might as well say what I feel . . . When I first met Kathy . . . I didn't think that my relationship had anything to do at all with power. I never even thought of power . . . control . . . And I find myself a little bit succumbing to what might be a control situation. That is, I obviously can't sit on a chair next to Kathy and discuss mathematical hierarchies of transformations, which is what a large part of my present work is about . . . Whereas it's very easy to discuss sexuality, because it's [a thing] we have in common. This automatically gives her a sense of power. And the fact that this for me is a public as well as a private domain, while for her it seems to be a public domain, is the second source of her power . . . It seems to me that none of this tape has anything to do with a notion of togetherness, with me and Kathy being together. But more about the fact that we seem to be in a very unfortunate and unhappy situation, and trying desperately to get apart.

After a short "commercial break," he appears naked and sprawled on a mattress for the next fifteen minutes, struggling to speak about the hierarchy of transformations as she gives him a consummate blow job: "I wonder whether I'm going to come while I'm desperately trying to hold on to my language . . . At the same time while I talk, I'm beginning to think that the words are sort of a defense . . ."And then he comes violently, loud and abandoned, and the scene ends.

"I can no longer use words such as love or fun," he says in a short denouement. And she adds: *I feel extremely tired and sad . . . I want to say that I'm scared . . . that you'll take the power away from my work. But I'm . . . right now I'm beginning to hate the words I, my, I, my, I, my. I can't think about my feelings.*

They showed the tape on March 18 at the St. Marks Poetry Project. Strangely, Len Neufeld's name appears beside Sondheim's on the schedule that night. *Endless meshes incest.* There was dead silence afterward. Vito Acconci was there. No one applauded or spoke except for Jackson Mac Low, who told them he thought "it was a very brave thing that you did."

And then she returned to San Francisco. A couple of months later, she'd write to Bernadette Mayer: *I just made this tape with Elly Antin in which we talk and since I hadn't told her all about what happened with Alan Sondheim in NY I told her on tape, it was great, it was REALLY NASTY and it's going to be played . . . Elly's going to take tape to NY to get played on WBAI so everyone will learn know what a shit Alan is I got my revenge.*

The Blue Tape played later at Yale, where everyone laughed. At RISD, they cried. "It depended on the first responder," Sondheim writes in his *autobiog.txt.* "Everyone followed suit; everyone was on an emotional edge." In 1977 it played at the Whitney. To Sondheim's horror, his parents drove in from Wilkes-Barre, Pennsylvania. "For them, the Whitney was a kind of validation."

"Worlds fall apart," Sondheim wrote. "Over the years, the split with my parents widened; how could they have seen that tape without total collapse?

"Bernadette didn't speak to me again. I was with her sister for a while. Vito and I stopped speaking. Around 1977 I moved out of New York and around 1990 I moved back. A lot has happened since then."

"I'd never been able to watch the tape; it was too painful," he wrote in 2002. "It still is."

Acker never spoke or wrote about *The Blue Tape*. In subsequent years she became increasingly occupied with questions of interpersonal power and control. She came to believe that sexuality formed the essence of selfhood, and she wrote about this over and over again. Acker died at age fifty. If she'd lived longer, would she have changed her mind?

* * *

I absolutely love to fuck, begins the first section of *I Dreamt I Was a Nymphomaniac: Imagining.* By the time she began this new six-part serial novella in June, her Black Tarantula mailing list had more than doubled. *I'm 27 and I love to fuck. Sometimes with people I want to fuck; sometimes, and I can't tell when but I remember these times, with anybody who'll touch me.* Except for financially, the first series had been a tremendous success in every respect. People now knew who she was. As she wrote to Bernadette Mayer early that summer, *[I] went to this party where all these people said they knew my work . . . so I felt totally fantastic.* As she'd later reflect, *When I was sending them out I had this community which I've never had since.*

Back in San Francisco with Peter Gordon after the draining collaboration with Alan Sondheim, she realized that she could continue her serial work, turning it into a personal praxis. She no longer wrote poems. She thought deeply about literary forms, but she didn't quite see herself yet as a "novelist." As she'd explain later, *I never thought I had imagination . . . I hated it really. I've never imagined anything. I've used texts, I've used friends, I've used memories but I've never created in that way . . . They've used the words "creativity" and "imagination" to place literature on a pedestal, which makes it both unavailable, and doesn't allow it to have the range it should have. I couldn't have cared less [about narrative development] in those days. I wrote so many pages a day and that was that . . . I would make a few other rules, such as you're not allowed to rewrite . . . It was task work.*

Once she'd established an audience as the Black Tarantula, she found the constraint of a circumscribed time frame—to begin and finish a work—very useful. Early that summer, she came up with a plan. For the first half of each year she'd continue her free-form personal writing, but from June through December she'd be "in production," writing serial pamphlets as the Black Tarantula.

Perhaps in the wake of her encounter with Sondheim, she was reading philosophy: Gustav Bergmann and Henri Bergson, although sometimes she mixed up their names. However improbable it might seem that such writing as *I wanted him to rip off my skin, take me away to where I'd always be insane* owes a debt to phenomenology and logical positivism, there's no doubt that Acker's readings of these thinkers helped shape her composition of the *Nymphomaniac* pamphlets.

In "Some Reflections on Time," Bergmann argued that since space and time are symbolized in language by descriptive, not logical constraints, they are not part of the world's form, but part of its content: "The world is not in space and time; space and time are in the world." Time, Bergson wrote, in *Time and Free Will: An Essay on the Immediate Data of Consciousness*, can only be truly perceived internally, and so it will always be altered and colored by memory. Consciousness, or one's internal life, is a duration that can be shown only indirectly through selective images and grasped intuitively. Such ideas were made manifest in numerous artworks throughout the 1960s and '70s. In 1969 Robert Smithson famously retraced the steps of a nineteenth-century explorer through the Yucatán, placing mirrors beside Mayan ruins and natural sites, and then photographing them. His "Incidents of Mirror-Travel in the Yucatan" was composed of nine photos and a descriptively speculative text: "A horizon is something else other than a horizon; it is closedness in openness, it is an enchanted region where down is up. Space can be approached, but time is far away. Time is devoid of objects when one displaces all destination . . . Yucatan is elsewhere."

In each of *Nymphomaniac*'s six sections, Acker composes a few pages of text collaged from her diaries and fragments of porn novels. And then she repeats, and repeats, and repeats them, like a fugue in the minimalist compositions of John Cage or Steve Reich or Terry Riley. It could be, as some scholarship has it, that repetition signals a "radical break from a dominant culture," that "defining oneself against a system inevitably will reproduce some qualities of that system." It could be, as Acker later explained in a 1989 interview with Ellen Friedman, that the work interrogates *what the reader remember[s] when you repeat something over and over again*, or it could be that it was a means of increasing her page count. All three possibilities are simultaneously plausible. In any event, while the collisions between Acker's "I's" in *The Childlike Life of the Black Tarantula* make the short work compulsively readable, *Nymphomaniac* is more explicitly experimental. Whatever interest the text holds lies in its construction.

I realized, she told Barry Alpert in their March 1976 conversation, *that the idea in* The Childlike Life *was very naïve . . . that it didn't go far enough . . . because I wasn't thinking about the nature of language . . . In* Nymphomaniac, *I started with this stuff about time. What I did is repeat things. I wanted to see if repeating would change things. I was searching for something. Trying to figure out how language works. It was harder to write than the first.*

She and Gordon produced the pamphlets at the Empty Elevator Shaft, a print shop and bookstore in Noe Valley.

In Part 4, "san francisco and . . ." she reframes the story of her break with Len Neufeld: *I told the guy I was living with I no longer wanted to fuck him. He told me to fuck or split. Then he started beating me up. I had to split fast. Either I could get a new apartment in New York City or split to California, the only other place I had friends. Either way I needed a lot of money . . .* She sent the pamphlet to Bernadette Mayer, who remarked to a mutual friend that she found it "polemic." When Acker heard this, she responded directly:

> *Dear Bernadette polemic hmmmm I don't know it all doesn't fit together anyway & polemics are supposed to fit together but. We'll get back to this I sure hate criticism.*

After rehashing the logistics of a St. Marks reading with Hannah Weiner that Mayer was arranging for her in the new year (this time, in the Wednesday-night slot for "established poets") she returns to the question:

> *I don't take criticism very lightly: Being new in SF where all poets are thoughtless due to Duncan & McClure claptrap & to being in NY where some poets still think etc I'm stating the case rather strongly, I'm sick of beautiful words word-phrases etc. Or politically which is why I have reservations about 4th* NYMPHO *tho since I ripped it off (all the* NYMPHO*'s by the way are totally ripped off but too boring to list books I've copied): A writer writes some great work which is great cause X reads it & X says right that's how things are. Image Pattern Form. Then X goes perceives & says yeah, just like the book. Image. Creating images . . . I don't know you see I suspect fascism. Telling people how to see. Extasy. I don't trust it. Better remain cool even boring present my shit say there it is take it or leave it. And open up. Possibilities for all kinds of language: "poetical" and mathematical & propaganda etc . . . Why not be polemic? Why be always the fucking same thing? Why do so many "poems" look & sound alike whereas when I go into a bookstore I see all kinds of shit & the writing don't look the same. Why shouldn't writing be everything? It's different times/time—*

beings too—as "Blue" Gene says, up to now everyone's been climax oriented, that's no longer feasible, why have beginnings ends better worse good bad divisions. So I send out stuff once a month so I have only 30 days to write print up send out each book so I force yourself to stop worrying whether it's good or bad. Though I worry about everything. That's no longer important. Just the why's important. And the opening up. Ideas are most important. Don't cover ideas with fancy writing. Blah blah.

This would be her next-to-last letter to Bernadette Mayer. The final letter, written to Mayer in Massachusetts after Acker had moved to New York, was more composed and distant: *Dear Bernadette, Good to hear from you and glad you liked the book— when's the baby due? . . . Did you like Connie's book? . . . How's Lewis?*

That summer of 1974, Patty Hearst sent out her seventh communiqué as Tania, and Gordon joined a local rock band, Butch Whacks and the Glass Packs. Butch Whacks were in demand as openers for such major bands as Boz Scaggs and the Doobie Brothers, so Gordon was often touring. He'd nearly finished his M.A. at Mills College, and the band had a month-long gig coming up in Chicago early in January. He and Acker were talking about moving to New York after that. *I now need the input*, Acker wrote to Mac Low. Jill Kroesen had already moved back to New York. Their apartment at 46 Belvedere had become a meeting place for rock musicians—*I'm not very interested I don't like coke for some reason I'm not fucking around any more. I got sick of fucking people who after three days bore me so I don't fuck anyone but Peter but then cause he's on the road a lot I'm horny*, she told Mac Low. She caught a six-week flu, read Brecht, considered studying German.

The poet Kenneth Rexroth, who'd been an early fan of Acker's work, attempted to get *The Childlike Life* republished with his friend Noel Young's Capra Press. Rexroth offered to write an introduction, but Young declined. As Acker reported to Jackson Mac Low in November, *It sounded too good to be true . . . Noel Young writes me I'm a lousy writer cause I'm "too green." I don't even know what that means . . . Depression. I wish all these shits would go to hell. I know no one's going to print them anyway. Except for Peter it'd be starvation.*

And then, on December 5, she received a letter from the artist Leandro Katz and the critic Ted Castle, founders and coeditors of the highly literary New York independent press TVRT (The Vanishing Rotating Triangle Press). "Dear Kathy Acker, Since you began issuing 'The Childlike Life' we have read each installment of your writing with great interest and pleasure . . . We are enclosing a check as a contribution to your work. . . . We would like to publish some of your work. It would be possible to republish *The Childlike Life* in one book, or perhaps a different work . . . There is no urgency in these propositions, but we hope to hear from you . . . Please let us know what you think of doing a book with us."

Since starting the hobbyist but prestigious press in 1970, Katz and Castle had published books by Guy Debord, John Ashbery, César Vallejo, and Nicanor Parra. Their letter is one of the very few pieces of correspondence Acker kept in her archive. In 1975 TVRT would publish *The Childlike Life* and *The Adult Life of Toulouse Lautrec*, Acker's third serial work.

Eventually a feud between Acker and these early champions of her writing would lead to the demise of the press. But the letter from Katz and Castle was surely a sign. When Acker and Gordon left for his Butch Whacks gig in Chicago that January, they would not return to San Francisco. Together or separately, they were determined to move to New York.

TASTING AND SPITTING

(1975–1979)

In Times as ours now, in a city with troubles we quite often feel like spitting, even vomiting. But today just two days after thanksgiving and shortly before Christmas we will be contented with spit. To spit of the junk of intake . . . spit of Junk-liquids . . . after a good taste, man, woman and child needs a relieve [sic].

—Lil Picard, *Tasting and Spitting*

Acker stayed with Peter Gordon for about a week at Chicago's Playboy Club, and then she traveled on to New York. Her friend, the poet Clayton Eshleman, agreed to hold on to her stuff at his San Francisco apartment until she found somewhere to land. At this point Acker and Gordon weren't sure if they were still actually together, but their plan was for him to join her at the end of the month wherever she was in New York. Which he did for a while and then left.

Acker's first stop was Bernadette Mayer's spacious apartment at 65 Second Avenue, where Mayer had moved after breaking up with Ed Bowes. She had set up Acker's reading with Hannah Weiner on February 19, 1975, at St. Marks and had invited Acker to stay at her place while she was in town.

Arriving at Mayer's five or six weeks before the event was, perhaps, a stretch. It's doubtful that Mayer intended her apartment to become the base camp for Acker and Gordon's move to New York, and the arrangement didn't last long.

Mayer was thirty years old. After an intense, brief affair the summer before with the poet Anne Waldman, she'd fallen in love with Waldman's long-ago former husband, the poet and novelist Lewis Warsh, who was then living with somebody else.

Astrologists tell us that the first Saturn return occurs between the ages of twenty-seven and twenty-nine. The planet Saturn— lord of chronological time, ruler of the bones and the skin, structure and form—takes about twenty-nine years to orbit the sun and return to the place where it was when a person was born. To astrologers, a person's Saturn return marks the time of adulthood. As the writer and astrologer Ariana Reines explains, "People have breakdowns and become suicidal in their Saturn return (and rock stars die) because of a lack of structure in their lives, which all of a sudden seems like it's going to kill them, or does." It's the time when people question how to live the rest of their lives.

By the time Acker arrived on the scene, Mayer and Warsh had already decided they wanted to have a child, and he'd left his partner to move into Bernadette's place. By the end of the year, they would marry, their first child would be born, and they'd move away from New York.

Gordon arrived from Chicago as planned, but the atmosphere in the apartment was strained, so he left. Acker's friendship with Mayer at that point was tense—it had never been fully relaxed—but she stayed on until things blew up at the end of the month.

As Acker would write in a letter to Ron Silliman, the trouble began when she buzzed a distraught Anne Waldman in from the street late at night. "Don't answer," Bernadette called out to

Acker from the bedroom she shared with Warsh. "It's Anne." They'd all just attended Anne Waldman's St. Mark's Wednesday-night reading of, mostly, poems about her and Bernadette's summer affair. By now it was well after midnight, and Acker ignored Bernadette's plea and buzzed Anne in anyway. Waldman had just had a huge fight with her soon-to-be-ex boyfriend Michael Brownstein, who, as Acker reports, told Waldman that "she had no right to reveal so many personal feelings" in her poems. Waldman, by Acker's account, was hysterical, standing out in the hall and begging to be let into the apartment because she had nowhere else to go.

Acker opened the door and begged Lewis and Bernadette to come out so they all could talk. Lewis gave Anne a valium, and then Acker and Anne sat in the living room for a while, until a loud crash rang out from Lewis and Bernadette's room. Warsh emerged from the room and told them both to get out. "Lewis, I just want someone to talk to," Waldman sobbed. "I have no one to talk to. I thought you were my friend." "Get out of here," Warsh replied. "Please, Lewis—" "You two—Get out." Acker walked Waldman home. By then it was three a.m. Kathy returned to the building and buzzed the apartment of another friend, the musician Rhys Chatham, who grudgingly let her in and said, "You can stay here tonight, but you can't stay any longer."

What's interesting about the incident of February 26—beyond the frisson of unearthing an arcane piece of gossip about these great poets' earlier lives—is the pains Acker took to record it. Replete with dialogue, the story unfolds as a three-page set scene in a long letter written to Silliman early that March. Sticking to the six-months-on/six-months-off schedule she'd maintained since *The Childlike Life*, Acker wouldn't start writing *The Adult Life of Toulouse Lautrec*, her third and last serial work, until early June, but she was already rethinking her methodology. She wanted to use a stronger narrative line in these new texts.

On the verge of her twenty-eighth birthday, Acker responded to her Saturn return wake-up call mostly through work. Now that she was officially part of the poetry world, she'd become bored, starting to see herself more as a novelist. But the question that vexed her in San Diego was still unresolved. How to write fiction without moving relatable characters through an invented plot? She despised the work of such literary fiction writers as Joyce Carol Oates and Donald Barthelme, who were revered at the time. Still, she didn't want to be stuck in the ghetto of "experimental" writing. She began looking toward nineteenth-century novels and contemporary mass-market paperbacks as models that might be adapted and then synthesized with her own free-form diary texts.

The Adult Life of Toulouse Lautrec, written in 1975 and published as a series of pamphlets by Acker and TVRT in 1976, was the final and most conventionally novelistic, technically adept of her three early serial works. She'd had misgivings about the second, *I Dreamt I Was A Nymphomaniac: Imagining*, as soon as she finished the work. As she wrote to Ron Silliman late in 1974, *Thanks for the money and especially for word "marvelous" about last book since I've been totally depressed about it decided in horrible mood it stinks because not crummy enough.* Finally she decided that since she'd started the serial series by writing through childhood, she'd conclude it as an "adult." *I even feel like an adult (huh) I mean the new book's called* The Adult Life of Toulouse Lautrec, she wrote to Silliman when she began it half a year later in New York.

* * *

For the next four months, until Peter Gordon sublet the artist Constance DeJong's apartment and Acker moved in, they couch-surfed at various friends' apartments, sometimes together, more often alone. For a while Acker crashed at the Fluxus artists Dick

Higgins and Alison Knowles' SoHo loft. Then she moved west to Richard Heyman's three-story brick building on Greenwich and Spring streets that housed the Ear Inn. Used as a weekend venue for experimental music performance and poetry readings, the bar was otherwise frequented by truck drivers from the warehouse district. Moving around lower Manhattan, Acker used TVRT's East Fourth Street office as her return mailing address.

Her discipline during these rootless months was, as always, formidable. Soon after arriving back in New York, she discovered the open dance/movement classes that were held in loft studios with wood floors and huge rattling windows, in apartments and theater spaces rented on an hourly basis by soon-to-be-legendary dancer/choreographers Simone Forti, Trisha Brown, and Kenneth King. No formal dance steps were taught. Each artist sought to convey his or her singular approach to the body and its movement through space. Kenneth King shared Acker's background in philosophy and Latin. His "grid dances"—in which the performers improvised moves within hypothetical lined grids on the floor—must have seemed to Acker like an embodied analogue to her own texts. In Forti's workshops, dancers crawled and ran and rolled from one end of a long, rectangular loft to another as if they were in a river, circumnavigating boulders. Dance became Acker's new passion, and she embraced the community's grueling regime of back-to-back classes preceded by two hours of yoga and followed by marathon jams. She read *The Thinking Body*, Mabel Elsworth Todd's treatise on ideokinesis, and pondered the difference between linguistic and physical consciousness. A friend got her a part-time job taking tickets at the dance/performance venue the Kitchen for $15 a week.

Acker struck up a sexual friendship with the younger composer Rhys Chatham. As she wrote to Ron Silliman: *I've also been fucking this other guy Rhys Chatham . . . but he's more idiotic & nonsensible & childish than me . . . We get along well tho: we leave* each other alone, *don't interfere in each other's lives, basically have nothing to do with each other.* She got pregnant and had an abortion. *O my god I'm pregnant! Should I stick a hanger up my cunt?* she wrote him around the same time TVRT released *The Childlike Life of the Black Tarantula*, her first "real," non–self-published book. But mostly, when she wasn't dancing, she read, wrote, and thought about writing.

I hate NYC. I totally hate NYC, she wrote to Ron Silliman in March 1975. *I hate the Protestant work ethic, the real apolitical coldness of the artists, the competition for what? . . . [M]y life's gone topsy-turvy . . . since I hit this town; so confused I couldn't write anyone for awhile but now writing you & the Antins . . . probably cause I'm running a fever today, so am at 1:45 a.m. huddled up in corner writing letters rather than dancing and/or writing.* Her first TVRT book, with Jill Kroesen's collage of a black tarantula superimposed over Acker's angular face, would come out in ten days, but this was a fact she downplayed. . . . *that's old stuff. Who's interested—*

Soon, though, her feelings about being back in New York would change.

By the beginning of June, she'd write to Ron Silliman, *NYC calming down, or me calming down . . . In spite of my everlasting hatred of this city . . . people band together, the art community's incredibly strong here. In SF I thought no one gave a shit about my books here I'm some kind of star, but that doesn't matter anymore well maybe cause I have it here: that recognition . . .* But that didn't mean she wasn't still lonely: *since no one's gonna give an inch, that defines the sex & emotional (love) scene: macho. I've even become incredibly macho to survive, like everyone else when I'm horny I go pick someone up why should I fuck a friend, when I can fuck a stranger, & either way don't want to get involved. After all I've got my work . . . so you see my pet how "work" is all important here . . .*

For almost exactly a year Acker would write Silliman long, detailed reports about her life in New York, telling him everything about who she was seeing, what she was reading and thinking, and the process she had devised to write *Toulouse Lautrec*. When Silliman's collection of poems *The Chinese Notebook* came out, she sent him a confusing response composed in a Department of Health waiting room where she was filling out forms to receive Medicaid. Her letter is mostly a critique of Silliman's new published work : *By the way, how do I "experience language directly"? I'll be damned if I can ever separate language from my use of it from my perceiving/desires . . . You're dealing with language in CN only in a certain way . . . How would you write a section of CN after fucking for 5 hours? After long yoga session? . . .* but she ends with a fan-girl P.S.: *I think* The Chinese Notebook *has made me fall in love with you. What'm I supposed to do about it?* As she finished each section of *Toulouse Lautrec*, she sent the printed pamphlets, or sometimes the early pages, to him. Her crush, or faux crush, on Ron Silliman—and, by extension, the intellectually fashionable language-oriented poetry group he represented to her—becomes the centerpiece of Part 2 in *Toulouse Lautrec*:

> *The night before I was going to Paris, I went over to Ron's house to see him once more and say goodbye to him. We talked for hours, again about writing . . . About midnight I said, "I'd better go." He says, "You can stay the night if you want to."*
>
> *I feel confused. I don't know what to do. I figure I should stay the night because I've been wanting to. I don't know how to approach Ron sexually . . . I walk into the tiny worm in which's his bed, leaf through his new work. It looks terrific. I turn around to him. He's larger than me. Is he as frightened as I am?*
>
> *I'm not used to seeing Ron like this . . . We take our clothes off . . . He's very tender to me.*

I want hot violent passionate sex. That way the intensity of my physical feelings will make me forget not have to deal with the person I'm with, the total confusion I'm feeling.

Ron's so gentle with me. I can't handle it. He wants to kiss my lips. I'm committed to going to Paris . . . I keep licking nibbling at, squeezing sucking, rubbing his cock so I don't have to look at his face . . .

I love Ron mainly because I love his work. I always fall in love that way. Ron's a great poet: His varied sensuous language reflects and questions itself. What emerges, finally, is a restless deeply-perceiving consciousness. A consciousness, finally, I don't understand. I adore him.

With the exception of *Nymphomaniac*, each time Acker worked on a project, she selected, perhaps unconsciously, a "silent partner" as her ideal reader: a confidant, always male, who would serve as an oblique addressee. Writing the diaries that would form *Politics,* she sent pages to Jerome Rothenberg. For *The Childlike Life*, she chose Jackson Mac Low. Her text for *The Blue Tape* was written directly to Alan Sondheim. As she prepared to start writing *Toulouse Lautrec*, Ron Silliman stepped into this role. Several years later, as she began writing *Great Expectations*, the emotionally charged synthesis of her writing experiments that became her first breakthrough book, she chose the British writer and translator Paul Buck as her addressee. *Don Quixote*, composed on the eve of her first commercial publication and mainstream success, was directed to the filmmaker and scholar Peter Wollen. But as soon as her first flush of fame hit, she stopped.

* * *

The New York *Daily News* wouldn't publish its famed headline—FORD TO CITY: DROP DEAD—until the end of October, but by the summer of 1975 the conditions surrounding the city's near bankruptcy were manifest everywhere.

Writing to Ron Silliman early that June, Acker described *the sense everyone has that it's doomed.* Standing in line for food stamps, one of her fellow recipients prophesized *"the government's gonna close off the cities within the next ten years cause they don't need the cities and they can't handle the incredible urban problems anymore . . ."*

50,000 city workers just got laid off, she continued; *. . . the city's badly in debt, it's gonna be a hot summer baby, no relief in sight . . . this knowledge . . . makes everyone act like he/she better grab do hold on do anything not only to survive but to enjoy all he/she can . . . Rome at its decay as we sail into the Middle Ages on some tiny raft . . . the artists say "I'm here because it's so exciting the art ideas excitement keep me working hard" but that's a truckload of shit they're just becoming the shit by saying that . . . the fact is: everyone with this impending doom rushing to survive & be happy means no one's gonna give an inch, people band together, the art community's incredibly strong here.* Acker, apparently, saw no correlation between the catastrophic municipal debt and a well-educated twenty-eight-year-old Jewish white girl availing herself of social welfare services . . . but at the time, nobody did. Throughout the 1970s, welfare, unemployment insurance, and disability SSI were the de facto grants that funded most of New York's off-the-grid artistic enterprises.

More than four decades later, it's almost impossible to imagine the texture of daily life during an era as wholly mythologized as 1970s New York. Memoirs and novels, photography exhibitions, ephemera, and archival blogs summon a vision of unrepeatable freedom and danger. And yet it's always the last call for the last avant-garde. Molly Crabapple's 2015 *Drawing Blood* describes her generation's adventures in the pre-Crash bars and clubs of '00's New York. Some of the most interesting recollections of the mid-'70s New York art world come from the artists Ross

Bleckner—"You know, the '70s were dull. Then there was a little bit of energized nightlife that was instigated by Studio 54"—and Chuck Close: "We would play this game where you would empty the contents of a salt shaker and make a thin layer of salt on the tablecloths. Then you would have to make a drawing of someone's painting or sculpture. Just drawing it with our finger. And everyone guessed within three seconds. It was amazing that everyone's work could be reduced to a few shapes."

In New York, Acker became close friends with Pooh Kaye, a dancer, choreographer, and filmmaker who'd go on to found the company Eccentric Motions, and the writer and artist Constance DeJong. DeJong had moved to New York with the idea of doing graduate studies in literature, but the classes were not to her liking, so she dropped out and worked as a waitress. She'd already started writing her first book, *Modern Love*, a fractured but highly narrative work that veers between stealth observation, crime, and generic romance in a female first person.

Although DeJong's early work was more seamless and less frenetically written than Acker's, it was driven by strikingly similar questions. How to write prose that engages the reader without relying on an archaic narrative structure where invented characters move toward greater self-knowledge through a coherent plot? DeJong did not see the world in this way. Reality was never coherent, and identity was fluid, unfixed. Both she and Acker were also radically feeling their way toward a means of depicting the position of straight women of their generation and class. Beneficiaries of second-wave feminism, they were equal participants in a culture that still played by macho, heterosexual male rules. What could they do with their freedom? The first chapter of *Modern Love* begins:

> *Everywhere I go I see losers. Misfits like myself who can't make it in the world. In London New York Morocco Rome India Paris*

I've started seeing the same people. I think I'm seeing the same people. I wander around staring at strangers thinking I know you from somewhere. I don't know where. The streets are always crowded and narrow, full of men. It's always night and all strangers are men.

. . . I think I have to have a past. I think too much. A common malady. I make a vow: restrain yourself, become more or less observant, use fewer French and/or fancy words. I have to watch myself. I was a seven-year dreamer. I live two, three, four multiple lives; I get distracted in these crowded narrow passages. I have to watch myself; it's not safe for a woman to be alone on the streets. Have to get off. I'll take someone home. Hey honey, come up to my place, I'll show you my best recipes. Do you have a lot of cash? Shameless at last. It's 1975 and I can say and do anything I want. I want to prove this . . .

DeJong was adamant that she wasn't a poet. She knew that her work belonged more in the art world, but no one else in the art world was writing serious fiction that entailed finding new compositional rules. Before meeting Acker, DeJong had been mailing her work to a list that she got through Art Services, run by Robert Ashley's wife, Mimi Johnson: a strategy almost identical to Acker's serial pamphlets, first mailed out to the Antins' list.

"At first," De Jong recalls, "I was really pleased to make Kathy's acquaintance. Because I found that we could talk shop. The writers I came across in so-called downtown New York weren't interested in language or questions about narrative or structure. People were just relying on whatever style came out of their heads, just using conventions. Kathy and I shared some interests in dismantling and examining the conventions, self-consciously using or not using them. We had that in common, and she was a great friend, because you can't sit around talking about verb tenses with everyone! Actually, almost no one."

The pleasure was mutual. Acker would mention DeJong in most of her letters to Silliman: *Connie's about the only person I can talk to about writing here*; and *My closest friend at this point is a woman named Connie De Jong [sic] who's an incredible & totally unknown writer . . . I feel I can learn a lot from her writing it's incredibly precise, i.e., so transparent its conceptions are clear;* and *I don't see writers anymore except for Connie;* and *Connie (De Jong) [is] a basically unknown or starting-to-be-known poetry-prose writer (I mean that she writes in prose but the sensibility is that of poetry, the definition I'm making here.)* They talked about starting a press, maybe even an independent distribution service together, through the nonprofit organization run by Philip Glass, DeJong's partner at the time. DeJong remembers having long conversations with Acker over cheap Polish food in restaurants across the East Village.

Pooh Kaye—*my best girlfriend here*, as Acker wrote Silliman—met Acker around the same time: perhaps through Jill Kroesen or perhaps at the Simone Forti workshops Kaye was co-teaching, or perhaps during Acker's brief stay at the Higgins/Knowles loft, where Kaye worked as a cleaner part-time. Years later, they'd discover that Kaye's father and Acker's mother were first cousins. Kaye, Acker, and Kroesen went to art openings, poetry events, parties, and art bars such as Mickey Ruskin's the Locale, sometimes in twos and sometimes together. Barnabus Rex, a 400-square-foot hole-in-the-wall on West Broadway, with a jukebox, pool table, and bar, was a popular hangout for such artists as Richard Serra (Acker to Silliman: *Maybe I should go fuck Richard Serra (there are hints of it in the air) and, as a friend of mine says, get beaten up*), Julia Hayward, and Boris Pearlman (a.k.a. Boris Policeband). The Austrian playwright Peter Handke, whose works had been recently translated, was known to frequent the bar during his trips to New York. Acker, like everyone else in her circle, was reading Handke enthusiastically. It's likely she was a regular at Barnabus Rex. By 1975, when Hilly Kristal turned CBGBs into a new music mecca, everyone also went there. The Ramones, the Talking Heads, Mink DeVille, the Patti Smith Group, and the Heartbreakers all played there that year.

After moving back to New York in 1974, Acker and Gordon's old friend Jill Kroesen, a.k.a. "Fay Schism," began dating Len Neufeld, Acker's long-ago ex. They married in February 1975 and Neufeld moved in to Kroesen's Kenmare Street loft. Acker became a frequent visitor and sometime houseguest, recruiting Neufeld to run errands and helping herself to food from their fridge. One of the songs Kroesen wrote at the time, "Insecure Girlfriend Blues, or Don't Steal My Boyfriend," was inspired by this situation:

> I had a boyfriend who loved me and he told me so
> You were so jealous you called him up on the telephone
> You talked about sex so he'd get turned on while he's talking to you
> You pretend yourself's my friend but you're just a selfish slutty
>   little fool

"I didn't like her," Kroesen recalls, "and I didn't like her art. I saw her . . . she was very charismatic and we were in the same art world, the same group of friends, but she was very selfish." Just as Martha Rosler found herself somewhat conflicted when Acker burst into her marriage with Neufeld, Kroesen couldn't entirely blame Acker; she seemed so fragile and needy. As Kroesen recalls, "She had this way that made you want to take care of her. She was very vulnerable, and brought out your maternal instincts in spite of yourself."

Preparing to write *Toulouse Lautrec* that summer, Acker immersed herself in books about the French belle époque, the revolutionary anarchist Peter Kropotkin, Paul Gauguin's journals, and American anarchist histories. She devoured the work of the poet-turned-novelist Blaise Cendrars. Sharing his taste for puns, she saw in his novels *an elaborate morality tale about the nature of the world. Fuck [philosopher Willard] Quine*, she wrote to Ron Silliman, *I need new material.* No longer much interested in conceptualist godfathers such as Bergmann and Bergson, she turned to the mass-market novels of Irving Wallace and Harold Robbins. Robbins's work was especially appealing. Years later, her attraction to Robbins, the "dirty old man of American letters," would prove almost fatal to her career.

Robbins's twelfth novel, *The Pirate*, had just come out in paperback. Its dense 372 newsprint pages mapped the fortunes of three Arabic/Jewish generations across the Mideast, Europe, and the United States between the cardinal points of sex and money, money and sex. With his descriptions of oil wars, speculation, colonialism, debauched jet-set parties, and revolution, *Robbins turns out to be the main interest*, she wrote to Ron Silliman . . . *his use of fact/fiction . . . the conception of writing . . . based on audience . . . all this in relation to American politics and existence, use of story narrative as myth (a source of common energy information) that again has politics advertising conceptual basis and the information! A range that no avant-garde person has touched, and a new way of writing opens.*

Transposing the lower Manhattan art world to belle époque Montmarte, the first installment of *Toulouse Lautrec* is a seamless pastiche of the 1969 Agatha Christie murder mystery *Halloween Party* and accounts of martyred nineteenth-century American IWW leaders and industrial strikes. Scenes from the lives of Vincent van Gogh, Paul Gauguin, and Toulouse-Lautrec are laced with pornographic digressions and relationship conversations between their girlfriends, who—like Acker and friends—had to walk a fine line between girlish dreams of true love and the social convention of emotionless fucking:

"He kept looking like he was about to jump me. He was real drunk, that's why he was letting some emotion show. This life's keeping us lonely, Giannina. What these artists really want are pillows. Nice soft sweet female pillows. We can't be that way. We've got our own work. We're waitresses."

"Each time I get hurt, I close myself up." . . .

"The trouble is we keep having images of what we want. We don't let our emotions take over."

"At the end of the party," I'm telling Poirot, "she was dead."

Writing in the first person as Toulouse-Lautrec, Acker asserts the same direct and emotional self-disclosure that ran through her earlier works:

I'm a totally hideous monster. I'm too ugly to go out into the world . . .

No one will ever fuck me because I'm a hideous cripple.

I don't know how to present my image properly. When I'm with people, I act either like a changing wishy-washy gook or like an aggressive leather bulldog. That's an image . . .

. . . He's putting his arms around me. For at least a moment I'll be able to relax. I'm deliriously happy. I'm thinking about how much and badly I'm going to get hurt. I'm going to get burned. I'm going to get burned all over. His arms hold me in this real warmth that makes the constant pain I feel go away. I'm no longer thinking . . .

"Reading this early work," observed the writer and critic Gary Indiana, "was like being stoned in a taxi speeding through an unfamiliar city." One can only imagine how *Toulouse* was read in the circumspect art world. Acker's work, from the beginning, featured cameo appearances by named and unnamed mentors and friends. Now she was part of a scene, one among dozens of people her age who drank at the same bars and crashed the same parties of older artists who seemed increasingly dull. *Seems like the 35–45 year old artists have copped out, I mean this, $'s destroyed almost all of their work*, she wrote to Ron Silliman. The work was completely *à clef*. Everyone who mattered would have known who Lautrec's waitress friends—and the male artist-boyfriends who tormented them—actually were. If mailing the first *Black Tarantula* pamphlets gave Acker an audience to write for, downtown New York gave her the characters to cast in an eighteenth-meets-twentieth-century chamber satire. *I'm interested*, Acker wrote to Ron Silliman, *in realism*.

She applied for a CAPS (Creative Artists Public Service) grant in the summer of 1975, proposing to travel to Haiti for extended research that would lead to a book. New York was intense and useful, but really she wanted what most writers want: enough time and money to read, write, think, and be left in peace.

* * *

Could she have really lived in New York on $15 a week? Fifteen dollars was about $68 in today's money, and even though she was not paying rent, it seems unlikely. Still, as DeJong recalls, except for writing and performing, Acker never worked. Most of their friends worked part-time as cleaners or waitresses or bookstore clerks, but "I never saw Kathy work a job. Ever." She told DeJong she was estranged from her family and that her father had killed someone after—or while—he was making his fortune on Seventh Avenue as a handbag manufacturer.

When Constance DeJong left to travel in India that summer, she sublet her East Ninth Street apartment to Gordon, and Acker moved in. *I just moved to [the] back room of Peter's place*, Acker wrote Ron Silliman that June. *I'm the live-in maid I earn $15 a* *week which is pretty good I can live on it, I have this gorgeous room covered with huge cloths yellow orange Mexican striped pale yellow covered by shawls . . . I hardly ever let anyone in here. Peter & I are getting along well, maybe cause we don't fuck anymore, we're really brother & sister, maybe cause the money's straight, which gets me into another political discussion . . .*

By now she was totally committed to her life in New York. She sensed that the city was about to become an energy center again. A cluster of artists, mostly her age and bored by hermetic conceptualism, was gathering. Her St. Marks performance with Peter Gordon in late July got a *terrific reception*, she wrote to Ron Silliman. *[W]hat's happening here that's interesting is not what's going to get to SF so easily . . . i.e. Laurie Anderson's realization that art . . . comes from the kinesthetic & emotive centers as well as the logical centers, me, [the poet] Ed Friedman, many of the composers . . . Peter, trying to make our work as available, as conventional (using conventions genres as information, especially political information) as possible; artists such as Willoughby, Scott [Chris] Burden Dan Graham banding together [to] make conscious the socio-economic-sexual-etc nature of this environment . . . conceptualism [is] dead . . . non-NYC artists tend toward provincialism not cause they're not in NYC per se, but because they keep thinking about NYC art scene . . . in this sense, it's necessary to come to NYC.*

Deep into work on *Lautrec*, she'd stopped attending dance workshops and classes. Mostly she stayed in her small fabric-draped room in DeJong's apartment, reading and writing. For a while she gave up on dalliances: *I got sick of the whole art-sex scene . . . better horny than bored. I just wish most people talked as well as they fucked . . . I don't want to be too close to anybody, but I do like being able to talk to people I fuck and fuck people I like talking to . . . I always want everything.* Her trips outside the apartment were forages for *more information I can use and some affection so I can keep on going on writing.*

A brief romance with the artist Joel Fisher late in the spring had ended badly. She wanted more, but he made it clear that he didn't want to make any commitments. Asking herself what, really, was the "more" she wanted, she started reading about Tibetan Buddhism, a discipline that occupied Philip Glass and many of her older contemporaries. Writing to Ron Silliman, she touchingly struggles to transpose the Buddhist precept of "nonattachment" to the "non-grasping" behavior her culture demanded of heterosexual females. *[I]t just became clear that the whole romantic falling in love business that I kept doing was actually a possessing desire.* Maybe wanting her affection reciprocated was part of the *'50s shit* she grew up with? *I mean romantic love doesn't concern love at all but concerns power.* Reading Govinda's *The Way of the White Clouds*, her heart opened up. *I stopped desperately wanting someone.* And then, suddenly, *all these artists started wanting to fuck me.* Having discovered The Rules, she began dating the artist Scott B.—*it's pretty good cause it's doomed to failure*—and making up fairy tales that she'd use in *Toulouse Lautrec #4*.

The fourth pamphlet, titled *The Creation of the World*, begins with Toulouse and the other male whores (Peter [Gordon], Rhys [Chatham], and Garrett) telling bedtime stories when their clients have gone home for the night. From there she cuts to a scene lifted out of Vietnam-era soft porn—*Come here you little bitch yellow girl . . . Come here gook twat . . . I've got the thing that's going to conquer your country*—that might remain forever uncited, unsourced. In the next section, "the true story of a rich woman: I WANT TO BE RAPED EVERY NIGHT!" the narrator introduces herself as Jacqueline Onassis and describes how she picked up a Georgia pimp's son for wild sex at a disco in Paris. Acker's formulaic descriptions and lurid sex scenes—in fact, the entire text—were copied almost verbatim from two scenes of Harold Robbins's *The Pirate*: *I was high. The private section of the*

Metropole was packed. . . . The heavy pounding of the rock group tortured my ears. I took another sip of wine and looked down at the crowd . . . After a moment I was screaming as I had never screamed before. Each orgasm seemed to take me higher than I had ever been . . . At the time, and until *Toulouse* was republished by Picador fourteen years later, her appropriation of Robbins's work seemed benign and hilarious.

When DeJong returned in early September, Acker did not want to leave the apartment. Sick with the flu, she'd just had another abortion and was deep into writing and mailing *Toulouse*. Eventually Gordon found them a place of their own at 341 East Fifth Street. It was a dark railroad flat, but it had an extra back room for Acker to write in. She made a sign for the door: DON'T DISTURB ME—I'M WRITING. Her regime entailed writing at least three pages a day.

Writing *Toulouse* #5—a text that conflated the hypothetical romance of James Dean and Janis Joplin with a critique of Henry Kissinger's doctrine of "limited war"—required extensive research. *I need a lot of info, each sentence now takes me almost a book of research*, she hyperbolized to Ron Silliman. While her work on *The Childlike Life* had been almost shamanic, using sex, drugs, and sleep deprivation to catapult herself back into the sensations of childhood, *Toulouse* was a more synthetic project. She was trying to locate the murderous heart of American culture by reciting its myths. She'd dabbled in genre when she wrote *Rip-Off Red*, her extravagantly noncommercial attempt at writing commercial porn. Influenced by her encounter with Alan Sondheim, *Nymphomaniac* had been composed as a phenomenological exercise, arranging found and original texts onto a grid and inflicting repetitions on them. Working on *Toulouse Lautrec*, Acker drew on these early experiments but aimed for a narrative style that spoke to and for her new group of friends. Even though process determined her through-line much more than plot, each *Toulouse* pamphlet built on the premises she'd explored in the last. If *Toulouse #4* presented a paradigm of language used solely as content, a material stripped of all *psychological crap*, #5 would extend the investigation into how language becomes propaganda, internalized. How is language used to shape myths? *It all ties in,* she wrote to Ron Silliman, *is one issue.* She read Stanislavski's book on method acting. Like Ron Silliman, Bruce Andrews, Charles Bernstein, James Sherry, Carla Harryman, and others who'd come to be known as the Language School poets, she pursued confounding thoughts about semiotic theory and the correlations between language and reality, mythology and meaning, but unlike the Language School poets, she wanted her thoughts to be manifested in compulsively readable prose.

By now she knew that *Toulouse Lautrec* would be her last serial. The form, she told Silliman, is *too narrow for me and imposes a way of writing I'm no longer interested in. Also, the problems I'm getting toward are too much for me to handle in these month by month writing sessions.* She was starting to fabulate more about being a novelist. Her work habits, she thought, were closer to those of a paperback writer. *Poets,* she told the poet, *hardly seem to do any work. Even a hack novelist works an eight-hour writing day.* Except for Ron Silliman and his Language School colleagues, the poets she knew were still *issuing non-thought baby pap . . . words of wisdom, baby pap, noble poems, who gives a shit?* While TVRT helped produce at least one of the *Toulouse* pamphlets, she wouldn't publish the entire manuscript until 1978, when TVRT's efforts were preempted by the more visible, prestigious-within-the-art-world imprint, Printed Matter books.

In her long March 1976 interview with Barry Alpert for Toronto's lit-zine *Only Paper Today*, Acker would explain how, while writing *Toulouse*, she suddenly had *enormous respect for people like Harold Robbins . . . they just wrote eight hours a day. I couldn't be that simple anymore. The simpler ways of investigating language, Ron Silliman and people like that, were . . . missing the point . . . They were doing what they were doing, but there was the much larger thing that was really right in the realm of fiction.* She was trying to distance herself from the poetry scene, even if that meant throwing her good friend Ron Silliman under the bus. He lived in San Francisco; there was a good chance he'd never see the Canadian zine.

That fall, Acker and DeJong approached the Kitchen with a proposal for reading together over two weekends. Until then, the Kitchen had no literary programming. It was a venue exclusively featuring dance, performance, and new music shows. DeJong and Acker had both read their work in clubs, and the event they proposed fell somewhere between reading and performance. DeJong made a postcard announcement for their late-October performances, and they each rehearsed their own set without talking too much about it. The night before the first show, Acker called DeJong and said, *You know, we really need to talk about the order.* They'd never discussed who'd go first or second, and DeJong hadn't thought about it. "And then," DeJong recalls, "Kathy said: *I'll just tell you that you don't want to go second, because what I'm doing is so amazing, you* cannot *follow.* The floor just kind of disappeared. Because, this is my friend. Oh, I see: not my friend. I think that was the initial— Thinking about it as a game board, that was Kathy's first move to winnow me out. But I was shocked. It was shocking. Until then, there weren't any indicators. When she wouldn't leave the apartment after the sublet was finished, I just wrote that off as a quirk. But this was an indicator." To this day, deep online, DeJong's second book, *The Complete Works of Constance DeJong*, appears on the website Fantastic Fiction as a work "by Kathy Acker." "I think," Eleanor Antin said when we talked in 2000, "Kathy, at that point, sort of chose Connie DeJong as an enemy."

DeJong went on first and received a standing ovation. The next week, Acker canceled her performances "due to an illness." Ten years later, after Acker left and then returned to New York, they'd meet again at another Kitchen performance. Acker was there with an entourage; by then she rarely went out alone. When DeJong went up to say hi, she turned her back and walked off.

* * *

Phil Glass brought his friend Rudy Wurlitzer to the opening night of DeJong and Acker's double bill. Wurlitzer was, and still is, an extraordinary writer. They sat on the floor next to DeJong's mike, leaning against the wall of the big, open room. Glass introduced Acker to Wurlitzer after the show. She must have already known who he was. "The novel of bullshit is dead," Thomas Pynchon wrote of Wurlitzer's 1969 debut, *Nog*. Embraced by the new Hollywood of the early '70s, he went on to write screenplays for Monte Hellman's 1971 *Two-Lane Blacktop* and Sam Peckinpah's *Pat Garrett and Billy the Kid*, released in 1973. These two films established him as the avatar of the "acid western," a genre he virtually invented. Ten years older than Acker, Wurlitzer, still at the height of his mainstream acclaim, lived in the East Village. His novel *Quake*—"one of the greatest novels ever composed about Los Angeles and death in the west," as Rodger Jacobs wrote for *PopMatters*—had come out from Dutton in 1974.

After that night, Acker sought Wurlitzer out and, as he'd later tell Constance DeJong, pursued him aggressively. Her attraction to him is understandable. Just as she'd begun taking herself seriously as a novelist, she met Wurlitzer: a mythic, complex, and established writer ten years her senior who, in his own way, had solved some of the compositional problems that plagued her. Wurlitzer's coming-to-culture was as unconventional and singular as his work. He'd started writing while working on an offshore oil tanker at age seventeen. Later, living on the island of Majorca, he'd learned "how to write short sentences" while working as a secretary to the British poet and novelist Robert Graves. Wurlitzer seemed to fulfill the ideal Acker had described to Ron Silliman a few months before, when she was longing to *[be] able to talk to people I fuck and fuck people I like talking to.* They began a brief, confusing affair.

A practicing Buddhist, Wurlitzer was fed up with his life in New York. The distractions, the gossip, the ethos of perpetual achievement and progress were all bad for his work. When he met Acker, he felt himself gripped by a spiritual crisis. The last thing he wanted was a binding romantic involvement, which of course brought out the romantic in her. She was already confused about the relationship between love, friendship, and sex. *I'm totally a romantic,* she'd written Ron Silliman three months earlier, *which makes me live too much in [a] fantasy world.* Prone to infatuation, she longed to meet someone stable enough to accept her excess emotion while remaining a friend. She sought understanding, acceptance, and love. *I guess that's what defines a friend to me: someone who can still be a friend while I go manically through romantic visions.*

Toulouse Lautrec #6, written during her involvement with Wurlitzer, cuts back and forth between the panic of romantic confusion and a diatribe on corporate capitalism:

Marcia realized she was a bum and didn't belong in this picture of Scott's success. Please tell me whether you love me or not. WHY DO YOU WANT TO KNOW? *I can't fuck anyone else cause I'm always thinking about you and I'm getting too horny.* I'M NOT IN LOVE WITH YOU AND I DON'T WANT A HEAVY RELATIONSHIP. I'M MORE OFF THAN ON. *I understand what's going on.* THIS IS CRAZY. WHY SHOULD I DEFINE MY FEELINGS FOR YOU? . . . *All I said was that I was stuck on you.* HOW CAN YOU BE IN LOVE WITH ME YOU'VE

ONLY KNOWN ME FOR A FEW MONTHS AND YOU'RE JUST A KID. I
DON'T BELIEVE YOU WHEN YOU TELL ME YOU LOVE ME.

She began to go crazy. A glance at the annual earnings of 220 men
in charge of some of America's largest corporations (there are no
women) shows them to be at the very top of the income pyramid.

Being in love transports the narrator into the kind of delirium
Acker enacted through sex in *The Childlike Life of the Black
Tarantula*:

Suddenly seeing something you've never seen before. You're willing
to compromise yourself for this person. Forget what you've just
thought. You don't have any more thoughts of yourself. You want
to know everything about the other person:

What was your childhood like?

What do you like to do the most?

Have you ever fucked any weirdos?

When did you start being an adult?

Writing under the influence of Ulrike Meinhof's famed *Letter
from a Prisoner in the Isolation Wing June 16, 1972–February 9,
1973*, which had recently been translated and was circulating
among her East Village friends, Acker continues:

Feeling lonely . . . Feeling almost cut to the bone . . . Feeling
gentle and soft (the second part.) Feeling incapable of doing any-
thing except reaching in this totally soft way. Feeling big large eyes
opening wider and wider. This part is all defense . . .
*   Feeling like a thing rather than living. Knowing that wanting*
a lover, wanting Scott back, is wanting to be dead again, wanting

one feeling so much that feeling becomes a thing, my possession. Knowing this but not feeling it all throughout my body.

* * *

I'm a CAPS finalist, Acker wrote to Ron Silliman ebulliently early that fall. Around the same time, she accepted the artist Lil Picard's invitation to appear in a duo performance at Stefan Eins's 3 Mercer Street gallery. Picard, like Acker, had progressed to the final round of competition for a 1976 CAPS grant. Picard's application was in Performance. Having no video documentation of her prior work, she decided to put on a show and invite the judges.

Born in Landau, Germany, in 1899, Lil Picard was a former cabaret artist. In her youth in Berlin she'd known the Dadaists Richard Huelsenbeck, Emmy Hennings, and Hugo Ball. In 1937 she and her husband fled the Nazi regime for New York, where she designed and sold outrageously high-concept hats in her own small Madison Avenue shop. Introduced to the Tenth Street galleries of the 1940s by her friend Patricia Highsmith, she shifted her interests to visual art and began making collages, "ghost-prints," and other works. Picard became a key member of the NO!art group, a transnational association of artists that included Boris Lurie, Alan Kaprow, Yayoi Kusama, and Jean-Jacques Lebel. The group embraced rebellion and stood against pop art, the celebration of consumerism, art world–market investment, and the amnesiac postwar consciousness that reigned in New York during the 1960s. *Railroad Collage* (1963), one of Lurie's signature works, places a pinup model atop a cattle car of Auschwitz corpses. But Picard's interests were wide. A fixture at Warhol's Factory, she knew everyone in 1960s New York.

By the time she met Acker at the Poetry Project, Picard was a rotund and bewigged seventy-six-year-old woman with bright red lips and a marabou feather boa: a living myth whom no one took completely seriously. Years later, Carolee Schneemann would acknowledge Picard's influence, describing her as "a free spirit . . . able to negotiate many different worlds because, as a woman, she was negligible." "I work," Picard wrote in 1974, "with the idea of destruction and construction, dematerialization and symbolic references . . . to the political, sociological, environmental situation and I try through Art and Self-Performance to help to achieve CHANGE for values of humane and spiritual conditions."

Picard's CAPS performance, staged at the end of November, would be called *Tasting and Spitting*. She told Acker she needed a girl to lie naked under a table, which at the time seemed like no big deal. It wasn't until two days before the event that Picard announced that they would follow a script and be in conversation together. When Acker arrived for the show, she found the plan changed once again. There was no table. Picard asked her to undress and rouge her nipples. And then, as Acker would later recall, *I had to sit naked right next to all these people I knew, and I didn't know them that well . . . The door was open . . . I was just sitting there naked freezing my tits off.*

Picard introduced Acker as the Black Tarantula, the star of the show, and then—in a somewhat Germanic inversion of Yoko Ono's 1965 *Cut* performance—invited the audience of artists to take sips of wine and spit on Acker. Dieter Froese went first. Judy Rifka upped the stakes by spitting into Acker's vagina. By the end of the evening Acker decided to reverse the roles by spitting on a *New York Times* photographer's camera. *Really*, she'd tell Barry Alpert several months later, *there are worse atrocities.*

* * *

Wurlitzer left New York for an indefinite stay in Mabou Mines, Nova Scotia, early in the new year. Acker didn't keep much correspondence, but his three thoughtful letters are preserved in her papers at Duke University. He writes to her about how open he feels, alone in the middle of a northern winter, "wind wrapping around the house, stars outside like silver bursts of rifle fire, drunk on rum, grass, huge blasts of arctic air, weeping and rolling in snow" and peeling off "all these excessive layers of skin, all the fucking culture." He needs intimacy; thinking about her makes his cock get hard; he needs his solitude. Acker's letters to Wurlitzer weren't kept, at least not by her. But eventually Wurlitzer writes that things are getting too weird, "way out of proportion and full of illusions, mine and yours." His short, final letter affirms his need for solitude. "Please, don't think my removal or isolation has to do with you. It doesn't at all, I think you're one of the best people I know. And I honor and respect and love who you are and are trying to be."

* * *

Acker received a 1976 CAPS grant that January, a generous stipend of $7,000 ($38,000 in today's money) that would allow her to travel to Haiti and live for a year. Picard's application was declined. Curiously, CAPS was the first and only grant or award Acker would receive during her lifetime. Initially she was too unknown to receive the kind of institutional support that many writers of her caliber enjoyed. Eventually she'd face an opposite dilemma: *I'm far too famous, notorious and the literary world is doing some major ostracism*, she'd email Ira Silverberg in 1996, when she'd been diagnosed with cancer and was looking for a permanent full-time job in an English or Creative Writing department, virtually anywhere.

* * *

"Maybe the party began at Max's, circa 1966, or at the Factory around '63 . . . In any case, by the mid-70s, the party was no longer an event but an institution, and pretty near the only one around . . . The night was dark, the streets were empty, the taxis were nowhere to be found, but there, all lighted up at the bottom of the alley, was the party. It was very, very loud . . . Friendships were forged that might last for hours, possibly days . . . Having fun was all very well, but what really mattered was to be seen doing so."
—Luc Sante, "The Party," *New York Times* October 5, 2003

In June, Acker left for Haiti just as she'd proposed when she wrote her CAPS grant. She stayed for most of the summer and began work on the novel *Kathy Goes to Haiti* when she returned. Adhering to her habitually strict schedule and her new taste for mass-market fiction, she wrote it very fast.

By now she'd established an active artistic career, traveling for readings and residencies at the alternative spaces on the East and West coasts that flourished in the U.S. and Canada during the Carter and Trudeau years. Among other 1976 engagements, she did a residency at the Western Front, Vancouver's artist-run alternative center. While there, she appeared on the *HP Radio Show*, hosted by the Western Front cofounder Hank Bull. They cowrote a song titled "Lady, Be Bad," dedicated to the "Western Front livers"—the loose collective of artists who lived and worked in the old Masonic lodge they'd converted to a complex of galleries, theaters, video labs, and apartments. Disciplined in her habits since her early youth, Acker forced herself to compartmentalize her writing time, separating it from the public work entailed in building her career.

Still, *Haiti* wouldn't be published until the end of 1978. Acker was finished with self-publishing. The serial novels had been part of her literary apprenticeship; she was a journeyman now. TVRT was still Acker's publisher, but—though it's unclear whose decision it was—they never brought out *Haiti*, and the book wouldn't be published until Willoughby Sharpe, *Avalanche* editor and general man-about-downtown New York, introduced Acker to his Canadian girlfriend, Judith Doyle.

Doyle was twenty-one years old. She worked at the Toronto alternative venue A Space and was a great fan of Acker's work. Doyle's friend Anne Turyn was just starting Top Stories—an influential pamphlet series featuring female narrative prose—at the exhibition and cultural center Hallwalls in Buffalo. With her friend Fred Gaysek, Doyle decided to publish *Haiti* with a new imprint they'd call Rumour Publications. The text would be interspersed with original block-print illustrations by the artist Robert Kushner, one of Acker's downtown New York friends.

Kushner and Acker met at the early-morning meditation sessions he and his wife held in their Leonard Street loft. Based on the teachings of Swami Muktananda, their chanting and meditation regime was known as *siddha*. The group met most mornings at six. Acker was on a late-night writing schedule at that time, often working until 5:30. While the others were just waking up, Acker used *siddha* to wind down her day.

She stayed in Toronto with Doyle for a couple of weeks for Rumour's *Haiti* book launch in February 1979. While there, she taught a "clinic" in the storefront downstairs and recruited Doyle and some of her friends to help her perform "The Scorpions," a piece that would eventually become part of her novel *Blood and Guts in High School*. *Haiti*, the book she'd come to promote, didn't interest her much. It was already part of her past. A photo taken at the A Space house shows Acker curled up on the floor in a fisherman's sweaterdress, socks, and black tights. Her chin rests on artist Andy Patterson's lap. Her shaved hair has grown out to a pixie. Acker's Toronto visit occurred less than two months after her mother's death—a time she'll later recall *passing in a void*—but in the photo, she looks healthy and happy. A sirenlike Judith

Doyle stands behind Patterson, wiping his forehead. Eyes closed in a trance with his head thrown back, Patterson looks a little like Robert Desnos in the famous surrealist photograph.

While in Toronto, Acker hooked up with Andy Patterson, an A Space housemate. Willoughby Sharpe was also around. Acker and the publisher spent a lot of time "yakking like bathrobe after-talk girlfriends," Doyle recalls. "She had this business-y side at the time, a kind of drag but also possibly a total reality. She was exceptionally bright, always thinking, alert, pissed off at one infraction or another. She was dominant. That was OK with me. I had no clue about what she aspired to—for me, she was at the summit of my small world . . . Her mom was on her mind a lot. How mean her mom had been, but how much she loved her . . . Acker's stance was girly, victimized, ruthless, cagey, business-oriented and unpredictable. You never knew where you stood. Always putting everything into the mean typewritten letter she wouldn't say to your face that becomes a read-aloud, or bit in a novel. Best friend, frenemy, total enemy, better than the sex gab-fest afterglow . . . I was in this role-playing game. I don't think she liked who she worked with long."

Republished by Grove Press in the *Literal Madness* 1988 anthology, *Kathy Goes to Haiti* tells the "story" of Kathy, *a middle-class, although she has no money, white girl, twenty-nine years of age,* who flies to Port-au-Prince on an indefinite vacation and has a hot affair with a local married drug dealer. The headline of James Frakes's *New York Times* review of the Grove edition sums up his estimation of the novel: *OOH OOH. AND THEN AGAIN, AH AH.*

By the 1990s *Haiti* became a book Acker sought to distance herself from. Setting this art world porn romp against an impoverished third world backdrop had become an embarrassment. In a 1992 interview with Rebecca Deaton, she would describe the novel as *a joke . . . a parody of a porn novel. I tried to write the dumbest book I could . . . I wrote the novel really to make* money—*they were buying porn novels at the time*. (Unconsciously or consciously, she was confusing *Haiti* with *Rip-Off Red* and *Nymphomaniac*, her 1973 and 1974 experiments.) Two years later she'd elaborate: [H]aiti *was written in] 73–74, and I got very bored writing a porn book, plus laws changed and they no longer had these little porn publishers. So I made up all these rules . . . I was very intrigued at the time by Raymond Queneau, by Cortazar . . . so I made up my own writing game . . . I did a grid, and everything was a mirror of each other . . . [I]t wasn't as amusing to write as I thought. So in retrospect, I'm not very fond of that book.*

Still, the hope she revealed to Barry Alpert in their 1976 interview is probably more to the point: *I want to do a big novel. I've changed . . . [T]he series novels I sent out were a three-year block for me, and in a way that's all one work. It's a development of one problem . . . And I feel I arrived at an end to the problem.* Written under the influence of Harold Robbins, *Haiti* was an attempt to compose a more or less continuous narrative spanning the lurid and glamorous worlds of sex, international politics, high finance, and drug use.

* * *

Until she sat down to compose the manuscript at the end of 1978, Acker never conceived *Blood and Guts in High School* as a continuous, stand-alone book. Neither a serial project nor a "big novel," the book was composed from an assortment of fragments and outtakes written and saved since she moved to Solana Beach with Peter Gordon in 1973 and began writing prose. The intricate pictograph dream maps she drew while she was writing *The Childlike Life* appear for the first time in *Blood and Guts*, preceding some fairy tales she'd composed but not used in *Toulouse #4*.

Teen gangs like the Scorpions had been on her mind since becoming involved with the downtown scene when she moved back to New York. In a 1974 letter to Ron Silliman, she gleefully wrote, *I'm becoming a rock & roll lyricist*, and copied her new "poem" for him:

NO MORE PARENTS NO MORE SCHOOL

NO MORE SOCIETY'S DIRTY RULES

SPREAD MY LEGS I'M SO POOR I WANT TO DIE

According to Judith Doyle, Acker saw punk as "this schoolyard nasty-girl desire thing." Composed in the wake of the hyper-narrative *Kathy Goes to Haiti*, *Blood and Guts* proposes a more aggressive and upbeat, less tragic form of rebellion than the schoolgirl conspiracies that unfold in *The Childlike Life*, drawn from her years at the Lenox School and the writings of Violette Leduc.

The Persian Poems—her ingenious, maybe real, maybe fake translation of such phrases as *Janey is an expensive child/But cheap* and *see my cunt!* into Farsi that form the middle part of *Blood and Guts*—was initially published in Sylvère Lotringer's 1978 *Schizo-Culture* issue of the magazine *Semiotext(e)*. *The Persian Poems* appeared again in 1980 as an artist's book illustrated by Robert Kushner that was also funded and produced by him as "Bozeau of London Press."

Early in 1978 Acker confronted, for the first time, the possibility that she might have cancer. Discovering a breast lump, she underwent a biopsy that turned out benign. Fear and dread of the disease course through the second half of *Blood and Guts in High School*: *[In] my life politics don't disappear but take place in my body*, she writes in the section following *The Persian Poems*. And further on:

Having cancer is like having a baby. If you're a woman and you can't have a baby 'cause you're starving poor or 'cause no man wants anything to do with you or 'cause you're lonely and miserable and frightened and totally insane, you might as well get cancer. You can feel your lump, and you nurse, knowing I will always get bigger. It eats you, and, gradually, you learn, as all good mothers learn, to love yourself.

By now she and Gordon no longer lived, or expected to live, as a traditional couple. Best friends and roommates, they had established completely separate lives. Still, that year they got married on a freezing February afternoon at City Hall. As Gordon recalls, the marriage was wholly Acker's idea. There was no reception, party, or other acknowledgment of the event.

To Gordon, "[Our marriage] was always kind of a mystery to me . . . I still wonder about it. Perhaps it was because . . . mortality had raised its head and perhaps there was a re-evaluation of the importance of the relationship." A more crass viewpoint would be that it was for insurance reasons. But even though he'd signed up for insurance, Gordon's employer neglected to pay for the policy, and they were stuck with the hospital bill.

Six months later they separated permanently. Gordon moved out of the apartment, into his East Sixth Street studio. They'd been together since 1972. Even though she'd been actively seeking a more—to her mind—suitable romantic partner for the past several years, Acker was devastated. The pain of their separation defines the comedic exchanges between "Janey" and "Father" in the opening of *Blood and Guts in High School*.

In Scene One, Janey's father—like Peter Gordon—has started casually dating a girl and discovered that he likes her. *Janey: You're going to leave me . . . Father (dumbfounded, but not denying it): Sally and I just slept together for the first time. How can I know anything? Janey (in amazement. She didn't believe what she was saying was true. It was only out of petulance): You ARE going to leave me. Oh no. No. That can't be. Father (also stunned): I never thought I was going to leave you. I was just fucking . . .* A series of tormented relationship conversations ensues:

Janey (searching for a conversation subject that doesn't touch upon their breaking up): What's Sally like?

Father: I don't know. (As if he's talking about someone he's so close to he can't see the characteristics.) We're really very compatible. We like the same things.
     She's very serious; that's what she's like. She's an intellectual.

Janey (showing no emotion): Oh. What does she do?

Father: She's hasn't decided yet. She's just trying to find herself. She's into music; she writes; she does a little of everything.

Janey (trying to be helpful): It always takes awhile.

Father: She's trying to find out everything . . .

Janey: Are you going to want to live with me again?

Father: I don't know right now. I'm really enjoying the emotional distance . . .

Janey: When do you think you'll know if you ever want to live with me again?

Father: Oh, Janey. You've got to lighten up. Things just got too entangled. Everything between us is still too entangled for me to be with you.

Janey: I see. That means no . . .

Father: Right now I just really like opening my door to this apartment and walking into my own space. I'm going to be here through September and then I'll see what my plans are. I don't think you should bank on anything . . .

"We were basically living separate lives," Gordon recalls. "Kathy had her own life and I had my own life, with Kathy in it. The relationship was not going to change, and I was now marked as a married man. I realized I had to get out."

The exchanges between Janey and her father comprise the first scenes of the book, but they were clearly the last to be composed. It could be that the disturbance of her final separation from Gordon prompted Acker to arrange this collection of outtakes and unpublished writings into a disjunctive but emotionally continuous work.

* * *

I think soon things are going to start happening again, Acker had written Ron Silliman in 1975 after arriving back in New York, and by 1978, she was right.

During that year, Eric Mitchell, Vivienne Dick, James Nares, and Beth and Scott B premiered new feature-length movies, shot mostly in each other's apartments on Super 8 film. Brian Eno released his compilation album *No New York*, featuring No Wave bands like the Contortions, DNA, Mars, and Lydia Lunch with Teenage Jesus and the Jerks. Robert Mapplethorpe and Patti Smith had a joint exhibition of their photographs at Robert Miller's Fifty-Seventh Street gallery; David Wojnarowicz began photographing himself behind a xeroxed mask for his series *Arthur Rimbaud in New York*; the Wooster Group performed *Nayatt School* at the Performing Garage; and the Mudd Club opened its doors at 77 White Street.

Acker's close friends at that time included the photographer Marcia Resnick; the writers Victor Bockris, Jeff Goldberg, and Gary Indiana; the dominatrix and writer Terence Sellers; filmmakers Bette Gordon, Becky Johnston, Michael Oblowitz, and Tim Burns; Semiotext(e) founder and editor Sylvère Lotringer;

Bomb magazine founder Betsy Sussler; the theater director Lindzee Smith; and James Grauerholz, who'd just begun working as a secretary to William S. Burroughs at "The Bunker" on 222 Bowery, a former YMCA.

As Gary Indiana recalls, "We all wanted to do as many things as we possibly could, all those readings and performances . . . because we had so much energy at that age. And drugs . . . Just about everybody converged on the same four or five places every night . . . At that time, a 'close friend' tended to be someone you did things in public with or met for drinks or whatever a little more frequently than other people."

That summer, Acker republished *The Childlike Life* and *Toulouse Lautrec* with Printed Matter books, an imprint founded by Lucy Lippard and Sol LeWitt and directed by Ingrid Sischy, who would go on to edit *Artforum* and *Interview* magazine. Unlike Ted Castle and Leandro Katz's inspired and hobbyist TVRT Press, Printed Matter had a real office, distribution, and staff. TVRT had already helped Acker publish *Toulouse* in pamphlet form. While they were preparing to produce *Toulouse* as a bound book, LeWitt proposed a Printed Matter "co-production" with them.

As Katz recalls, "Ted Castle and I worked very hard designing the project. The publication was going to be funded by Sol [LeWitt]. I did one cover, and Bill Wegman did the cover and illustrations for *Toulouse Lautrec*.

"We thought Sol was doing this to help both TVRT and Printed Matter. But after the two books came out, Ingrid called me and Ted to a meeting and made us sign an agreement saying we had no claim to the publications. I think Kathy decided to have Ingrid handle the hatchet. We ended up with fifty copies each of the books, if that.

"We were very upset, and I guess that was the end of TVRT. Things were changing. It was the start of the '80s . . .

For me, it was not a question of money, but loyalty. I stopped speaking to Kathy."

* * *

Acker finished the *Blood and Guts* manuscript sometime in the fall of 1978. On August 3 she wrote her old friend Lafayette "Lafe" Young, the proprietor of San Diego's Bargain Books, that she just had to *rewrite first 60 pages [of the new book] in the next few weeks before I blow up into out . . .*

Acker's friend Becky Johnston was then working full-time as the publicist for Urizen Books. Founded in 1975 by veteran publisher Michael Roloff, Urizen built an impeccable reputation publishing translated works by such international writers as Peter Handke, Augusto Boal, and Julia Kristeva and by American writers like Sam Shepard and Michael Brodsky. Roloff was in close touch with the downtown New York world, and when he and his partner, Wieland Schulz, decided to launch a downtown New York list, Johnston gave them Acker's *Blood and Guts* draft. At best, they were ambivalent. Schultz hated the book, but Roloff, although he "didn't exactly love it," realized that "it struck a nerve with the downtown crowd." A contract was signed, but Acker pulled out when Roloff suggested omitting *The Persian Poems.* As Acker complained to Lafayette Young, *Michael Roloff is a sexist creep and HE WANTED TO REWRITE THE WHOLE THING!*

Still reeling from the controversy surrounding *Toulouse* and *Great Expectations,* she told Young, *I've never had to deal with publishers before, and it is not a pleasure.* Suffering again from PID, she was in bed reading Robert Louis Stevenson and Sir Walter Scott, enjoying the way they made her world "into pageantry." By then, all she could think of was leaving for Mexico on August 17: *I want to be anonymous & write. I've saved up, by this time, borrowed $300, and am leaving.*

In a 1979 letter to *Sun & Moon* magazine editor Douglas Messerli, Acker reports that her new novel BLOOD AND GUTS IN HIGH SCHOOL *will be out from Stonehill in July.* This negotiation dragged on for two years, but it was never to be.

By this point Acker might have prevailed on such art world supporters as Robert Kushner or Sol LeWitt to publish *Blood and Guts in High School,* but she did not. Mainstream commercial publication seemed just a heartbeat away. While Acker's talk about her career in letters to friends at this time became more circumspect, her ambitions are disarmingly strewn across the opening pages of *Blood and Guts: I'm beginning to have some fame success, now women want to fuck me. I've never had women want me before. I want everything. I want to go out in the world as far as I can go;* and *I have to work as hard as possible so I can get enough fame then money to get away from here so I can become alive;* and, regarding career, *There are two levels. It's not that I think one's better than the other, you understand, though I do think one is a more mature development than the other. Second level: It's like commitment. You see what you want, but you don't go after every little thing . . .*

As Michael Roloff would later reflect, "What looked like the 'greening of America' in that neck of the woods metamorphosed into the wildest kind of neo-liberalism down in Tribeca and the East Village."

* * *

When *Blood and Guts* was finally published by Picador in London and Grove Press in New York early in 1984, its aggressive charm and dizzying sweeps between high culture and low would turn Acker into a post-punk icon for the Bush/Thatcher years. Fragmented, bratty, and raw, the book took on new life as a mass-cultural object that would not have occurred had it debuted in 1978 with Urizen or a smaller, more exclusively literary trade press. She was the first to admit that *Blood and Guts* was conceived more as a collage than as a continuous text. As she'd later explain in a long 1991 interview: [Grove and Picador] *got the end mixed up. They got the last two chapters in the wrong order. No one noticed! I told them they're in the wrong order and they said, Have a glass of champagne. (laughs) So I guess it's not the most tightly structured . . .*

Acker wouldn't set out to write another "big novel" until December 1979, when she began *Great Expectations* in the wake of her mother's suicide and her grandmother's death. Arguably her best work, Acker's 1983 *Great Expectations* was the novel she worked on for the longest time, and the shortest of all of her subsequent books.

In it, among other things, she finally exacts her revenge upon Peter Gordon for finding a girlfriend he likes. *Dear Peter,* she writes:

I think your new girlfriend stinks. She is a liar all the way around because her skin is yellow from jaundice, not from being Chinese like she pretends. She's only pretty because she's wearing a mask. You're hooked on her tight little cunt: it's only a sexual attraction I know you're very attracted to sex cause when you were young you were fat and no girl wanted to fuck you. What you don't know is that this cunt contains lots of poison—not just jaundice—a thousand times more powerful than the coke she is feeding you to keep you with her—especially one lethal poison developed by the notorious Fu Manchu that takes cocks, turns their upper halves purple, their lower parts bright red, the eyes go blind so they can no longer see what's happening, the person dies. Your new girlfriend is insane and she's poisoning you.

> *Love,*
>
> *Rosa*

Had her publishers listened to her, the final sentence of *Blood and Guts*—*Shall we find our way out of all expectations?*—would have been repeated within the title of her next book, *Great Expectations*, creating a kind of prose sestina.

But by then her image was everywhere—*have a glass of champagne!*—and it would no longer matter that much.

A PERSON OF
GREAT EXPECTATIONS

(1979–1983)

Happy are those ages when the starry sky is the map of all possible paths—ages whose paths are illuminated by the light of the stars. Everything in such ages is new and yet familiar, full of adventure and yet their own. The world is wide and yet, it is like a home, for the fire that burns in the soul is of the same essential nature as the stars; the world and the self, the light and the fire, are sharply distinct, yet they never become permanent strangers to one another.
—Georg Lukacs, *The Theory of the Novel*

Written continuously over eighteen months while Acker moved between New York, Seattle, San Francisco, and back to New York, *Great Expectations* begins when the narrator positions herself in time:

On Christmas Eve 1978 my mother committed suicide and in September of 1979 my grandmother (on my mother's side) died. Ten days ago (it is now almost Christmas 1979) Terence told my fortune with the Tarot cards. This was not so much a fortune— whatever that means—but a fairly, it seems to me, precise psychic map of the present, therefore: the future.

There is no space, only time. Her recital of dates and the tarot card spread are attempts to lock down an emotional flow. Acker was thirty-two years old when she began writing this text. Newly orphaned and twice divorced, she was now as alone in the world as she'd always felt. Two things about these opening lines stand out.

First, there's her use of the colon, repeated throughout the book: a punctuation mark that separates an introductory clause from a phrase, amplifying or explaining the preceding thought. But in *Great Expectations*, a book that, above all, enacts a working through of grief by way of strands of knowledge and consciousness, the colon is used as a summoning. A signature of Acker's presence and style, the colons in *Great Expectations* simultaneously establish the narrator as an authoritative guide and draw us more closely into her train of thought.

In *Great Expectations*, the colon functions as a slap, a jolt, an epinephrine shot that yanks the sentence—and by extension, us—from grief's downward drift into the present time. *Consciousness just is: no time. But any emotion presupposes differentiation. Differentiation presumes time, at least BEFORE and NOW. A narrative is an emotional moving.* And: *Do I care? Do I care more than I reflect? Do I love madly? Get as deep as possible. The more focus, the more the narrative breaks, the more the memories fade: the least meaning.* Sometimes Acker's colons are used to sequentially ground cascading logic chains into orderly sequences. At the same time, they draw us into the narrator's emotional world, moving each phrase toward greater intimacy: *I feel much better after I cry: more aware of who I am, more open. Great Expectations* chronicles a cosmological self-interrogation. The colons are ladder rungs, helping us get a grip, catch a breath, find something real to hold on to within a continuous drift.

Compressed into 122 pages, *Great Expectations* cuts between fragments of plagiarized text from sources that include (but are not limited to) Charles Dickens, Pierre Guyotat, Pauline Réage, Ben Jonson, Propertius, and Marcel Proust. But despite its textual breadth, the novel is set and bracketed in real time, recording its own composition and charting the narrator's passage through these borrowed texts.

A narrative is an emotional moving.

Acker's work in *Great Expectations* is a summation of the conceptual investigations she'd begun with *The Childlike Life* six years earlier, in 1973. Of course, the compositional problems Acker pursued during those years weren't hers alone. They belonged to the lingua franca of conceptual art. The phenomenological effects of repetition, disjunction, patterning, chance, and grids were pursued in more abstract, distilled forms by some of the poets, musicians, and artists who were her mentors and friends.

Bernadette Mayer's 1972 photo-and-text project *Memory* transported conceptual art's clinical investigations of the effects of expanded duration into a more sensational realm, "one that appears explicitly personal and autobiographical, fraught with memory and subjectivity . . . Whereas the very intensity of surface detail . . . paradoxically atomizes personal experience into an endless flow . . . its authorship is distributed among various functions that don't necessarily cohere into a single self," as the art historian Liz Kotz wrote. Acker's 1974 *Blue Tape* collaboration with Alan Sondheim, in which she tries *to find out what the structure is, or structure of intentions were, behind my remembrance*, owed a great deal to Sondheim's phenomenological research, which in turn was inspired by projects by Robert Smithson, Donald Judd, and Dennis Oppenheim, who used the philosophical writings of Maurice Merleau-Ponty as a primary source.

As Acker would later explain her compositional process in writing *Great Expectations*,

I wanted some kind of enactment with something called actuality. What seemed to me to be the reality when I started to write was process. And that's why I started writing the way I do. In the beginning I didn't know about context. I was interested in process . . . I became interested in context, and in other texts and in their flows . . . so that was Great Expectations, so it was all this process of other texts, and that led to context. It was about an environment. I was influenced by Bob Ashley's music at the time and Bob was doing environmental music. So I thought I could do environmental text. That I didn't need a centralized plot or centralized characters.

Written on the cusp of the new decade, *Great Expectations* at once summarizes artistic experiments of the past twenty years and announces a changing of guard. In this sense alone, it's a classic. Acker brazenly juxtaposes her investigation into the structure of consciousness—the sort of investigation that defined conceptual art—with extreme pornography, diatribe, parody, gossip, and trash, which had become the staple diet of New York's new guard downtown art crowd. Driven by grief, Acker's writing turns grief inside out and then proceeds to use it as a channel for larger investigations. *I realize that all my life is is endings. Not endings, those are just events; but holes. For instance, when my mother died the "I" I had always known dropped out.* Feminine and hyperfeminized, *Great Expectations* is memorable mostly for the way it directly transmits emotion and thought.

* * *

Except for a younger half sister, Wendy Alexander Weiss, from whom Acker was estranged, she had lost all her immediate family in the two years before she began writing the book.

Her stepfather, Albert Alexander, died of a heart attack in January 1977 at age sixty-one. He left his widow, Claire Weill Alexander, with an estate valued in his probate will between $3,000 and $10,000. This was an alarmingly small amount of money to sustain Claire's upper-middle-class Manhattan lifestyle. Since the birth of her first child when she was twenty-two, she'd never worked.

Described in *Great Expectations* as an unremarkable drunk *who didn't even know who Dostoyevsky was*, Albert was nominally employed as the manager of a garment business once owned by his mother-in-law, Florence "Florrie" Weill.

By all accounts, Albert Alexander wasn't highly ambitious. He dropped out of college when he was nineteen to manage a clothing store. This decision was most likely prompted by his marriage to Emily Alexander that year and the birth of Richard, their son. In July 1943, when he was twenty-seven years old, Albert was drafted into the army for the remaining years of World War II. He divorced Emily in October 1946, when Claire was four months pregnant with Kathy. There are no records of how Claire and Albert met. He was nine years older than Claire; his surname, Alexander, was the same as her father's first name. Most likely, Claire knew Albert then as an older and married family friend. Even though he was not Acker's biological father, Albert's name appears on her birth certificate. He recognized her as his daughter for the rest of his life.

As Acker would write over and over again—and as her surviving relatives concur—Claire became pregnant during a brief relationship with Donald Lehmann, a German-Jewish businessman from Buffalo. Claire was then twenty-one. When she told Lehmann that she was pregnant, he fled. Albert promptly ended his marriage to Emily and began a new life with Claire. No record exists of their marriage. When Florence Weill disposed of her late husband's glove manufacturing business, she did the right thing by making Albert's continued employment a condition when the business was sold. As Acker describes the situation in *Great Expectations*,

> *Daddy's drunk and he's still whining, but now he's whining nastily. He's telling my mother that he does all the work he goes to work at six in the morning and comes back after six at night (which we all know is a joke cause his job's only a sinecure: my mother's father gave him his first break, a year ago when the business was sold, part of the deal was my father'd be kept on as "manager" under the new owners at $50,000 a year. We all know he goes to work cause there he drinks and he doesn't hear my mother's nagging.)*

Pooh Kaye, one of the first friends Acker made in 1975 when she moved back to New York, confirmed the legend of Albert's employment. Eventually, before becoming estranged, Acker and Kaye would discover that their grandmothers were sisters, making them second cousins. Acker's mother, Claire, and Kaye's aunt Louise had been best friends during their youth.

Unlike the figures of the disappeared father, her mother, and her grandmother, Acker's stepfather appears only briefly throughout her work. A shocking aside in *Great Expectations* casts him as her rapist: *When O was 17 years old her father tried to rape her when she told him he couldn't rape her he weeps "your mother won't fuck me, those boys don't respect you enough, I'm the only man who's respecting you."* Yet as P. Adams Sitney surmised, this incident is almost certainly derived from the time Albert returned unexpectedly to the family apartment and walked in on the fourteen-year-old Acker with one of her boyfriends in bed. Later, in *Pussy, King of the Pirates*, he's *this man who was kind to me, gentle and stupid.*

I know, Acker writes in *Great Expectations*, *my grandmother hates my father*. Florrie, highly organized and dutiful, was also by all accounts venal and calculating while Albert was *so gentle he didn't exist.* Nevertheless, Florrie upheld an ongoing moral obligation to him for rescuing the helpless, impractical Claire and sparing her granddaughter the shame of being an illegitimate child. Throughout their lives, Florrie, Albert, and Claire remained, if nothing else, geographically close. The Alexander family apartment at 400 East Fifty-Seventh Street was a short walk to Florrie's rooms at the Dorset Hotel on West Fifty-Fourth.

* * *

The trauma of the disappeared father is a theme Acker pursued throughout her writing, from *The Childlike Life* to her last published novel, *Pussy, King of the Pirates.* In *The Childlike Life,*

> *My mother tells me my "father" isn't my real father: my real father left her when she was three months pregnant and wanted nothing to do with me, ever. This husband has adopted me. That's all she tells me.*

The story is told exclusively from the daughter's point of view in all its many iterations. But then again, perhaps the greatest strength and weakness in all of Acker's writing lies in its exclusion of all viewpoints except for that of the narrator. As William Burroughs wrote, with great precision, in his blurb for Grove Press's 1983 publication of *Great Expectations,* "Acker gives her work the power to mirror the reader's soul."

How does she do this? Acker had no shortage of female contemporary writers throughout the 1970s. Outside the downtown New York scene, Jayne Anne Phillips, Margaret Atwood, Ann Beattie, Alice Munro, Janet Frame, and dozens of others published semiautobiographical novels with strong female narrators. But, shaped by their interactions with others in naturalistically described situations, the presence of their narrators was wholly relational. While these women were widely respected for their achievements as writers, they never sought or attained the iconic status of Great Writer as Countercultural Hero that Acker desperately craved. Until she achieved it, no woman had.

In *Great Expectations*, Acker worked deeply under the influence of such Beat-era icons as William S. Burroughs and Alexander Trocchi and the French modernist writers and thinkers Georges Bataille and Pierre Guyotat. Sometimes described as "philosopher-artists," these writers conveyed their narrators' internal lives with startling primacy. And so, by extension, whatever pain and emotion they felt was not theirs alone. They offered themselves as receivers for cosmological information transmitted via their works. "In my writing I am acting as a map-maker, an explorer of psychic areas," William S. Burroughs wrote.

Defending his work at the 1962 Edinburgh Writers' Conference, Trocchi proclaimed himself "a cosmonaut of inner space." Written against history and time, Trocchi's 1960 novel *Cain's Book* dispassionately records a few months in his life as a remorseless heroin addict. His narrator states, "When I write I have trouble with my tenses. Where I was tomorrow is where I am today, where I would be yesterday. I have a horror of committing fraud."

A special issue of Sylvère Lotringer's journal *Semiotext(e)* devoted to Georges Bataille appeared in 1976, and Harry Mathews's translation of Batailles's 1928 classic *Blue of Noon* came out with Urizen Books the following year. Acker and Lotringer were close friends and lovers between 1977 and 1980. Years later, she would credit him widely for introducing her to French theory and "giving her a new language" through which to explain her existential and literary sense of fragmentation, multiplicity, and disjunction. Lotringer taught Georges Bataille in his Columbia University "Sex and Literature" graduate seminar; no doubt he and Acker discussed Bataille's work and thought.

The first line of Bataille's *Story of the Eye* could easily have been written by Acker herself: "I grew up very much alone, and as far as I recall I was frightened of anything sexual." *I don't write to express anything*, she'd write in a 1979 self-interview in the French literary magazine *Dirty*, named after the "Dirty" character in Bataille's *Blue of Noon*. *Everything is material . . . culture is more and more a rag-bag . . . I use material that is commonly described as "autobiography." There are lots of emotions to draw from, and I love working with emotion because I love shock.* Acker was the first female writer to so relentlessly pursue the artfully naked "I" of French modernism. In fact, she'd go on to "plagarize" Bataille in *Great Expectations*:

> *I never wanted you, my mother told me often. It was the war. She hadn't known poverty or hardship: her family had been very wealthy . . . My father, a wealthier man than my mother, walked out on her when he found out she was pregnant . . .*

The story of the missing father is retold at least three times within *Great Expectation*'s 122 pages. In a "political" faux diatribe about the Trilateral Commission, she writes,

> *Three different power groups: the owners of the North-Eastern banks, the top-ranking military, and the Southern oil producers and distributors control the American government. The female artist doesn't know who her father is. Three months before she was born her father had abandoned her mother . . .*

In therapy with the Marin County past-lives regressionist Georgina Ritchie during the last months of her life, Acker embraced the suggestion that her mother unsuccessfully tried to abort her two months before she was born:

George: When you were seven months in the womb, your mother tried to abort you using something to do with heat, a method common in those days.

Electra: I know this.

George: The abortion didn't work because you were meant to be born . . .

Was this metaphor or memory? Transformed into myth, the facts of Acker's childhood shift slightly throughout her writings. Sometimes the story is told through the veil of plagiarized texts. Nevertheless, her birth father's disappearance will haunt her writing for the rest of her life. *Since I never knew you, every man I fuck is you. Daddy*, her narrator O states in *Pussy, King of the Pirates*. Still, from at least age twenty-six, when she discussed and transferred the myth of the disappeared father onto the less-than-willing Alan Sondheim in *Blue Tape*, Acker knew her father's full name, his address, and his place of employment. Clearly, she made a decision not to contact him, but this decision is absent from all her work.

* * *

By the time Albert died, Claire Alexander had no occupation or income except for occasional gifts or loans from her mother, and these were becoming more scarce. Still, in the first months of her widowhood, she discovered Studio 54. Opened that year by Ian Schrager and Steve Rubell, Studio's clientele included Jackie Kennedy Onassis, Andy Warhol, Bianca Jagger, Truman Capote, and, occasionally, Claire's daughter Kathy. Luc Sante recalls Acker standing outside, heckling socialites as they walked through the door, but there were times when Studio 54 became one of the stations on downtown New York's nocturnal sweep.

During the day, Claire drank, took diet pills, and shopped. Checks bounced, her department store credit cards were declined, and she was behind on her rent.

Broke and depressed, on Christmas Eve 1978 Claire checked into the Hilton Hotel a few blocks away from her house and took an overdose of barbiturates. She was fifty-three years old. It had been almost two years since Albert's death. As Pooh Kaye recalls, "Late in 1978, Kathy called to tell me that she was talking to her mother again, and her mother wanted to invite the family to a dinner." Kaye's father, the attorney Clifford Kaye, had maintained a close but covert friendship with his first cousin Claire.

"The dinner was to be a big event, except on the night before it was to take place she checked into the Hilton and overdosed. The cause, beyond her profound depression, was her state of bankruptcy. She literally could not afford the dinner. Apparently she had asked for money from Aunt Florrie, who turned her down. The tragic thing is how little time Kathy had with her mother after years of alienation."

Sylvère Lotringer recalls running into Acker sometime that night, when she was distraught, calling police and hospital wards in search of her mother. He still regrets telling her not to worry, that everything would turn out all right.

In *Great Expectations*, Acker writes,

Mother was a real actress . . . I had no idea until after the end that she was spending all of her money and, then, that she was broke . . . She madly frittered away money. Suddenly surprisingly, she asked me if I wanted gifts and she bought me three copies of a gold watch she liked. At the same time she owed three months' rent, two of her bank accounts were closed, all of her charge cards had been revoked. The 800 shares of ATT grandma had given her were missing.

Like the myth of the disappeared father, the story of Claire Alexander's suicide will be paraphrased in all Acker's subsequent works. Sometimes the event is recalled several times within the same text. Over the years, from book to book, only the date of her mother's death and the name of the hotel are slightly changed. But in all these accounts some facts are left out. If Florence held financial control over Claire, that control was selective and punitive, as it often is within families of means. As broke as Claire was at the time of her death, she still had a live-in maid. She left her apartment on December 24 determined not to be found and revived.

Other friends of Acker's vaguely recall her frantic search for her mother, which went on for days, even weeks. Still, the coroner's preliminary cause of death "pending further review," was dated December 26. Acker's half sister, Wendy, identified their mother's body. In *My Mother: Demonology*, Acker writes, *I remember that night when I learned that my mother had suicided, Christmas Eve, I didn't cry. For that night I rocked back and forth. I have no memory of the next month or two, except for the funeral.* Pooh Kaye thinks she recalls that "it took some time for Kathy to find out about it. Kathy may have been in her usual ambulatory state of housing and there was no way to reach her immediately . . . But Kathy could have called her sister, her mother's maid, her grandmother or my father to calm her fears if she did not know what happened to Claire." And then again, her friend and sometime lover Jeff Goldberg recalls, "[Kathy] called me up to tell me what had happened and I went over. I think it was Christmas day. My memory is that the city was very quiet and very few people were out. When I got to her apartment she wasn't distraught or crying. She seemed sort of numb. She asked me to take her to a movie. I thought it was weird, and questioned whether that was really a good idea under the circumstances. She got angry and threw me out."

The narrator of *Great Expectations* spirals back and forth through time, driven by grief. Living in an abrupt self-imposed exile in Seattle between May and November 1980, which none of her New York friends fully understood, Acker found herself awash in dreams and limitless time. "The problem," the narrator of *Cain's Book* decides, "has always been to fuse the fragments of eternity, more precisely, to attain from time to time the absolute serenity of timelessness." Trocchi attained it with heroin; Acker found it through grief. *Timelessness versus time. I remember it was dusk*, begins the second section of the book. And, later: *Timelessness versus time . . . There is very little money available to poor people.* The experience of time is completely internal, bound by emotion and thought.

* * *

The first section of *Great Expectations*, "I Recall My Childhood," begins with a paraphrase from the Charles Dickens book: *My father's name being Pirrip, and my Christian name Philip, my infant tongue could make of both names nothing longer or more explicit than Peter.* Abruptly, the narrator leaps forward more than a century:

> *Ten days ago (it is now almost Christmas 1979) Terence told my fortune with the Tarot cards. This was not so much a fortune— whatever that means—but a fairly, it seems to me, precise psychic map of the present, therefore: the future.*

Childhood, for Acker, is a wondrous foreign land, and the movement toward it is more toward arrival than a return.

The second curious thing about the beginning of *Great Expectations* is that Acker's real-time narration begins with a tarot spread.

When I started writing this book, I asked Geoffrey Cruickshank-Hagenbuckle, a poet and scholar of tarot, to tell my fortune with tarot cards. He was in New York City; I was in northern Minnesota. He emailed a list of instructions, tasks to complete before he cut the deck: "slice a vegetable or piece of fruit; bury a coin; put some scent behind one of your ears; burn something small and drink a glass of water." But, on the other hand, Geoffrey said, "There's nothing ritualistic about this. Nothing is a must. Time flexes." Among the cards he laid out in the magic square were Justice, Temperance, and Death. "Do not over-react," he advised. "Don't get drastic."

"Tarot is totemic magic," Geoffrey said. "The cards don't tell us what will happen: they show us what to do. They are objects to think with. The spread is more a picture than a story. Everything happens at once. There is no empty time. Time with Tarot is not abstract, ambiance or ether. The cards are less psychology or personality than a plan of action. It's like pulling up a map when you get lost. *The cards make time happen.*"

Snapshot of a moment: The card reading that begins *Great Expectations* positions the narrator's movement through time like a pin on a map. In the next eleven pages she'll career between self-analysis, phenomenology, dreams, an Algerian war battle scene from *Eden Eden Eden* by Pierre Guyotat, childhood memories by turns burlesque and tender, and a pastoral scene of New York: *New York City is very peaceful and quiet, and the pale gray mists are slowly rising, to show me the world . . .*

Driven by grief, ambition, and fear, after positioning herself in present-day time, the narrator launches herself on an epic traversal through memory, literature, culture, and alien worlds. As Acker writes, *There is no time; there is.*

* * *

If the narrator of *My Mother: Demonology* is to be believed, Acker spent the beginning of 1979 in a daze. Still, she was determined to have *Blood and Guts* published by an established trade press.

Sometime early that year, she signed a contract with Stone-hill Communications, founded by former *Rolling Stone* editor Jeffrey Steinberg in 1971. His father, Harold Steinberg, was the owner and publisher of Chelsea House Publishers, acquired in the 1980s by Infobase Publishing. Best known for its 1975 publication of *Inside the Company*, Philip Agee's notorious CIA exposé, Stonehill was less formally known as a tax shelter. The company boasted a prestigious high-countercultural list, with titles by Aldous Huxley, Helmut Newton, and Christina Rossetti and the *Cocaine Papers* of Sigmund Freud. In May 1979 Acker told *Sun & Moon* magazine editor Douglas Messerli that *Blood and Guts* would be out from Stonehill by July. By January 1981 she'd write Terence Sellers *I've taken* Blood & Guts *away from those junkies at Stonehill.* Steinberg would die later that year, age thirty-four, in a Long Island car crash.

Messerli had asked Acker for a contribution to his *Sun & Moon* magazine, and she sent him a short piece called "Girl Gangs Take Over the World." It was the start of a new book that begins as she cuts back and forth between scenes of her life in New York and Gillo Pontecorvo's 1966 film *The Battle of Algiers.* She's writing as "Omar":

> *Here in New York, every morning I wake up, I don't want to be awake. I have to persuade myself to wake up. I have to use my will to get food in my mouth because my heart sees no reason for anything.*

> *. . . I, Omar, live alone in a room. I almost never leave my room. I am lonely out of my mind sometimes. A lot of this time I worry a lot about money because for the last three months I have owned about ten dollars a week I am two months behind on rent I hate all other people . . .*

Omar is trapped in an ambivalent romance with "Kader." Like Andy Patterson, Acker's fling during the Rumour Publications launch, Kader lives in Toronto.

In a section called "CUNT," she writes for the first time about the events leading up to her mother's death—

This is the way THE CUNT my mother committed suicide:

THE CUNT ate at the most expensive restaurants in New York City. It purchased five copies of every expensive piece of clothing it liked. It bought needlepoint designs at $300 a piece. It rode in taxis and hired limousines. THE CUNT ran through $300,000 of its husband's life insurance money and the money THE CUNT its mother gave it in two years. The closer THE CUNT came to no money, the more frenzily it spent.

—and her ongoing confusion about sex and relationships:

Whenever a cock enters me every night three nights in a row, I ask myself regardless of who the cock belongs to should I let my SELF depend on this person or should I remain a closed entity. I say: I'm beginning to love you I don't want to see you again. The man thinks I'm crazy so he wants nothing to do with me.

By June, she abandoned the project. Eventually "Girl Gangs" appeared as the chapbook *Algeria*, published by Aloes Books (London) in 1984. Stuck in New York for the rest of the summer, she wrote a new story, *New York City in 1979*, that would be published in 1981 by Anne Turyn's Top Stories and resulted in the first and only award Acker ever received, a Pushcart Press prize.

Written as and about "Janey Smith," the persona she'd continue to use in *Blood and Guts, New York City in 1979* perfectly captures the end-of-the-decade zeitgeist in downtown New York.

Janey, a woman *who has sexually hurt and been sexually hurt so much she's now frigid*, meets Johnny, *a man who wants to keep everyone and everything who takes him away from his music off him*. Nevertheless, *As soon as Johnny sees Janey he wants to have sex with her. Johnny takes out his cock and rubs it*. Meanwhile, *All of New York City is fake is going to go all my friends are going crazy all my friends know they're going crazy disaster is the only thing that's happening*. Outside the Mudd Club, *A girl who has gobs of brown hair like the foam on a cappuccino in Little Italy, black patent leather S&M heels, two unfashionable tits stuffed into a pale green corset, and extremely fashionable black fake leather tights heaves her large self off a car top* and starts a fight with the bouncer. Johnny and Janey discuss her career: *You want to be as desperate as possible but you don't have to be desperate. You're going to be a success. Everybody knows you're going to be a success. Wouldn't you like to give up this artistic life which you know isn't rewarding . . . You know you want to get away from this media world*. To which Janey replies, *I don't know what I want now. I know the New York City world is more complex and desirable even though everything you're saying's true*.

Uptown, Janey's grandmother gives her a check for $10,000 and tells her to buy shares in AT&T. *You can fritter it away if you want . . . If your mother had invested the 800 shares of IBM I gave her, she would have had a steady income and wouldn't have had to commit suicide*. Janey and her friends discuss art and feminism. Intertitle: *INTENSE SEXUAL DESIRE IS THE GREATEST THING IN THE WORLD*. Janey and Johnny go on a date. They go back to her place and fuck. She comes when he enters her, but *he's moving too quickly to keep Janey coming*. When he comes, *he pulls the black pants he's still wearing over his thighs because he has to go home*.

Speaking for nearly every straight girl in late-'70s America, Acker concludes the story: *At the door to Janey's apartment Johnny's telling Janey he's going to call her. Johnny walks out the door and doesn't see Janey again*.

New York City in 1979 records a wonderful confluence between Acker's hard-won, fragmented, but sharp sensibility and her environment. By now a principal actor in NewYork's downtown scene, Acker feeds the scene back to itself, aware that she's both a protagonist and chronicler of the new art world's weird chamber drama. Transporting emotion and sex from the realm of the female-abject, she proposes a new universal that is—to borrow a line from the poet Ted Berrigan, Acker's contemporary and friend—"feminine, marvelous and tough."

* * *

The summer of 1979 continued into September. Acker wouldn't get out of the city until early October, when she traveled to Amsterdam to appear at the One World Poetry Festival. Then in its second year, One World was renowned as a kind of countercultural summit, hosting Beat and like-minded poets from all over the world.

When the British poet and translator Paul Buck was invited to read at One World that year, he checked the program notes first. William Burroughs, Brion Gysin, Heathcote Williams and Michael McClure would all be there, but it was Acker's name that made him commit. He'd discovered *The Childlike Life* at Compendium Books, the London bookstore that served as a de facto club for avant-garde poets, post-'68 theorists, and punks. His friend Nick Kimberley, a bookseller there, had asked Buck if *he* was the real Black Tarantula? Buck was a fan of the French high-lit crime books published by Série Noire. Like Acker, his writings were steeped in crime, murder, and sex.

He was instantly hooked. When Buck arrived at the festival, he asked everyone, "Where's Kathy Acker?" They became fast friends right away. Buck published a literary magazine, *Curtains*, in which he introduced virtually all the twentieth-century "transgressive" French writers to readers in the UK. An unofficial emissary between avant-garde writers in Paris and London, Buck had been instrumental in promulgating the work of Maurice Blanchot, Bataille, Laure, and his contemporary, Pierre Guyotat, beyond France. Acker had recently heard about Guyotat's book *Eden Eden Eden*, a horrific account of the Algerian war conveyed in one endless, hallucinatory sentence. Published by Gallimard, it was hard to get hold of outside France because it had been partially banned, despite the entreaties of Roland Barthes, Philippe Sollers, and Michel Leiris. Acker was thrilled to learn that Buck knew Pierre Guyotat and had followed his writing for years.

On the festival's marathon opening night, Acker took the stage after Gregory Corso. She was one of the handful of women invited to perform at One World. Several nights later she read with the poet Ed Dorn. That year, to everyone's disappointment, Burroughs and Gysin made themselves scarce. Acker made sure that Buck understood she had nothing in common with Corso and Dorn or the other "post-Beats," who by now looked like shambling old hippies. She was there *to make further connections*. Her eyes were fixed on the future, and Burroughs, Bataille, and Pierre Guyotat were the writers she most closely identified with.

The festival passed in a happy blur of readings, impromptu meetings, and drinks for most of the invitees. Burroughs and Gysin stayed in a superior hotel, compliments of the festival, but Acker could rarely be found in the budget accommodation where she and the rest of the poets were housed. She told Buck she'd made plans to hang out with Lou Reed and Peter Gordon, who had Amsterdam gigs at the same time. Still, she and Paul Buck found time to have long, deep conversations about writing. Before leaving, they visited the artist Caroline Gosselin, who cast plaster mold masks of their faces.

* * *

Travel to Europe in 1979 was expensive, and Acker was in no rush to return to New York. Through Sylvère Lotringer and James Grauerholz, she already had a few contacts and introductions to writers and editors in Paris. Paul Buck had agreed to read at the Pompidou Center on November 11, so they made plans to meet up in France.

Acker's first stop in Paris was Gérard-Georges Lemaire's apartment in Montparnasse. A translator and editor, Lemaire was best known for his work with William S. Burroughs and the prestigious contemporary Éditions 10/18 imprint he edited for his friend, the publisher Christian Bourgois. Acker had met Lemaire in New York the year before at Sylvère Lotringer's Nova Convention, a three-day countercultural summit that reintroduced Burroughs's work to downtown New York. Most likely they'd been introduced by James Grauerholz, who'd just become Burroughs's secretary, but prior to that, he'd acted as an informal agent for Acker and other downtown New York friends. As the Stonehill saga dragged on, Lemaire talked about publishing *Blood and Guts* with 10/18. Acker arrived in Paris that fall expecting to have the book published by the prestigious imprint, but within a year the deal collapsed when she and Lemaire had a falling-out.

Sylvère Lotringer recalls Gerard-Georges Lemaire as "part of the clique-ish Parisian milieu, mostly the *Tel Quel* entourage. He was tight with the then-powerful Christian Bourgois, who published the two Burroughs/Gysin volumes he put together. He wasn't exactly discreet, but he did do some decent work introducing the Beat writers in France."

Lemaire had already translated Ezra Pound, as well as Allen Ginsberg and other Beat writers. According to Buck, "Lemaire was a fast translator, not always so good when he was translating Ginsberg and Pound, if you get my drift. Typewriter translating."

During the days, maybe weeks, when Acker stayed at Lemaire's rue Paul-Fort apartment, he translated *The Childlike*

Life into French while she trawled his vast library. She discovered *Écrits de Laure*, the posthumously edited writings of the remarkable woman best known then (and now) as the girlfriend of Georges Bataille. The Change group had published Laure's writings in Paris three years earlier, in a slender volume containing Laure's writings bracketed by a collection of strangely apologetic essays by Georges Bataille, Jérôme Peignot, and Marcel Moré about her life and work.

Acker connected immediately with the obscure and overinterpreted Laure. While Lemaire translated Acker's early work, she found a dictionary and began freely transcribing Laure's tormented letters to her married lover, Bataille:

> *Dear Georges, . . . When we first met I thought you didn't notice me because I'm invisible so I said whatever I wanted to . . . Sometimes I want to break off everything with you because I hate you so much I want everything is your way:*

and

> *G explained in no way would he ever jeopardize the situation between the woman he was living with and himself. I said I didn't interfere with marriages I wasn't interested in them. Even though it was the first time, our bodies worked well together . . . The next day I wanted to see him again and wondered if I would.*
>
> *Two days later he phoned me had had tried to phone me*
>
> *no feelings involved . . .*

Laure's work was a revelation. Here was a true antecedent. Laure's texts were steeped in an avant-garde sensibility, but they were female, highly specific, and emotionally direct. Acker might have written these letters herself. In a sense, she already had.

Beginning with her ex-husband Bob Acker, most of her romances were with men who were already attached. A few left their partners for her, but most of her lovers did not. Writing to and from her own life, Acker, until her death, was drawn to the heightened emotional pitch of doomed love. Torment, she found she could write from. Boredom, she could not. Did Acker's pursuit of attached partners stem from her father's abandonment, or was it merely bad luck? Given Acker's extreme force of will and intelligence, both seem unlikely.

Just as the twenty-three-year-old Acker trained herself to heighten the emotional pitch of her diary by deleting conjunctions and adjectives, throughout her life she consistently sought situations that would result in disruptive intensity for all parties involved. Almost all the memorial tributes and essays penned in the wake of her death by her friends speak of her "vulnerability." Yet, like the rest of her writing and life, her vulnerability was highly strategic. Pursuing a charged state of grace, Acker knew, in some sense, *exactly* what she was doing. To pretend otherwise is to discount the crazed courage and breadth of her work.

Excited at discovering Laure, Acker mailed the first pages of her translation to Paul Buck from Paris. She would publish this work in a London magazine piece in the early '80s as "Translations of the Diaries of Laure the Schoolgirl." But Bataille's and Laure's ghosts would continue to move through much of her subsequent writing. She returns to Laure's letters in her 1993 novel *My Mother: Demonology*. This time Bataille becomes "B," short for "Bourenine," a cipher for her ex-lover Sylvère Lotringer.

Acker's next project at Lemaire's apartment was to translate his copy of *Eden Eden Eden*. "She worked hard on the Guyotat," Paul Buck remembers. "Freely, of course. She is finding what she wants in it. What Guyotat intended is not necessarily captured . . . But she worked hard on it, with a dictionary."

She hadn't begun writing *Great Expectations* yet, but in less than six months her translation of *Eden* would move from her notebooks into the book. Back in New York early in January 1980, she'd send Paul Buck the first pages of *Great Expectations*. In them the narrator juxtaposes an homage to her mother with whole swaths of Guyotat's *Eden*:

> *My mother often told me: You shouldn't care if an action is right or wrong; you should totally care if you're going to profit mone-tarily from it.*
>
> *The helmeted bowlegged stiff-muscled soldiers rample on just-born babies swaddled in scarlet violet shawls, babies roll out of the arms of women crouched under POP's iron machine guns . . . the driver's studded heel crushes*
> *As he pulls hair out the back of this head on to the sheet metal, some stones*
> *blow up*
>
> *My mother is the most beautiful woman in the world.*

* * *

When Paul Buck and his partner, Glenda George, arrived in November, they were eager to introduce Acker to their Paris friends. Among them was the poet Jean-Pierre Faye, who belonged to the Change group. A breakaway group from *Tel Quel*, Change was committed to advancing a "real" poetics that reflected the frag-mentation of contemporary life as it was lived. Faye was a close friend and sometime collaborator with Jerome Rothenberg, Acker's old crush and mentor. In Paris, they met as equals, but if she was excited about this, she was too circumspect to say so.

Acker attended Buck's reading in the Beaubourg with Faye and other new friends. He'd been invited to read from his translations of modern French poets, but when the Pompidou declined to pay as agreed, he read a piece by Ulrike Meinhof instead. This was written by Meinhof while she was in solitary confinement at Stammheim prison, and Buck read fragments of the same text Acker had paraphrased in *Toulouse Lautrec*—

Feeling your head exploding. Feeling your brain on the point of bursting to bits. Feeling your spine jammed up into your brain and feeling your brain like a dried fruit. Feeling continuously and unconsciously like an electric wire . . .

—in honor of the Baader-Meinhof Group member Faye had brought along to the show.

Acker told Buck she'd stayed on in Paris into November to perform in the Festival d'Automne. Buck can't remember ever attending that performance, and, searching the well-archived schedule for that year, Acker's name does not appear there.

Still, she made a big impression in Paris that fall among the Bucks' friends. When they invited her to a cocktail party thrown by the British ambassador, she arrived at his palatial apartment with one of her New York friends. She and Jill Kroesen—who actually *did* perform at the Festival d'Automne—were wearing ripped jeans and distressed black leather jackets. They'd either forgotten—or never had—official invitations to the soiree. When they were stopped at the door, Acker pointed at Buck, burst past the bouncer, and climbed over a table to give him a hug. Everyone wondered, Who *is* this woman? The Bucks were flattered and charmed.

In a short 2005 essay published in *Les Lettres Françaises*, Gérard-Georges Lemaire reflects on Acker's stay with him that fall in Paris. His description of the thirty-two-year-old Acker strangely echoes Georges Bataille's descriptions of Jane Lazare in *Blue of Noon* . . . a character based on the philosopher

Simone Weil, whom Bataille both admired and loathed. As Lemaire writes:

One fine day, she came to Paris and stayed a few days in my rue Paul-Fort apartment. There was something very restless about her. She was overly sensitive, as if she was always on the defensive. Relations with her were always difficult, for no good reason. I wasn't able to get close to her—or I didn't feel the need or desire, who knows? Anyway, a kind of ragged friendship grew over time. So long as you didn't try to find out who was behind the mask of the wild, poisonous punk (and you didn't have to be a genius to quickly perceive the fragile woman who lived on a razor's edge.) Above all, she maintained a troubling contradiction between the appearance she'd chosen, and the writer she wanted to embody. The two didn't match. And her literature suffered, by design, from this tension.

After leaving Lemaire's apartment, Acker stayed in St.-Germain-des-Prés with Jean-Jacques Lebel. An artist and cultural entrepreneur, Lebel belonged to philosopher Félix Guattari's group of friends. Lebel thrived on transgression. His living room walls were graced by a collection of original black-and-white photographic prints of women's assholes . . . mementos of his other guests.

During these weeks in Paris, Acker enjoyed a brief affair with Jean-Jacques Schuhl, a writer who then lived with Ingrid Caven, the famous Fassbinder actress. *I asked the cards,* Acker writes on the first page of *Great Expectations,* about *future boyfriends. This question involved the following thoughts: Would the guy who fucked me so well in France be in love with me? Will I have a new boyfriend?*

All in all, her first Paris trip was a tremendous success.

* * *

Acker's grandmother Florence Weill died in her New York apartment on October 26, 1979. She was buried in the Weill family plot in the Rodeph Sholem Congregation cemetery in Brooklyn. Wendy Weiss identified her grandmother's body and signed the death certificate. Pooh Kaye thinks she recalls seeing Acker at Florence's funeral, but this seems unlikely. Acker was verifiably in Amsterdam and Paris throughout the fall, and quick trips across the Atlantic were not common then. Acker definitely attended Claire's funeral, but she probably didn't learn of her grandmother's death until December, when she returned to New York.

Florence's relation to her granddaughter Kathy had always been a confusing mix of disapproval and sincere respect. The third daughter of Austrian immigrants who owned a York Avenue butcher shop, Florence was known as the most driven, astute, and financially ambitious member of her extended clan. Like Kaye's mother, Hortense, she married well. Florence's husband, Alexander Weill, owned a successful glove manufacturing business that they sold at just the right time. She was less than thrilled when her granddaughter married Bob Acker, a lower-middle-class Pole. Florence, Pooh Kaye recalls, "had a great business head and she was stingy as a Scrooge," sending miserly birthday and holiday checks to children within the family. Aunts consulted Florrie to appraise their jewelry; uncles asked her for stock tips. Within days of her sister Hortense's death, she badgered her brother-in-law for deep discounts on her late sister's jewels. Still, when Acker was virtually disowned by Albert and Claire, Florence paid her tuition during the two years she attended Brandeis. She disapproved of her granddaughter's choices but admired her brilliance, accomplishments, and drive.

Writing just a few months before Florence's death, in *New York City in 1979* Acker parodies her grandmother as a retired courtesan, juggling her remaining johns while playing the stock market. Shades of Colette's *Chérie*: *Nana's apartment rooms are tremendous, too big for her tiny body . . . Thick silk daybed spreads ivory-handled white feather fans hanging above contrast the black and-red "naturalist" clown portraits in the "study" that give an air of culture rather than of call-girl.* Giving her granddaughter Janey a $10,000 check, she scolds, *Now I'm going to tell you something, Janey. Invest this. Buy yourself 100 shares of AT&T. You can fritter it away if you want. Good riddance to you. If your mother had invested the 800 shares of IBM I gave her, she would have had a steady income and wouldn't have had to commit suicide. Well, she needed the money.* In *Great Expectations*, a lawyer at her mother's funeral shakes the narrator by her jacket lapels and asks, *Where are the 800 IBM shares?* Typical of Jewish comedy, most of Acker's burlesque family routines center around money, hubris, and sex. Throughout the first part of her life, virtually all the names of Acker's husbands, lovers and friends, mentors and art world associates are Jewish. In mid-twentieth-century New York, Jews were the culture industry's dominant force.

After Florence's death, Acker became a person of modestly "great expectations" in the Dickensian sense. Florence left behind an estate of just under $1 million (about $3.3 million in today's money), most of which was to be divided equally between her granddaughters Kathy and Wendy. Each would receive a lump sum of $100,000, and the rest would be placed in fifteen-year residual trusts. Throughout the time Acker was working on *Great Expectations*, she was waiting for the estate to clear probate and her funds to come through. The threat and promise of inheritance course throughout the novel like the River Styx. Paraphrasing a Virginia Holt romance, Acker writes:

> *My father had left me all his possessions and I was, by the world's accounting, a well-to-do young woman. I owned a large house in Seattle. The rest of the money, since it was tied up in stocks and bonds and lawyers' incomprehensible papers, only meant that I*

was no longer untouchable . . . I knew I was no longer a person to a man, but an object, a full purse,

And, again:

Is my lover trying to murder me? / Is my lover trying to get my inheritance? . . .

My husband wants me to put my inheritance in a joint bank account and draw up a will in his name.

In a conversation between the narrator and her lover Clifford in Seattle:

: I'm going to murder you, honey.
: I don't want you to murder me.
: But I want money and you've got it.

Clifford continues in soliloquy, [*My girlfriend*] . . . *had become sick so she could deny me. This means the sicker she becomes, the more I have to rip her off.*

Florence Weill named Pooh Kaye's father, the attorney Clifford Kaye, and his law partner Samuel Gordon as joint executors of her estate. Writing to Paul Buck from New York during the last days of December 1979, Acker complains, *Money from my grandmother's will doesn't come through till* [*sic*] *August,* but settlement of the estate eventually took a much longer time.

Pooh Kaye recalls a furious string of letters sent from Acker to Pooh's father throughout 1980. She either didn't understand or refused to accept that funds couldn't be disbursed until the will cleared probate. Clifford Kaye's control of the estate was a maddening reminder of Claire's dependency on Florence. *Clifford* (the name she also gave in the book to her Seattle truck-driving lover), *my father's best friend,* and *Mr.*

Gordon appear throughout *Great Expectations* as spectral figures of legal authority.

Desperate to return to New York from the West Coast, by the end of 1980 Acker began begging Pooh Kaye to intervene with her dad and get him to release $10,000 that she could use as a down payment on an apartment. Recalling, perhaps, that Kaye had once supported herself in New York cleaning lofts, Acker offered her the cleaning supplies left behind in her dead grand-mother's apartment in exchange.

Their friendship ended soon after that—not directly because of Acker's insulting bequest (although it couldn't have helped)—but because of a shared romantic interest. As Kaye recalls, "Kathy just had to make love with every man she saw. Everyone—hus-bands, lovers, heartthrobs—anyone that someone she knew was involved with. It was a territorial thing, as it is with many hyper-sexual people." She recalled the title of Jill Kroesen's song to Acker: "Don't Steal My Boyfriend."

Florence's furniture, jewelry, and personal effects were divided between her two granddaughters. Acker chose a pair of white silk upholstered chairs. She would keep these chairs for more than a decade, alternately storing and shipping them, together with her library, as she moved from New York to Seattle to San Francisco to New York to London and then back again in 1991 to New York, where they remained until 1996, when she finally sold her empty, expensive East Twelfth Street condominium. She'd be too sick to retrieve them by then.

* * *

Acker returned from Paris to New York and her dumpy East Fifth Street apartment in early December 1979. The place hadn't changed. It was exactly as she'd described it in *Blood and Guts: A three-room apartment; a fourteen by nine room, two seven by nine rooms, and one more fourteen by nine room which contains toilet, bathtub and stove. Usually no hot water or heat . . . Garbage covers every inch of the streets.*

While she'd been away, a fat sheaf of legal documents arrived in the mail. "The Accounting of Samuel Gordon as the Executor of the Estate of Claire W. Alexander" showed that her mother had died with $23.69 left in her checking account. The furniture in her childhood home had been auctioned off to cover the funeral bills, and her grandmother Florrie had paid $1,500 to get Claire's jewelry out of hock. Acker gave Jeff Goldberg the papers. She couldn't bear keeping them, nor could she throw them away.

The shock of her grandmother's death while she'd been away gave Acker a new sense of urgency, and her encounters with writers in Europe during those months helped to affirm the avant-garde modernist lineage that ran through her work. By Christmas she'd write the Bucks here *I am back in USA & hot on new book*.

Two weeks later, sick with the flu, she'd send them the first chapter of *Great Expectations* along with a detailed report on New Year's Eve at the Mudd Club. Assaulted by an acquaintance, she is saved by club owner Steve Mass, and they go back to his place to do coke. She declines his advances, has breakfast with him, and then goes home to read Dickens and Husserl.

She'd already shared her translations of Laure and Pierre Guyotat with Paul Buck. Like Jerome Rothenberg, Jackson Mac Low, Alan Sondheim, and Ron Silliman before him, Paul Buck would become her close correspondent and first reader for the next eighteen months as she worked on the book. He replied to her letters with constant encouragement and sometimes with poems of his own. But unlike his predecessors, Buck never enters the narrative, and none of its parts are addressed to him. She and Paul Buck never have sex. Her relation with him remains a friendship, and she'll dedicate the fourth chapter of *Great Expectations* to him and Glenda, his partner.

Buck saved their correspondence for more than two decades. In 2004 he published her letters—together with texts he composed in response to her work after her death—in his book *Spread Wide*, a posthumous homage to their friendship and literary exchange.

By mid-February 1980 Acker finished and mailed Buck "I Journey to Receive My Fortune," the next section of *Great Expectations*. The section included "open letters" to God, Peter Gordon, Sylvère Lotringer, Steve Maas, and Susan Sontag. I saw her read them at a Mudd Club performance she did with Gary Indiana on Valentine's Day. Her performance that night was indelibly charming and brazen. In a 1977 reading videotaped at the Western Front in Vancouver, Acker sat on the floor, unremarkably dressed in a T-shirt and jeans, with thick rimless glasses and a bowl haircut. Three years later, her presence is vastly more calculated: standing in a white spotlight wearing a tight leather skirt, she reads quickly, aggressively, tossing off outrageous insults to her well-known addressees with a quick nod to her audience. With porcelain skin, deep-red lips, eyes made even wider with heavy black makeup, she's both of this crowd and above it. She writes to a "David," who bears a striking resemblance to Rudy Wurlitzer: *Your explanation that you gave up writing your visions in order to do commercial Hollywood script writing because you needed Francis Ford Coppola's $150,000 when you receive huge monthly estate checks rivals a university professor's essay on the similarities between Moby Dick and Nazism. At least a university professor really has to make a living . . . The only thing I resent is when you were doing everything to force me to fuck your Tibetan guru and I had bad gonorrhea.*

After the performance, she'd write to the Bucks: *my dear husband Mr. Gordon just phoned me how dare I mention REAL NAMES during my performances especially his girl friend's cause her twat is sacred . . .* But perhaps the most shocking of all was her note to

Sontag: *Dear Susan Sontag, Would you please read my books and make me famous? . . . I now see my delusions are more interesting than anything that can happen to me in New York. Despite everyone saying New York is just the most fascinating city in the world. Except when Sylvère fucks me.* In one breath Acker demolishes the most respected—in fact, the only—American female public intellectual in an era when such things still mattered, and establishes herself by default as her punk rock successor: *I wish I knew how to speak English. Dear Susan Sontag, will you teach me how to speak English? For free . . .*

I'm having this weirdo affair with Sylvère (Lotringer), Acker reported to the Bucks in her mid-February letter. *I cancelled twenty dates in a row with him cause I'm such a lobotomy case and I might feel something . . . but the minute I NOTICE him, you know, not just treating him like shit . . . he says "Oh I hate feelings" "Oh I want everything to go fast and disappear" . . . so I have to be nastier and cleverer and fool around more than him: it's a great battle . . .*

Her next letter, written several weeks later, continues: *My head is gone cause this thing with Sylvère keeps getting I don't know what it's getting of course it's not ROMANCE or ANY WORD cause I'm a cripple and he's so tough . . . but meanwhile I might end up dead and not from extasy though extasy sure goes with it. I walk into the gym to work out and the women STARE at my back . . . Maybe I will end up dead. But . . . who cares S&M doesn't go beyond the bed unlike the usual relationships where it's all S&M outside the bed . . .*

Lotringer has no recollection of these BDSM sessions. As he recalls it, since meeting in 1977, they were continuously involved within the context of a promiscuous scene, but he felt closer to her than anyone else he went out with. "It was something else. In my eyes, it was not just about having an affair. She was a writer, and I was interested in writing."

Still: the third section of *Great Expectations*—all *porn*, as she'd write to the Bucks—includes long appropriations of text from Pauline Réage's *Story of O* and *Return to the Chateau*. Characteristically, Acker shatters Réage's erotic, somnambulant spell with phenomenological questions that, in this context, feel electrically urgent: *WHERE DO EMOTIONS COME FROM, ARE EMOTIONS NECESSARY, WHAT DO EMOTIONS TELL US ABOUT CONSCIOUSNESS?* There is willed pain—*He shows her his whip./ One of his hands lies on her left shoulder*—and there is the other pain, that's inescapable: *NOT ONLY IS THERE NO ESCAPE FROM PERCEIVING BUT THE ONLY WAY TO DEAL WITH PAIN IS TO KILL ONESELF TOTALLY BY ONESELF.*

When she moved to London and became, as she'd dreamed, truly famous, Acker would pursue BDSM in her writing and life to a point where sexuality became essentialist, almost religious, the path toward a unified being through violence enacted in solemn rites. No longer moored to any social relation, let alone artistic scene, sexuality became the means of both finding and losing one's self. Her remark to the Bucks—*S&M doesn't go beyond the bed unlike the usual relationships where it's all S&M outside the bed*—would be repeated almost verbatim fifteen years later in an email to McKenzie Wark.

* * *

In late March, *I Dreamt I Was a Nymphomaniac: Imagining* was republished by Traveler's Digest, a small imprint run by her friend Jeff Goldberg and his partners Andrew Wylie and Victor Bockris. *Nymphomaniac* was the last of her self-published serial works to be republished. *Everyone loves it*, she wrote to the Bucks, *and social social social more work I love work but I am so worn down dear . . .* Meanwhile, Robert Kushner's self-financed edition of *The Persian Poems* finally appeared, though he and Acker were no longer friends. "I have been trying to remember how Kathy reacted to the book. And I can't," Kushner said. "She had stopped being interested in meditation, and her life seemed to be filled with difficulties and perhaps I withdrew a bit at that time? I don't remember having much contact . . ."

With readings scheduled in San Diego, San Francisco, and Seattle, Acker left New York for a month in mid-April. But this tour would turn into a two-year flight. She'd made tentative plans to read with Paul Buck in London in June and then travel to Paris, but these plans were shelved once she arrived in Seattle. She'd given a reading at Art in Form, an alternative space run by a group of young women who owned a handful of galleries, record stores, and bookstores in Belltown. At the tail end of the grant-rich Carter years, Art in Form was a popular stop on the West Coast tour trail, with an impressive roster of visiting artists and writers. The venue's 1980 schedule, with talks and performances by Stuart Sherman, Charlemagne Palestine, Simone Forti, and Tom Marioni, reads like a who's who of the era's U.S. art world.

While in Seattle, Acker met Jim Logie, a truck driver/painter who lived in a storefront at 111 Bell Street. They embarked on a maddening five-month affair that would shape the midsection of *Great Expectations*, "Seattle Art Society." In a postcard to Jeff Goldberg dated May 28, 1980, Acker writes,

Aren't going to make it back to NYC—too expensive & I want to stay out here. So here I am: it's flipping my mind . . . NYC might have got me famous but it was killing me. I have to make a bid to see: apart from male-given media given-categories. I have to learn what nature is. Even if I die unknown. I mean, otherwise, I've done nothing. There's only one life. Stay in touch with me sweetie you're my friend . . . I know you're going to understand this move. I have to do what I have to do—love, Kathy.

She leaves out the part about meeting Logie, who'll become the bad boyfriend "Clifford" in *Great Expectations*. As Annie

Grosshans, who ran the bookstore and was then Jim Logie's primary girlfriend, recalls, "He was quite present on the Seattle cultural scene for a few years before Kathy arrived, and then off the radar after she left. He liked women, although there was an opportunistic quality to him. He was a heat seeker, and no doubt that was a component of his bond with Kathy, because she was a force." Or, as Acker would write of Clifford in *Great Expectations*, he was *a very good artist . . . who wants the world to be as it is in the center of his art. All the artists recognize this goodness. He's very animal especially his wiggling ass he's such a great fuck.*

She decided to give up the East Fifth Street apartment. In a July 24 letter, her friend Terence Sellers writes, "Okay, first of all your moving out caused all kinds of waves, people shrieking you were nuts, David E. calling me in despair that he'd have to get 900 boxes for your 72,000 books, general hilarity when your ceiling fell in on Grandmother's white silk chairs! We never did find out if all your stuff made it out there . . . Jeff Goldberg looking wan at your name. Come back, goomba girl."

To the Bucks, Acker writes, *Jeffrey's no longer talking to me cause I'm living in Seattle with a MAN so there go those royalties . . . and besides . . . I'm in love: this one's rough too cause I am definitely not used to sharing anything with anyone, but he's a good man, god-damnit he works as a teamster . . . Things weird in this country . . . looks like Reagan's gonna be President, everyone scared, crazy . . . We plan to move to Europe by December. But things good out here; am seeing slowly how fucked up I've been NYC years: no more normal person, media jetset hype faster faster*

But soon she was bored. Seattle was just like New York, only smaller. *I've been absolutely miserable here in the boonies with no one to talk to,* she wrote to Jeff Goldberg by the end of August. "Seattle Art Society" includes a brilliant pastiche of her new, ingrown world, superimposing Belltown gossip onto Madame de Lafayette's chamber novel *La Princesse des Clèves*: *[Clifford] lives in Seattle. He's fucked every woman artist in Seattle. All these women artists are still in love with him. A new woman artist who's more famous than these other women artists cause she's from New York City comes to Seattle. All the artists love her cause she's still living outside that community, isn't yet competing. She marries M. de Cleves so she can stay away from New York City.*

The women artists in Seattle were less cynical. Creating an artistic community with ties to Seattle's activist and organized labor scenes, they didn't see Acker as competition. "We as women and as Belltown shopkeepers were glad to have her presence in our community and her books in her store," Annie Grosshans recalls. Her friend Laura Millin adds, "We were very excited and welcoming when she arrived." Soon she and Jim Logie were making plans to buy a house outside of Paris or London once her inheritance cleared.

The idyll didn't last long. One month later she'd write to the Bucks, *Seattle is bleak and horrible and I believe I'm too old and rotty to live with anyone.* And to Jeff Goldberg: *Seattle is worse than the people in SF. There are no good restaurants under $10 people aren't obsessed artists they're phoney-polite to each other & macho hulks walk the streets. I don't talk to anyone.* What had she been thinking? *The love relation here in Seattle has gone blotto . . . it's like having a baby & I'm not even stable enough to be one & I can't afford someone less stable than me,* she wrote to the Bucks. By the end of September she tells Goldberg, *there's been a violent outbreak, and I'm scared. He's going to Paris right after Christmas so everything will end without violence if I just don't do anything precipitous.* Writing about her Seattle sojourn in *Great Expectations* after she'd left, the picture becomes even darker:

> *Red everywhere. Red up the river, where it flows among the green pines and old mining camps; red down the river, where it rolls defiled among the tiers of the shipping and dock pollutions . . . Red*

on the rain marshes, red on Queen Anne Hill . . . Red the artist's hand not from paint but from striking his lover's face out of repressed fear.

The raw afternoon is rawest, and the red is most red, and the streets are filthiest on the part of Bell Street next to the river where I lived in fear of my lover for six months . . .

Living with him was living with hell. He never relaxed. He was always like an atom bomb. He thought he was delicate feminine because when he got drunk (relaxed) the only aspect he could perceive was overwhelming self-insecurity or fear.

The only anchor in her life then was her work on *Great Expectations*. *Now*, she wrote Jeff Goldberg, *it is very slow, and sometimes painful in that I have to work very hard at it and* MAKE *it but it is always this way isn't it if you make everything from the beginning . . . and in this place where nothing is given (. . . NYC so much given but so crazy frenzied cannot build, and I need to write real now . . .* In Seattle, the grief she'd displaced since her mother's death finally took hold:

My mother is the most beautiful woman in the world. She has black hair, green eyes which turn gray or brown according to her mood or the drugs she's on at the moment, the pallor of this pink emphasizes the fullness of her lips . . . Her body is equally exquisite . . .

and

I realize that all my life is is endings. Not endings, those are just events; but holes. For instance when my mother died, the "I" I had always known dropped out. All my history went away. Pretty clothes and gayness amazes me.

Invited that August to teach at the San Francisco Art Institute for six weeks at the end of the fall, she saw the brief job as her ticket out. By the end of September, counting the weeks until she could leave, she sent the next part of *Great Expectations* off to the Bucks. But after San Francisco, where would she go? Her money still hadn't come through, and she couldn't afford to move back to New York. *Dear Jeffrey*, she wrote, *I miss you so much I can't bear it. I think I must be crazy escaping all over the place when we're so alike and like each other it's ridiculous and it's stupid for me to be scared all the time just I've had so many deaths . . . I've just finished typing the first two chapters of the next section of* Great Expectations *which is taking a long time cause it has to be just right . . .*

No doubt she was lonely. Leaving Seattle on November 19, she wrote a postcard to Paul Buck: *Rain rain rain right here (no, outside window) where I'm standing in Seattle airport, waiting to go to SF—no home, (yet), not going back to NYC cause I can't afford it . . .* Alone in the airport and panicked with no one to phone or not enough change for the long-distance call, she was leaving the city she'd fled to five months before.

* * *

Acker's first stop in San Francisco was the Noe Valley home of her friend the writer Bob Glück. Almost immediately she began an affair with the conceptual artist Howard Fried, who directed SFAI's new media program and was her boss. Fried extended her contract into the following year, but the relationship didn't last long because he had a long-standing girlfriend. *One slit wrist & PID as usual are the leftovers . . . I think all I care about is intelligence,* she quipped in a postcard to Goldberg in January 1981. This romantic debacle would provide material for the last section of *Great Expectations*, in which the narrator becomes the Roman courtesan Cynthia. Fried is cast as the poet Propertius, who *decides he doesn't want to fuck Cynthia again.*

Acker makes no mention of her inheritance in her correspondence after leaving Seattle, but it's likely her money came through that January. Beginning in February, she finally rented her own apartment in SoMa, a few doors away from New Langton Arts, a nonprofit art and literary center. In *Great Expectations*, Propertius derides her character, Cynthia: *If you're obsessed for me, bitch, you're going to drink blood—you now living off your grandmother's capitalist hoard though blowing more.* Fear of repeating her mother's overspending and outliving her money haunts Acker's subsequent writing. As it turned out, this didn't happen. But had Acker lived longer, it certainly could have.

After receiving her money, Acker sent Goldberg a terse postcard about his edition of *Nymphomaniac: As I remember our agreement . . . though you seemed unwilling to sign a contract was that I'd receive 25 copies & a certain amount of money. I can understand that I won't receive the money, but I'd like to get the other 10 copies . . . I don't like feeling ripped off.* This note marks the end of their correspondence.

Living alone for the first time in nearly a year, Acker set out to finish *Great Expectations* before her thirty-fourth birthday, which was coming up on April 18, 1981. Writing to Paul Buck, she confides gleefully how she's cast Fried as Propertius and herself as his girlfriend Cynthia, *who was, according to me like I'm some Latin authority hee hee, a whore.* Propertius pines after Cynthia: *This is my poem to your cunt door, Oh little door/ I love you so very much,* but she rejects him: *Well, everyone wants to fuck me I tell you I'm sick of this life.* She tells him about her mother's funeral, and concludes:

I do everything for sexual love.

. . . When you reject me, I'm gonna die in front of you. In the long run nothing's important. This is the one sentiment that makes me happy.

Please be nice to me.

After leading her on, Propertius abruptly decides to stop sleeping with Cynthia because he has a girlfriend. Cynthia and her friends, the whores Danielle and Barbarella (a character inspired by Glück), complain about boyfriends, but Cynthia proclaims: *I need sex to stay alive.* The text tumbles into a fragment of Colette's *The Pure and the Impure* and then back to Pauline Réage. Propertius thinks Cynthia's a whore because she has a career, while his girlfriend is pure. Waiting outside his door and rejected, Cynthia cuts her arm with a razor and barks like a dog. Swooping through all modes of being, in *Great Expectations* Acker compresses the dizzying switches between high and low culture she pioneered in *The Childlike Life* into an elaborate fugue composed in a fugue state.

Although she failed to complete *Great Expectations* before her birthday on April 18, by late May, Acker sent the Bucks her last manuscript pages. *I'm about to collapse . . .* she announced. *After 20 hours a day non-stop one very tired ex-writer who has no other life left and really can't gossip about anything cause there's nothing to gossip about no evil sexism no hurt feelings not even champagne has finished one novel* GREAT EXPECTATIONS *. . . and one two-year portion of a weird life. This one involved running away.*

Blood and Guts was still in limbo. More than six years had passed since TVRT published *Toulouse Lautrec*, and Acker knew she needed to publish a new book.

She decided that summer, against her better judgment, to self-publish *Great Expectations*. She didn't want this to look like a vanity publication, so she advanced funds for her new friend V. Vale to produce it under his San Francisco RE/Search imprint. The arrangement was a minor disaster, with only three hundred copies produced, but—as she told the Bucks—*the book's getting great reviews! The first really good reviews I've gotten.*

When RE/Search finally completed the book, Acker moved back to New York. She sublet her friend Ingrid Sischy's loft in the fish market district at 228 Front Street. Acker's friends threw her a launch at the Mudd Club. By March 1981 she rented her own large, newly renovated loft in a Lower East Side building owned by the artist Jenny Holzer.

Like many downtown New York women, Acker had begun the new decade by working out in a gym. Now she set out to train seriously. She booked sessions with the celebrity body-builder Lisa Lyon, whose book, *Lisa Lyon's Body Magic*, had come out the previous year. Lyon was a close friend and collaborator of the photographer Robert Mapplethorpe. Most likely through Lyon, Acker met Mapplethorpe and had her first series of pro-fessional portraits taken by him. A 1982 portrait shows Acker wearing an artfully deconstructed hand-knit sweater. Her fingers taper into long, manicured nails and a slim feather trails down to her shoulder from one of her multi-pierced ears.

By now her appearance and bearing, even her accent, had changed. George Quasha, her old friend or acquaintance from the Washington Heights Len Neufeld and Jerome Rothenberg days, was struck by her transformation: "Everything changed. Somehow she'd transitioned from being another poet, someone we knew, to being a personage. Very elegant, very composed, very deliberate." In New York she asked Quasha to republish *Great Expectations* with his more established Station Hill Press. Although he found Acker's new image irritating, he admired her work and complied. In the fall of 1982, the Station Hill edition of *Great Expectations* arrived in a handful of downtown bookstores, its cover graced by an invented blurb from Alain Robbe-Grillet: " . . . the most completely unified work of art Acker has yet produced. . . . its unified shape . . . fulfills the sort of demands that Sterne or Canetti make of the novelist." A real quote provided by the theatrical genius Richard Foreman appeared on a whiteboard outside the bookstore on St. Mark's Place: "Reading Kathy Acker is like playing hopscotch with a genius." Her exile was over. Within the square mile of the East Village and the Lower East Side, she was becoming a myth. And, at the time, the Lower East Side was a quadrant of culture beamed all over the world.

* * *

Senior editor Fred Jordan returned to Grove Press early in 1983 after a five-year hiatus at Methuen Books. Jordan had joined Grove almost three decades earlier after a casual meeting with founder Barney Rosset that took place in a Grand Central Station bar. Jordan arrived in the United States after the Second World War after being interned in a camp for people displaced by the Nazi regime. When Jordan met Rosset, he was employed as the editor of a trade journal about scrap metal and waste paper sales. Soon he became instrumental in building Grove Press's prestigious list, editing books by Samuel Beckett, William S. Burroughs, Amiri Baraka, and Jack Kerouac and overseeing Grove's journal, *The Evergreen Review*.

Jordan's first job at Grove that winter was to come up with a fall '83 list. His years at Methuen had taken him out of Grove Press's high-culture/underground loop. Looking around the office in the "slush pile" near the editor's desk, he saw a big stack of books that Acker, or one of her friends, had sent to Barney Rosset. "This might be good," Jordan thought. He took them home and found them "interesting, unusual, in many ways, remarkable." Her work was steeped in Grove's avant-garde lineage, but at the same time it reflected the abrasive Lower East Side early-'80s zeitgeist. At the time, his decision to take a chance with her work didn't seem that monumental. "You have to realize, it's all pretty routine. I remember my problem was what do I publish next week or next month," Jordan recalls. "You have a schedule to fill, and you think, what can I get, what can I put in there? It's much less strategic than it appears afterwards. At that time, you think: What do I have? What's in my drawer, what can I publish?"

At Jordan's behest, Grove acquired rights to all the books that sat around Rosset's desk for an advance of $5,000 (about $12,000 in today's money). It never occurred to Jordan to edit her work. "I assumed," he explained, "that her writing was 'difficult.' It was something that happened in her mind, not mine. You know? It was a construct of her mind. Therefore, I would think that not everything has to be clear. It would never occur to me to go to Samuel Beckett and say, 'what do you mean by that?' To me, that is sacrilege. If he has written it, or said it, or thought it, my job is to try to understand it."

Jordan would maintain this scruple throughout their long and happy relationship, which continued through 1995, with *Pussy, King of the Pirates*, her last full-length work. He decided to lead off in late December with *Great Expectations* because he found it the most accessible of all Acker's works. From there, he'd follow up with *Blood and Guts in High School* in the following season, spring '84. For the *Blood and Guts* cover, he'd use a nightmarish drawing by RAW artist Sue Coe. Coe had already established herself as an East Village Georg Grosz, and Jordan thought it might be good to conjoin their two sensibilities, which spoke, in different ways, to their time.

I've been bought up by some dumb publisher for $5,000, Acker wrote to the Bucks late that spring. George Quasha recalls getting a Demand for Reversion of Rights from Acker's attorney, to which he consented, although "I would have agreed if she'd asked me herself."

I have to work as hard as possible so I can get enough fame then money to get away from here so I can become alive, Acker had written in *Blood and Guts* a few years before. Her great expectations were about to be realized.

Acker's letter to Paul Buck announcing her acquisition by Grove Press would be her last. Soon she'd move to London, but she never saw him. Still, he didn't feel snubbed. "I lived out in Maidstone," Paul Buck explained, "and didn't come in a lot, as no money. And she was always on the move. So it kind of fizzled out. Nothing against her, it's just she was too busy making her career and connections. I understood."

My mother committed suicide and I ran away, Great Expectations *concludes.*

My mother committed suicide in a hotel room because she was lonely and there was no one else in the world but her, wants go so deep there is no way of getting them out of the body . . . I ran away from pain. What is, is. No fantasy. Pain. Just the details: the streets, the green garbage bag a bum's sleeping next to, a friend, too much time no time, too much to eat not enough to eat, going to a movie with Jeffrey I don't know if the world is better off worse than it has been I know the only anguish comes from running away.

FICTION

(1983–1990)

And after a while you learn that fiction becomes reality.
—Kathy Acker to Melvyn Bragg, *The South Bank Show*, 1984

"What we want to look at is the hard edge of a tough, fashionable, self-conscious group, now at the top of the New York avant-garde art world," the renowned British arts broadcaster Melvyn Bragg somberly told ITVS viewers on April 1, 1984, at the start of a *South Bank Show* episode devoted to Kathy Acker. "There are great riches there and the competition is very rough. Kathy Acker and the group around her are at present leading the pack . . . [She's] just been published for the first time in this country. Her book, called *Blood and Guts in High School*, has attracted considerable attention, and remarkably sold out within a couple of weeks of its release."

The South Bank Show, a series of hour-long documentary portraits of prominent artists, musicians, and writers, aired in the UK on Sunday nights throughout the 1980s. Bragg's previous subjects included Paul McCartney, John Berger, Francis Bacon, Jean Genet, Woody Allen, and Francis Ford Coppola. Everyone in the UK who cared about culture watched it. *South Bank* came on right after the cult favorite *Spitting Image*, a satirical show that featured grotesque, scary puppets.

Producing this profile of Acker, Bragg and his ITVS crew followed her for several wintry December days around some of her past and present New York haunts—Times Square, Gold's Gym, David Salle's and Robert Mapplethorpe's studios—and her renovated Eldridge Street loft, where she talked with him about her writing, her life, and her friends. Throughout these interviews Acker—highly composed, focused, and calm—sits before Bragg on an overstuffed gold velour couch. Messy, overflowing bookcases line the walls. She wears a black goat's-hair vest over black leggings and a sweater. Her bleached hair is buzz cut, and her multiply pierced ears are adorned with gold rings and studs that match her gold-veneered upper front tooth as well as the couch. Her red nails match her red lips, and her large eyes are enhanced by thick half lines of black kohl at the base of her lids and under her lower eyelashes. Her gestures are sparing, controlled, but each time her hands move, her bracelets and three enormous rings that cover most of her fingers flash in front of the camera.

The South Bank Show mattered, and Acker's improvised script and performance is masterful. As she tells Bragg, her return to New York from the West Coast sprang from *a resolution to look for some stability that wasn't in any way oppressive to anybody.* She leaves out the parts about her bad boyfriends and her grandmother's money. Dismissing all peer competition, she explains, *There are almost no novelists my age who are doing anything besides second and third generation Philip Roth—they're just imitators.* Rudy Wurlizer, after all, was a whole decade older, and although they were already writing and reading their work in downtown New York, her friends Lynne Tillman and Gary Indiana wouldn't be commercially published until the late 1980s.

As Acker speaks about the neighborhood—*the last poor section left of this part of Manhattan . . . this building up to three years ago was the main building where a lot of the junk trade happened, in fact in this apartment there were thirteen murders*—the camera cuts to the street to capture scenes of indescribable squalor. As the image cuts back and forth between her messy-but-comfortable loft and her walks through the city, she reads excerpts from *Blood and Guts*, *Great Expectations*, and *Don Quixote*. Bragg's montage clearly depicts the rugged formation of the Great Writer.

Outdoors, Acker wears a black jacket, black boots, a black wool hat with earflaps, white gloves, and an improbable long Comme des Garçons white linen tunic. *I think*, she tells Bragg, *in a lot of ways, my books are just mirrors*. Juxtaposing the aspirational glamour of mid-'80s alternative culture with scenes of the unreconstructed underclass misery that became a ubiquitous backdrop to the Bush/Thatcher years, Bragg's documentary itself functions exactly this way, by holding a mirror to Acker's mirrors.

Fifteen years later, the filmmaker Todd Haynes would draw a similar contrast, albeit more critically, in *Velvet Goldmine*, his 1998 faux documentary on glam rock. In *Goldmine*, Haynes cuts from the brightly lit, lavish musical spectacle onstage at Madison Square Garden to a shivering crowd dressed in cheap stocking caps, parkas, and scarves outside the arena.

Rephrasing the goals advanced by Jean-Pierre Faye and the Change group in Paris a decade earlier, Bragg explains, "Kathy Acker feels that the disjointed, angry style of her writing is a reflection of the fractured world she lives in. Her experiments arise out of a dissatisfaction with present-day literary forms, which in her opinion are no longer adequate to describe the modern world."

When the *South Bank* interview aired that April in the UK, its effect was phenomenal. "I can't tell you," the writer and critic Michael Bracewell recalls, "the impact that the film had. Nothing like that had ever been seen in London, in Britain. To have an hour of TV devoted to you—I mean, at the time, other subjects on *The South Bank Show* would have been people like Sir Ernst Gombrich. In those days, to have a *South Bank* documentary made about you was to canonize the subject as part of the cultural establishment. Not like today, where anybody who's been in *Cats* can be a subject of a TV documentary. It was a very big deal. And I think that that moment in the spring of 1984 set the tone for how I would come to perceive Kathy: that she was already a star. And the idea, even, that a writer could be a star on a frequency that seemed similar to that of a pop star, was revolutionary."

By the time the show aired, Acker no longer lived in the rough New York neighborhood she was identified with. She'd moved to London in January just in time for her Picador book launch.

* * *

Pan/Picador published *Blood and Guts*, together with *Great Expectations* and a shorter work, *My Death, My Life by Pier Paolo Pasolini*, in a single volume on February 10, 1984, for an advance of 2,500 GBP (about $9,000 in today's money), but no one involved recalls how this happened. Picador's London release dovetailed with Grove Press's December 1983 publication of *Great Expectations* in the U.S., but neither Sonny Mehta, Picador's former editor in chief, nor Jacqueline Graham, Picador's in-house publicist, remember just when and how Acker's work came to them. Ira Silverberg, who then worked as Grove Press's publicist and would later become Acker's agent, is sure that "the two companies pursued publishing her separately. Likely, deals were done on either side of the ocean at different times."

In December 1982, at least two months before Fred Jordan discovered her books in Grove Press's slush pile, Acker wrote her friend, the British artist Jonathan Miles, *Picador is definitely publishing me.* Her reputation in London had been steadily building since early that fall, when she performed with Heathcote Williams, Roger McGough, and Michael Horovitz in the first annual Poetry Olympics and alone at other venues. *City Limits*, a popular London newsweekly, covered her visit extensively, and Cynthia Rose interviewed her for a *New Musical Express* profile that would be published in January. During that fall 1982 trip she'd had meetings with Picador and discussed future projects with producers of the Almeida Theatre in Islington and with Channel 4, the soon-to-be-launched independent TV station.

In New York, Acker would always be one among many downtown New York artists and writers, but within the relatively insular London scene of the '80s she was shocking and singular. Acker's books, associated with the downtown New York scene that emerged in the '70s, were well known and respected. But compared with the visceral gross-out chic work of such younger contemporaries as Lydia Lunch, Nick Zedd (director of *They Eat Scum* and *Geek Maggot Bingo*), and Richard Kern, by 1982 Acker's books no longer seemed all that "transgressive." Meanwhile, in the UK, where "high" literature was both revered and highly exclusionary, Acker's unique mix of erudition, high fashion, and porn made her sensational. And for a while this was freedom. The Grove Press edition of *Great Expectations* received no major coverage. Even *Blood and Guts*, published by Grove a year later, received no more than a capsule *New York Times* book review that declared it "abusive toward women . . . not so much harrowing as pathetic."

During the same months in London, her name and her image were everywhere, from guest TV talk-show appearances to interviews, profiles, and fragments of gossip in *NME*, *The Observer*, *The Face*, and *The Guardian*. As she'd later tell Sylvère Lotringer, [*T*]*he move to England, as far as things like career matter, which they do, was fabulous for me . . . In New York there was no where to go . . . no way to make more money, no way to get more established as a writer.*

Acker's initial entrance to London was greatly facilitated by her friendship with Rosetta Brooks, a British writer and critic.

Brooks moved to New York shortly after founding *ZG*, an innovative alternative glossy transatlantic magazine that fused art and new writing, music, and politics. Known and respected in London, Brooks soon became friendly with *Bomb* magazine founder and editor Betsy Sussler and others in Acker's circle. In New York between 1982 and '83, Brooks acted informally as Acker's agent.

During Acker's fall 1982 trip to London, she met Brooks's friend Jonathan Miles, who was then *ZG*'s London editor. They had a brief affair that continued by letter and phone between November and January.

In the torrent of letters sent to Miles from New York, Acker performs her familiar routine of romantic anxiety, but she's also aware of her new and increasing stature. On December 16 she sends him a telegram—*ACTING MAD. ARE YOU MARRIED. MISS YOU TERRIBLY*. Four days later, after receiving a postcard that seems distant and cold to her, she confronts him: *your postcard makes me feel like I've been trying to make something out of nothing . . . By my age I should know about affairs and all that stuff tho really I don't . . . How can you or anyone bitch about America the life here when you don't know how really ghastly it is—the absolute brutality— what sort of lobotomies one does to oneself to survive . . .*

Their lives are different: *I've never lived in a squat and I buy lots of dresses*—but when he responds to her note, she feels like *I have someone to talk to am talking to again.* Several days later she writes, *I try to stay open to you, but . . . you didn't actually seem that interested you seemed and still do seem to me like another guy who's balancing a number of girlfriends . . . yet you step into my life (more delicate than my cunt) whenever you please and leave whenever you please without saying anything to me.* Still, her letters to Miles are laced with career updates. Channel 4, she tells him, wants to film her performance in London the next fall. She works out almost every day at the gym, has lunches and dinners with friends, and shops for expensive groceries: *braised cabbage in juniper berries,* two kinds of vinegar and some beautiful red lettuce and red peppers and tiny yellow squashes all at exorbitant prices. The anniversary of her mother's death looms; on Christmas Eve she weeps and burns a black voodoo candle. She's trying to finish *My Death, My Life . . . Pasolini* for the Picador book, but *suddenly all the gigs, everything's coming to a head, and I'm thinking Oh, now I'm a bad writer*. Throughout all of this, her ulcer is bleeding.

The text of *Pasolini* (later republished in *Literal Madness*, her 1988 Grove Press anthology) will include a transcript of the ACTING MAD—ARE YOU MARRIED? telegram she sent Miles on December 18 and an account of their 1982 meeting in London—*I met him by accident . . . The next day we fucked. I wasn't expecting anything to happen . . . All we did was fuck. The minute we saw each other we fucked. It wasn't that we didn't have anything in common . . . The next day we saw each other in the afternoon, but I had to see the TV people that night. And the next day I had a dinner date and couldn't take him along. You know how it is . . . When I got back to New York . . . I phoned him. I haven't heard from him since I phoned. I sent him a telegram . . .*—alongside a discourse on nominalism.

A few days after New Years, before the correspondence breaks off, she tells him *I have to make all my living as interesting to myself as my writing.*

* * *

Cynthia Rose's *NME* profile came out in January 1983. Beneath a half-page, three-column photo, the subtitle reads "New York novelist KATHY ACKER has a longtime cult following which is now giving way to fame, both in the art world and on the rock/poetry scene." Speaking to Rose, Acker wonders aloud *why all these people are suddenly paying me all this money to do my stuff in all these countries* and why *they seem to be getting so much from it,* even though she's *not big enough for them to clap just over who I am*. The scene in New York is dead. *Since that community broke up, it's been hard. You work 20 hours a day, you see everyone in terms of your work, boy it's nuts.*

By now in their mid-30s, many of Acker's downtown New York friends had begun settling down and living in couples. Raw lofts were converted to co-ops, and club nights gave way to intimate dinners. Summer homes in the Hamptons or upstate New York were rented or bought; hardly anyone stayed in New York during July and August. Those who remained single made plans to travel in Europe or rent apartments in Provincetown, returning by Labor Day in time for the start of the new season. Others, who'd failed to attain this bourgeois-bohemian lifestyle, left New York permanently.

That year, Acker spent the summer in London. She'd booked a few readings, relieved to be out of New York and probably reasoning that whatever shows she did there would be good pre-publicity for her Picador launch the following February. Her first stop was the one-bedroom flat of the cultural historian Barry Miles and his partner, Rosemary Bailey, a journalist. Acker was not a good houseguest.

As Miles recalls, "It sounds brutal to say 'threw her out,' but the fact is, we had to . . . We did not have a spare room, so she slept on the couch in the living room. Shortly after moving in with us, we introduced her to [filmmaker and scholar] Peter Wollen and they began an affair—in our living room. Peter was still with [filmmaker and scholar] Laura Mulvey at the time, and as she was also a friend, it caused us a bit of anxiety because . . . Laura was unaware of what was happening. Because of this, it meant that their affair was conducted entirely in our flat. It was an intense, loud affair, and it meant that Rosemary and I couldn't use our living room as they were either necking or fucking, or having the kind of intense conversation that other people cannot join into.

"In addition, Kathy was not very aware of other people or their needs . . . not just because of Peter, but even when he was not there she would choose to do yoga in the middle of the room when we had friends over, never wash up her dishes, and, possibly, worst of all, fill the flat with the smell of patchouli oil . . . I remember one day Rosemary ran screaming from the flat, yelling she couldn't stand it anymore. Kathy was completely unaware that anything might be amiss."

She packed her wardrobe—"very dramatic sort of London-style post punk outfits . . . unraveling dresses where one of her breasts might be visible" —and moved on to stay with another friend, Chrissie Waite. The story repeated. Waite asked her to leave after two or three weeks.

"Kathy," Miles continues, "was very much someone with an eye for the main chance . . . I didn't get the impression [she] was curious about London . . . She was obviously aiming to impress, to please, to be liked, but felt that she had to make a tough impression. This meant she talked all the time, it was hard to get a word in edgewise. This may be why she and Peter didn't last as a couple, because Peter liked to have his opinion known as well . . . I think her interest in Peter came mostly from his status in the intellectual circles she moved in. She very actively sought out people who were well-known or influential, and had something of a reputation as a self-promoter, which in New York happens all the time but in London is viewed with opprobrium.

". . . I felt that because the people she met spoke English, she thought they shared many of the same views, whereas that is not the case. Britons and Americans, even those who are part of the downtown New York art scene, do not necessarily see eye to eye because they come from such different backgrounds."

There's no doubt that Miles was right about Acker's ambitions. But she wanted much more from Peter Wollen than just social connections. Wollen, who co-wrote Antonioni's great 1975 classic film *The Passenger*, was also a gifted filmmaker and one of the most brilliant critical theorists of his generation. A pioneer of cinema studies, he was among the first to apply semiotic and psychoanalytic theories to critical readings of narrative film. As he writes in his essay "The Hermeneutic Codes," "I believe it is necessary to try to understand the mechanics of narrative if we are to discover different modes of story-telling rather than pursue an utopian and pointless project of dispensing with narrative altogether. Any counter-language must be preceded by a meta-language." Wollen's ideas are seductively close to the notions of narrative Acker arrived at intuitively. Like many highly intelligent people, Acker saw her "self" as a composite. To make her "self" larger, she sought to cannibalize the intelligence of others whenever possible. *How close can I get to someone, where we become each other? Being human is too boring and difficult*, she'd written to Alan Sondheim nine years before. In her 1984 *Artforum* essay, "Models of Our Present," Acker cannabilizes the "morphological analysis" Wollen deploys in his book to brilliantly giddy, confounding effect, juxtaposing her descriptions of a Jenny Holzer and Lady Pink mural with dense mathematical formulae.

* * *

Back in New York by the end of August 1983, she began a feverish correspondence with Wollen that she'd eventually transcribe and expand in *Don Quixote*, her next full-length book after *Great Expectations*. As in Acker's earlier writings, fragments of her letters to Wollen collide with other original and plagiarized texts in a witty conjunction of longing, assault, and lament. In Section 2, "The Poems of a City," Acker intercuts her Latin translation notes with lines from a letter she'd written to Wollen:

Fulsere quondam candidi tibi
Soles,
Cum it hurts me to remember I
Did act up today, a way of
Saying "I'm not perfect," forgive
My phone call, venitabas quo
Puella ducebat (on a leash:
Leather Rome)
Amata nobis quantum amabitur   *The first future tense. What*
Nulla.   *do words really say: does this*
                                  future propose future time?

The letters themselves are much stranger. Unlike the strategically confrontational, highly composed letters she'd sent Alan Sondheim, her letters to Wollen ramble on like a diary mailed inadvertently. He doesn't want Acker to call, as he's still living with Mulvey, but her need for connection implodes through this veil of discretion. She pours herself glasses of wine to celebrate Wollen's occasional calls and then describes how the wine tastes and what the glass looks like. She tells him what she had for dinner—*salad and pulpo, thick red blood sauce—lots of dry white whine* [*sic*]—*at Ballato's for supper*—and reports on the weather, overheard conversations, her career, and her feelings. Most of all, she tells him what she is reading: Pinter and Brecht, Phillipe Sollers, Cioran, John Clare, Catullus, Propertius, Samuel Melville, Husserl, Strindberg, James Joyce. Like Laura Mulvey, Wollen attended Oxford University, and to the extent that he appears in these letters at all, it's as a higher-class adversary who she hopes to impress. The letters are littered with Britishisms; she adopts the words *proper* and *quite* and resolves to say *phone* instead of *call* because she needs to be more *particular, not American-like language sloppy.*

Have to stop being a sentimental lump, she writes him on Halloween night, 1983. . . . *translating bits of Propertius and Catullus and concentrate on this time stuff, deep conceptual business no changing quivering emotions: reminiscent of Descartes' dualistic world? Well, of course as always, I'll end up (begin and continue) doing exactly what's pleasure—is this being a female? They didn't train me properly in the schools.*

Still, when Wollen asks what she thinks of his forthcoming book, *Readings and Writings: Semiotic Counter-Strategies*, she's dismissive. In her first letter she filibusters about David Bowie, her typewriter problems, and what she's making for dinner. Later, responding to a conversation they'd just had on the phone, she advises, *Writing, Peter, not only demands but also causes the free excretion of the word. Talk about desire. About everything. You've got to know, darling, and not just theoretically* . . . which seems like an odd response to Wollen's meticulously clear and well-argued theoretical writing.

Because by then she was lost. On the verge of becoming a famous writer just as she'd dreamed, she knew she had to come up with another book soon, but she could not find the drift; the conditions were changing. What was the process, what was it she'd done all those years? *Writing is being so calm now, all about grandparents which of course is about nothing or rather flux, cause memory (equals disappearance) not only desire but all mentalities predicated on at edges of nothing absences. That texture is very calm. Mmm, the wine tastes good.* Because Wollen possessed *mental capacities [that are] at least as sharp and rapid as mine*, she could fabulate him as her best and her worst interlocutor. *Want . . . establish or be nature, that fullness, I must get there, out of this endless selfishness a problem with always watching oneself . . . the autocratic autistic world that I MUST penetrate into nature. The model is: if there are no conjunctions there can be no disjunctions. More simply: as in my life, absolute right; but the methodological rigor is absolutely meaningless. So what will happen with this meaninglessness . . .*

She started out thinking that the first section of *Don Quixote* would approach Nature by tracing the writings and life of the nineteenth-century British agrarian working-class poet John Clare. Clare famously ended his life in a mental asylum. But, she found, *Everything's again wrong, doing the easy stuff; now every-thing has to be rethought. No more cut-up. Why? Why? I want the hollowness that isn't cut-up. I know why? Do I? Maybe that's what to turn back on, explore. If it's not expressing, I'm on a rampage against expressing, then of course I can write anything and always write which is total freedom; now.* And yet the last thing she wanted was freedom: *Nothing coheres. No structure no model. Where to rip off from. No peace. Poor old mind mole. It's never not cohered before. I want a story! There is no story. It's a cry . . . I based it on John Clare and it's a cry. One scream. I'm going crazy. Should I make it John Clare's life? No cohesion anywhere.*

All eyes, it seemed then, were on her: *The books are coming out, I have to go farther and be absolutely clear and steadfast: quick virtuosity teenager passion is no longer useful or interesting. It's the choice, not identity, but choosing: that reverberation . . .*

Conjunction, disjunction. Husserl, Melville, Descartes. She was hoping to write her way into a void: a state of hollowness she felt inside and out that might still *lead to all possibilities.* And yet—*the anxiety to name it constricts. Is knowledge the same naming. But then there's that name naming Peter Peter Peter Not constricting, Gertrude Stein's nominalism. I'm scared . . .*

Don Quixote wouldn't be published until 1986. It was the last of her books that would draw so extensively from a correspon-dence. She finished the book in London sometime between 1984 and '85. By then she'd scrapped the John Clare/Nature idea. Wisely, she leads off burlesquely instead, transforming the abor-tion routine she'd developed in *Blood and Guts* into broad comedy: *Having an abortion was obviously just like getting fucked . . . They stripped us of our clothes. Gave us white sheets to cover our nakedness. Led us back to the pale green room. I love it when men take care of me.* The narrator of *Don Quixote* attains knighthood by having an abortion but choosing romantic love as her quest anyway: *When she was finally crazy because she was about to have an abortion, she conceived of the most insane idea that any woman can think of. Which is to love . . . By loving another person she would right every manner of political, social and individual wrong: she would put herself in those situations so perilous the glory of her name would resound.* The puke-green paper hospital gown becomes her knightly armor. To Don Quixote, *having an abortion is a method of becoming a knight and saving the world . . . According to what she had read about the ceremonial of the order, there was nothing to this business of being dubbed . . . except a pinprick . . . When she woke up, she thanked them for her pain and for what they had done for her. They thought her totally mad; they had never aborted a woman like this one.* This was a brilliant conceit. Legalized in the United States since 1973, abortion was characterized then, as it is now, as the most painful decision a woman can make. Like many of her friends, Acker had had at least five of them. As Maureen Howard wrote, reviewing the book for the *Los Angeles Times*, "We have all been there . . . Unless we have been wrapped in cotton wool or sent to the nunnery, we are fully prepared for [Acker's] sexual and political extremes."

After receiving her abortion, the narrator sets off in pursuit of her love object, whose name is Peter: *When you talk to me on the phone I'm hurt and maddened by your lack of sexual and emotional communication . . . I'll mold my love for you . . . Time's the main non-allower. I can't touch your cock right now because one event can't be another event . . . Three thousand miles now between the events of you and me, or three hours . . . Time's killing me.*

From here, the book ranges around familiar themes: childhood, abandonment, Henry Kissinger, the Fun City sex show, Bataille's Laure, and elite private girls' schools. Appropriating a scene from de Sade's *Juliette* in a section titled "Reading: I Dream My Schooling," she deploys the same strategy of textual repetition she'd used in *Nymphomanic* ten years before. But in *Don Quixote*, Acker's narrator grapples seriously for the first time with the limits and possibilities of a same-sex relationship. *My decision to be with women only didn't heal the initial sickness: why I had let myself be treated so badly . . . Since I didn't want to sleep with women, sleeping with women couldn't endanger me, didn't touch the ranting, raving, unknown.* It's only when she enters the leather dyke scene that her narrator learns something new. In a long section paraphrased from de Sade's *The Crimes of Love*, the characters Villebranche and De Franville are locked in the infinite loop of a power exchange, the self-perpetuating Hegelian master-and-slave dynamic. Gender is no longer fixed; both characters are referred to by double pronouns. *Whatever her (his) confusions, De Franville knew she (he) had never felt such sweetness: sweetness and gentleness had never existed in the realm of love.*

In the mid-1980s, London's lesbian BDSM world became the nexus of urgent feminist debates about sex and pornography. Should pornography be condemned for its exploitation of women or embraced as a means of liberation? The leather dykes who gathered at the Vauxhall Tavern and the Bell in King's Cross were, of course, diametrically opposed to the puritanical bent of post-Marxist feminism. Acker would have been drawn to this scene if for no other reason than its support of her writing. *I have no self . . . Don Quixote's* narrator declares farther on in the book. *I'm forced to find a self when I've been trained to be nothing. Therefore, I perceive that physical pain, if it doesn't scare me because it's happening without my expectation and consent, helps out and enlarges sexual excitation. I won't,* Acker writes, *go against the truth of my life which is my sexuality.*

Acker's work, up until *Don Quixote*, is full of depictions of sex. Sex as a psychological displacement, sex as a power play and social comedy, sex as the glorious sexual revolution's default means of exchange, sex as the empty signifier of vacant pornography. But in *Don Quixote*, Acker moves toward the essentialist notion of sex that will define the rest of her work.

* * *

I have to make all my living as interesting to myself as my writing, she'd told Jonathan Miles early in 1983. During the six years she stayed in London, Acker would become more deeply involved with BDSM, as well as with tattooing and bodybuilding. Her image became increasingly elaborated, even baroque. In a black-and-white London portrait taken in 1983 by Chris Garnham, she has her back to the camera. Dressed in a tailored but flowing white linen shirt, her face is in profile, and an artfully razored line on her buzz cut flows across her jeweled ear to the base of her neck from her forehead. In her interview with Melvyn Bragg for *The South Bank Show*, Acker described being photographed as *the same sort of play I do in my writing with identity . . . because an image is rigidity, and I'm always interested in seeing an image being able to fluctuate to another image. Or my identity fluctuate to another identity. And this is one way I can do it.* "I remember sitting with her on a sofa at a party and looking into her face," Leslie Dick wrote, "with its harsh makeup and amazing punk hair, peroxide blonde then with brown burn marks on it as if it had been seared with a branding iron, and recognizing this spectacle as a mask that she peered out from behind, or within, oddly like a little girl."

In a 1984 profile on Acker, Rosemary Bailey describes her as a "writing, talking, dressing challenge to any established ideas about anything . . . She will wear wide, wide boiler suits over zipped and frilly nylon blouses, t-shirts exquisitely slashed, sinister silver jewelry of cockroaches and skeletons." As Acker told Bailey, *Street fashion is where the art is for poor people. I can't afford to buy a painting so if I get some money I go buy a dress.* Two years after Acker's death, the photographer Kaucyila Brooke would produce *Kathy Acker's Clothes*, a series of 154 photographs of the dead woman's dresses and T-shirts, trousers and jackets, lingerie, blouses, and shoes. In 2006 the writer Dodie Bellamy would curate an exhibition of some of these clothes. "How to summon the spirit of a shopaholic?" asked Derek McCormack, reviewing the show:

> In 1988, I saw Acker read . . . in Toronto . . . She was wearing Vivienne Westwood, from the Fall & Winter 1988 collection . . . A man's coat. Grey pinstripes broken up by blocks of black. Sleeves were detachable . . . The coat's references include gladiator garb, motorcycle jackets, roller derby uniforms. Mad Max might have worn it to the office. When Acker moved, the pads parted, revealing her tight and tattooed muscles. On the bottom, she wore bondage pants.

Allowing herself to write no less than two pages a day, she continued producing books while immersed in these other things.

* * *

Picador rented her a Marylebone flat for three weeks in February 1984, and she didn't go back to New York. She'd already contracted to purchase the leasehold to a large one-bedroom flat at 87 Riverview Gardens, one block south of the Thames. The Hammersmith neighborhood, known as Barnes, was traditionally artistic and pricey. "I went to a party in that mansion block in the nineties, hosted by a Russian émigré who had lived there for yonks," Matt Fox recalls. "Fantastic original art on the walls from the old country. Many of the guests were from the block . . . A very sophisticated bunch." In New York, the performance poet Darius James packed and shipped Acker's belongings: china and knickknacks, books, jewelry, clothes. *THE BOOKS AND MANU-SCRIPTS IN THE CASE TO THE LEFT OF MY DESK ARE IMPORTANT AND MUST BE SENT TO ME IMMEDIATELY*, she told him, *ALONG WITH THE FILE CASE IN THE CLOSET AND ALL THE CONTENTS OF THE WRITING DESK . . . No news—am getting accustomed to the isolation here. I love the river. Moving is hell on the psyche. But—in the long time—it's good here.*

The writer and human rights activist Nathalie de Broglio was nineteen years old, unemployed, and living in London when she answered a small classified ad in *City Limits* early in 1984: "Women Writers—Meet Up." There was no name, just a date and a phone number.

I showed up at the flat and rang the bell, and there's Kathy Acker at the door—it just stopped me. There must have been about ten or twelve of us, all very young. Kathy had wine out and we just talked. Her flat was just boxes of books, she'd just moved in. It was pure altruism. I guess she was looking for contact, to see what was going on. It was completely informal—just a get together, just hanging out. We would talk about books. We talked about William S. Burroughs' *The Third Mind*. And we went out, we'd go to a club or a pub together.

We were talking about London, how male dominated the culture was. Kathy was thirty-seven. I'd been in Paris, but I grew up in London. My father was active in the apartheid movement, and we moved to Hammersmith as well. Everything at that time that was being done, the boys were doing it. There were very few girls that were doing something anywhere, among the people I knew. Still, I wanted to try. Which was why Kathy was so important to London. You had this massive class thing in the culture, it's coming back today, where the only people you hear from have been to Oxbridge and private schools.

Kathy loved reading, and she loved the street scene. She was very erudite. She had lots of piercing in her ears, black hair, rosebud lips, and big boots. She didn't come across as this big person, she was very on the level. You could talk to her about things.

We had three or four meetings, and then it stopped. Maybe we were too young for her, or she just got into something else. Kathy was definitely reaching out to all points at that time in London, she was enjoying herself.

Bette Gordon's breakthrough independent feature film *Variety*, for which Acker had written some scenes and received a full screenplay credit, premiered in London in May 1984, and then Kathy was everywhere.

As Michael Bracewell recalls, "Suddenly, here is this astonishing American woman, incredibly glamorous and punky, kind of street. But obviously at the same time, talking an intellectual language that in London at that time was like being from another planet. The British literary scene then, as now, was moribund and boring. And there Kathy was, suddenly connecting the idea of being a writer to all of these points in subculture. And then to points in critical theory, which none of us had ever even heard of . . . She very swiftly became the ambassador to this London post-punk scene of an international idea of what an avant-garde might be. And she made the idea of applying critical theory to writing seem incredibly cool.

"When she first came to London, she would encourage young writers, she'd invite people around to her flat. Kathy was very, very generous . . . But the interesting thing was, she was incredibly private about her background. We only found out

later that she was from a quite wealthy New York background . . .
I suppose we naively thought that if you'd had a documentary
made about you on *The South Bank Show* and you were a famous
writer, then of course you were rich.

"When Kathy did a reading in those days, it was a big deal.
And she was such a good performer. She could really vamp it up.
The whole kind of New York street voice, the jewels, the whole
show . . . I remember she had a ring. I asked what is it, this ring?
It's like a lump. And she said, Oh, it's a model of a dying city.
And when you looked at it closely, I think it went over two
fingers, it was like lots of melted skyscrapers, it was like a
postapocalyptic cityscape. And things like that just seemed at the
time so powerful. It sounds corny now. But at the time it seemed
like, this is truth—

"In the end, I just couldn't deal with the gravitational field
around Kathy. I'd be working in an office at a fairly low level, and
Kathy would ring my work number. And if Kathy wanted to
talk, she wanted to talk. And that could be ninety minutes. She
had no concept of the fact that if you were working in an office
and you had a boss and you were taking a ninety-minute personal phone call without somebody having died, you were gonna
get into trouble . . . It just reached a point where, I suppose, I
went into a total aversion to everything that I associated with her
world . . . all that scarification stuff. More and more, she wanted
to go to extremes.

"Kathy's importance, Kathy's moment of greatness was
almost less in terms of her writing than her embodiment of a
constellation of influences . . . [S]he did an enormous thing,
which was that she single-handedly in London connected people
who bought records to people who bought books. And nobody
had done that before. There had not been a writer, a contemporary writer living in our midst, who united the world of pop
culture and music and post-punk to the world of literature, let

alone the world of critical theory. And that, I think, was the zenith—that was her imperial phase, I think."

* * *

"I AM, AM I?" by Don Watson, *NME*, August 25, 1984:

Eyes bulging from a head framed by tufts of newly bleached hair, dressed in pure white, Kathy Acker looks frail and very vulnerable standing on the ICA stage . . . [in] a performance accompanied by members of Psychic TV . . . What Acker presents her audience with is in fact only herself, the rest is a jumble of vague forms, derived in this case from the language of the official, of the political activist and of the "scared little shit," with the semiotics of the monster movie thrown in for good measure.

Her distinction is that she gives the horror a very human face. Eventually as the reading reaches its slow climax her very fragility becomes more powerful than the bombast we might have expected of her.

Where Burroughs, old enough to remember before the video age, is able to analyse it, Kathy Acker, caught up in the middle of the barrage, is able only to reflect it. Her wisdom is the wisdom of uncertainty. She is not the writer of the future, but one of the writers to the present—which is something not to be overrated or undervalued.

Until Acker's arrival, Laurie Anderson had been downtown New York's most prominent cultural ambassador to London. In the summer of 1981 Anderson's eight-and-a-half minute song "O Superman" improbably rose to the top of the UK single's charts. *What bugs me about Laurie,* Acker told Rosemary Bailey—without being asked—in her 1984 interview for *The Face, is she is someone who could push a lot harder. She doesn't have to be a nice little Midwest white girl. She never touches sexual material. It's never really political, it's just very smart semiological stuff basically.*

I asked English people why they thought there's been such a big to-do about me in your country, she reflected to Don MacPherson that year for the *Guardian*. *I mean it can't just be a woman writing about sex. There's not that much sex in my books really.*

* * *

The play Acker discussed writing for the Almeida Theatre never transpired, but in July 1985 the section of her still-unpublished novel *Don Quixote* based on Frank Wedekind's 1904 *Lulu Plays* was adapted for a collaborative Institute of Contemporary Arts (ICA) theater project called *Lulu Unchained*. Directed by the young fringe theater director Pete Brooks and written by Acker, *Lulu* was, as the press release had it, "a blazing reinvention of Wedekind's *Lulu Plays* with a live score that disembowels Berg's opera. It's as if you're on the threshold of Room 101 or at the portal of Bluebeard's castle. *Lulu Unchained* looks at how art makes violence safe."

Acker fictionalized her production biography—"KATHY ACKER IS NOT ONLY WHAT HER PUBLICITY HAS LED YOU TO BELIEVE"—in ways that are hard to fathom. She described her mother, Claire Weill, as a "translator" who committed suicide in 1979, a year after her mother's actual suicide. Her ex-husband Bob Acker was "also a student of Herbert Marcuse," and Bette Gordon's already released *Variety* was a forthcoming work "to be filmed in a Channel 4/German TV production."

"ICA in row with writer over script," London's *Theatre News* reported two weeks after the opening:

An angry novelist has been told that it is too late to disassociate herself from a new show at London's Institute of Contemporary Arts.

Kathy Acker, described as a "fashionable post-punk novelist" demands that her name should be removed from the credits of Lulu Unchained which opened last week, claiming that her script had been cut drastically before the production reached the stage.

But ICA theatre director, Michael Morris, claims that she not only complained too late but also got the wrong end of the stick.

The show had been intended as a collaboration of four different people, of which Acker was one . . .

Her name could not be taken off the credits because she had complained after the publicity posters had gone up all over London and the critics had seen the show.

Three weeks later, she appeared as a commenter on Channel 4's evening news.

THIS IS HYPE CITY! Acker complained to Marc Issue in *Blitz* magazine that September. *It isn't as if now and again a paper writes about you—they all write at once and you're trendy—for a week. They like to manufacture people here . . . If someone wanted to make themselves a lot of free publicity here, they could do it. It wouldn't be extremely difficult. If you've got a little bit of money behind you for the right advertising . . .*

But these fears of a short shelf life were somewhat exaggerated. Acker remained trendy in London for at least one more year, until she became painfully, publicly, extremely unfashionable.

* * *

Don Quixote, Acker's first significant work to be published since her commercial breakthrough two years earlier, came out from Paladin Books in May 1986. By now she was a fixture in London. She belonged to the Groucho Club, founded by publishing trendsetters Liz Calder and Louis Baum as a modern riposte to the traditional stuffy men's club, where select women would be automatically welcome. Moving between high culture and low, she performed with Genesis P-Orridge and played chess with Salman Rushdie. Early supporters were now more than ready to question their initial enthusiasm. Was she the enfant terrible genius they'd declared her, or merely a fraud? In an *NME* review titled "Genital on My Mind," Duncan Webster observed, "Acker seems most daring in her unique combination of an overblown and embarrassing romanticism (the tortured, alienated mad artist) with a reduction of culture (Cevantes, Shakespeare, Oedipus, Jane Eyre) to banality. It's like reading some lecture notes . . . written by a bored student, with genitalia and 'I love Peter' doodled in the margins. Thomas Hobbes makes a guest appearance as the Angel of Death but the novel is not really nasty, brutish or short enough." Robin Chapman, writing for the *London Review of Books*, described it as "a dead-eyed romance, indebted to Burroughs rather than Cervantes . . . There is plenty of sado-masochism, bags of centrist anarchism, and built into the text as well as the title, the enervating get-out clause that what we are reading is really just a dream for author and reader alike." Still, these high-lit slams served only to enhance Acker's renegade reputation. Her name appeared regularly in gossip columns ("kinky scribbler Kathy Acker is due to record a single with kinky noise combo Swans"); she interviewed leading writers, wrote the preface to a book of Robert Mapplethorpe's work, and performed with Georgie Fame and the band Lindisfarne at the Edinburgh Fringe Festival.

Grove Press published the book in the late fall of 1986. This time, the disparity between critical acclaim for Acker's work in New York and London reversed. Except for a thoughtful discussion of Acker's work in Michael Davidson's long *New York Times* essay on avant-garde writing early in 1985, there'd been virtually no major coverage in the U.S. of her first two Grove Press books. But on November 30, 1986, the novelist Tom LeClair gave *Don Quixote* a stunning full-length review in *The New York Times*. Describing it as a "literary trash compactor" not unlike Cervantes's Renaissance work, LeClair saw the book as the product of a new era, "collapsing with hammer thumps and electronic whine the fictional containers—the genres, stories and characters—from which we take nourishment and, Ms. Acker says, sup poison." Acker's "scarified sensibility, subversive intellect and predatory wit," he concludes, "make her a writer like no other I know." In a sidebar conversation with Lori Miller, Acker explains, "I write by using other written texts, rather than by expressing 'reality,' which is what most novelists do. Our reality now, which occurs so much through the media, *is* other texts."

Almost two decades later, David Antin's ad hoc workshop technique—*Go to the library! Steal! You can write about anything in the world that you want, except somebody else knows more about it than you, and it's already in a book in the library!*—as channeled by Acker was presented as something almost mainstream. Throughout her career she described herself as a pirate, but she was also a time traveler, smuggling avant-garde histories into the media culture of the 1980s, which—except for the absence of complete connectivity—isn't so different from the one we inhabit today.

* * *

I think Don Quixote was an end for me, Acker told Angela McRobbie in a 1987 ICA video interview. *I wanted to wrap up the New York art world . . . And now I'm in England, I don't know, to me it's a little pretentious . . . I think I'd begun to question the avant-garde. . . . The new work is science fiction and part of the senseless . . . It's got no theory behind. All my books had such theory behind! ... And I'm having a lot more fun with it than I've had in a long time.*

Beyond the content of their conversation, the contrast in demeanor and appearance between McRobbie and Acker in this videotaped interview dramatically illustrates Acker's distance from mid-'80s British political feminism. Six years younger than Acker, McRobbie was best known at that time for her essay "Settling Accounts with Subculture," a feminist critique of Dick Hebdige's 1979 book *Subculture: The Meaning of Style*. Wearing black trousers and a long-sleeved white shirt buttoned up to the neck, McRobbie reads from a carefully prepared list of questions. Acker appears to listen intently. Occasionally she frowns or raises a ring-studded hand to thoughtfully prop up her chin. She wears a black leather headband around a red buzz cut, velour leopard-print leggings, and an enormous deconstructed black leather jacket with sharp gladiatorial ruched shoulder wings. Her eyes are lined underneath with her now-trademark thick half lines of black kohl. Acker's presentation is at once affected and earnest. Enhancements to her biography—*I went first to Brandeis, but then I transferred because of someone named Herbert Marcuse* (as if the Marxist scholar McRobbie had never heard of the famed New Left philosopher) *to UCSD*—are now repeated across scholarly papers on Acker as fait accompli.

By that time Acker knew she'd have to come up with something new if she didn't want to remain known as the "post-punk plagiarist" for the rest of her life. She could no longer ignore the impasse she'd reached when she wrote *Don Quixote*. She'd averted disaster that time by reprising more than a decade of original work into one volume. In vaudevillian terms, *Don Quixote* was the production number of Acker's oeuvre to that point, with Peter Wollen cast as the offstage interlocutor.

Count Zero, the second novel in William Gibson's *Sprawl* trilogy, was published in 1986. The first volume, *Neuromancer*, published in 1984, had opened the door to a new kind of novel that was at once narratively coherent and blissfully free of the kind of naturalistic depictions of domestic middle-class life that defined British fiction. Brilliant, inventive, and gracefully written, *Neuromancer* opens with one of the most memorable first sentences in late-twentieth-century fiction: *The sky above the port was the color of television tuned to a dead channel.* As Cory Doctorow writes, the book is "a vividly imagined allegory for the world of the 1980s, when the first seeds of massive, globalized wealth disparity were planted, and when the inchoate rumblings of technological rebellion were first felt."

During the mid-1980s a group of younger writers in London, including Neil Gaiman, Geoff Ryman, Mary Gentle, and Alan Moore, hung out at the München Café off Charing Cross Road and began defining themselves as a generation of sci-fi and fantasy writers. Acker was tangentially part of that group, and one of its influences. As she explained to McRobbie, *Because there is no underground movement [in London], a lot of the sort of non-Oxbridge writing goes into science fiction. It's the one place that you're allowed to do everything you can't do in what almost looks like the social realist novel.*

Grove Press sent William Gibson a copy of *Don Quixote* in 1986, and he responded directly to Acker, enthusiastically: "You're really an astonishing writer, Kathy Acker. I hadn't read you before. I'm really happy you like my work." Six weeks later he wrote her again to say he'd like to use a line from *Quixote* in *Mona Lisa Overdrive*, the book he was working on then. "I like to think," Gibson joked, "of academics having to go back to the text to put it in context."

Acker returned the compliment, importing two scenes and most of the plot from *Neuromancer* into *Empire of the Senseless*, the new sci-fi work she'd discussed with McRobbie. Gibson's "Panther Moderns" become Acker's "Moderns"; "Sense/Net" becomes "American Intelligence," or AI; and the *Neuromancer* character Wintermute is reborn as Winter. In *Empire*, the characters Thivai and Abhor break into a CIA library called MAINLINE with the help of a terrorist group called the Moderns. MAINLINE is a central control network that contains its own memory. Abhor and Thivai's search for a biological construct named Kathy is also a search for the MAINLINE code, which turns out to be the following statement: GET RID OF MEANING. YOUR MIND IS A NIGHTMARE THAT HAS BEEN EATING YOU: NOW EAT YOUR MIND. *Empire* was intentionally written in a crude pulp fiction style. The word *cunt* appears at least forty-four times, and the book contains various depictions of BDSM, incest, child sex, and insurrection.

After Don Quixote I got sick of whatever I was doing, Acker later told Sylvère Lotringer. *At one point, I thought there was a real need to examine certain things, because there was so much hypocrisy. But it really broke down, especially after Watergate. Everybody now knows what's happening. They might not want to see it, but certainly all the information is out in the open. You don't have to keep examining everything to see how it works, people sort of know. They just don't give a damn. And I thought . . . what was needed now is to start constructing . . . I became very interested in myths. What I tried to do in* Empire *was to start to make a kind of myth that would be applicable to me and my friends.*

She was lonely a lot of the time.

Sometime in 1986, on a plane to New York, Acker met the man she'd describe to her friends as "the Germ" or "the German." An account of their meeting appears toward the end of her next full-length work, brusquely composed in the tone of a police procedural, first published in 1990, *In Memoriam to Identity*.

When they got off the plane, "the German," a journalist, followed her back to the apartment where she was staying. After drinking too much and telling her about the beautiful German woman he was in love with, he initiated a BDSM scene. She'd always been drawn to the idea of power exchange. Descriptions of BDSM scenes—some lived, some imagined, others borrowed from literature—had appeared in all her work since *Great Expectations*. But this time the play was more global: *Proceeded to tell me to do various things. Masturbate with my fingers. Then, talk. Ordered me to come. Repeated these instructions. Sometimes watched me and sometimes left my bedroom, sometimes for a long time. Felt I was entering into my privacy, myself . . . Sometimes hurt me by pressing on my clit or asshole skin with fingers. While hurting me naked in front of open windows in my kitchen, asked me if I wanted him to leave, I had the choice, and I said "No" and I was coming. Back in my bedroom, told me no man had ever given me so much, not sure what I meant, wanting to go to sleep, my body started shaking as if it had had too much cold.*

They spent three nights in New York together. On the last he announced that he was married. *Walking back from the restaurant . . . a habit (part of me) knew all about men, a man who had a wife and a girlfriend beside me. "Go to hell" . . .* and then, *[he] shoved me up against the locked glass door, winter, thrust a hand under and up my leather coat, sweaters, down wool tights, as much as he could get in, my cunt hurt. "Come." "You bastard."* She came. *Now, maybe now*, she surmises, *I'm reliving childhood because now I'm strong enough to handle it. German is presenting me with rejection and absence; this time rejection and absence won't kill me.*

Always at least half-believing she was dead.

Acker's relationship with him would continue for the rest of the time she lived in London, almost four years. She had casual lovers, but her connection with him was consuming, even, in fact most of all when, when he wasn't present.

The journalist, whose name was Rainer, lived in Hamburg with his wife and child. He was an editor and cultural correspondent for the German newsweekly *Der Spiegel*. Rainer wrote about things of great interest to Acker and most of her friends: religious cults, dive bars, socialist politics, the squatting movement, and video piracy. Sometimes they'd make plans to meet for a week in another city, and then he'd leave early, abruptly.

> Decided she would make an attempt to get what she wanted by arranging to see the reporter. Decided he would be at a certain news conference . . . and persuaded . . . a homosexual friend of hers to invite her to the conference.
>
> Upon telling the reporter that she had been invited to this conference, arranged to spend a week with her there.
>
> As soon as they met in Berlin, informed her he had to fly to London the next day to interview Yoko Ono. Who wasn't in London.
>
> When Airplane upset (fear covering anger), instructed her he made all the rules.

Speaking to Barbara Caspar in 2007, Ira Silverberg recalled, "They had a very, very intense emotional relationship to one another. And he had trained her to have an orgasm at his command. And her most successful story was sitting on a bar stool somewhere in Germany in a hotel bar and he was across the room. And he gave her the signal to have an orgasm. And apparently she had multiple orgasms as this man was across the room. And this was triumphant to her, entirely triumphant, and the true sign of a great relationship. And I just remember thinking, God bless you . . ."

It was fun sometimes, and then it was not. *Expecting. That night, before flying to Germany, stomach blew outward, immense pain in right side of stomach, fever. Knew why . . . Every time phoned reporter from Hamburg, he sounded increasingly unfriendly. The more unfriendly sounded, the more her fever increased, the more she begged him to love her.*

By this time she was working out at the gym five times a week, pushing herself to and beyond the point of muscular failure, and the discipline of it was affecting her writing. *Where are you left—in a text, in your body—when control breaks down?* Acker's work and celebrity made her a role model to younger women. In London, bodybuilding was still an underclass sport. Most likely it was at the gym where she discovered tattooing. Acker got her first three tattoos during the months she was working on *Empire*. As she explained in a 1987 video interview with four starstruck young women as they sat next to a pool in Gothenburg, Sweden:

> *At the end of the book . . . the woman makes up her own sign. She says—it's based on the highway code cause I was taking my motorcycle test—I hate all these rules, I'm gonna make up my own signs. So she makes a tattoo . . . of a sword going through a rose. And the rose to her is like a cunt. And then she says no, and then underneath is a scroll. And the scroll says, anarchy and discipline. And she decides that the sword and the rose are her cunt, that her and her cunt, that she is both things. So that any pain is the pain that she is taking on and deciding is hers. So I went to Dennis and said, I want this tattoo. And I showed him the picture. Dennis is my tattooist. And I said, I want you to do this picture I drew. And he said, No, it's tacky. [laughs] . . . So what he did is he did his version of it, which is this rose, which is piercing itself. And the rose twines around itself and comes through. And it's a story about that.*

"Myth dealing," Lotringer observed in his conversation with Acker, "is essential. Myths aren't just a narrative you can identify with, they're meant to mobilize. They're a powerful emotional bond. No society can do without them . . . I think it's part of the Black Tarantula syndrome. One of the ways of making your work legitimate is to work it through yourself. If you are not the 'I,' but the 'I' becomes you, then you have it to offer as some sort of performance . . . [But] what happens when you're a dealer of myths [is], you become myth. Genet, Pasolini, Artaud, Rimbaud, Burroughs, they all went through that. But that was mostly before media. Now you don't even need a real biography—sex, drugs, jail, murder, madness. All you need is, what?—tattoos?"

Empire of the Senseless was published in London by Picador in May 1988. Except for Jeanette Winterson's passionate defense of the book in a Sunday *Times* end-of-year survey, the response in the mainstream press was derisive: John Melmouth, *The Independent*: "Nasty and cantankerous, it is unredeemed by a moment's wit . . . Kathy Acker's new line in post-punk fiction is petulant, otiose, maudlin, sentimental, undisciplined, and incoherent. Otherwise, it's fine. If this sounds like unconsidered, red-necked hostility to the avant-garde it should be qualified by the recognition that Acker has done interesting work in the past." Lachlan Mackinnon, *The Guardian*: "On the surface the book, with Persian inscriptions, amateurish drawings and a cast of transvestites, junkies, gay bikers, mutants and brutal policemen, with its emphasis on used needles, blood and faeces, leather, discarded condoms, tattoos, pleasureless sex, incest and dreams of brutality reads like a verbal cartoon. Everything in it is vaguely recognizable but seen through a hallucinating vision of surprising sentimentality . . . *Empire of the Senseless* is in the end a very dated work." Danny Karlin, *London Review of Books*: "[T]he main impression is of a performance both turgid and trivial . . . Acker makes the mistake of taking herself seriously here, as though 'ultimate outrage' were not a commodity being peddled by her agents and publishers as assiduously as 'towering genius,' 'warm humanity,' or 'delightful touches of wit.' . . . The reader sits in a kind of narrative dentist's chair, where being talked at is worse than being operated on." Jan Dalley, *The Observer*: "Kathy Acker's new novel is aptly entitled: *Empire of the Senseless*. Since the success of *Blood and Guts in High School* she has simply turned up the volume on a senseless, not to say meaningless, sequence of lurid images, randomly juxtaposed . . . Acker's volume knob is now on max, but there's no record on the turntable: that excruciating noise is just the needle screeching across the rubber mat." Even *New Musical Express*, one of her early and staunchest supporters, joined the attack: "*Empire* trails its Acker-patented sub-Burroughsian, pseudo-Theatre-of-Cruelty entrails from page to page, a wounded lame dog of a novel that makes up for in gratuitous nonsense what it lacks in originality. In short, more of the same old story . . . Some wag recently dubbed Acker 'the most important bad writer of the '80s' and this tome is proof, if needed, that her critical reputation is inversely proportional to her creative ability."

One night she was walking around the city with Rainer. He told her to take her clothes off under a bridge, and she did it. He teased her skin with a knife. She knew then—thought she knew then—that he might kill her, and she was shocked and upset that the idea of her death made her feel peaceful and happy.

In England, Acker later told Sylvère Lotringer, *the media had made this huge image of Kathy Acker. But this media image is so much this kind of sexual image . . . I'm sure there are tons of Kathy Ackers. I'm very well known there and I get tons of work. But to say that they like what I do? No, I wouldn't say that. They fetishize what I do.*

Opinions about Acker's later work, expressed after her death, are conflicting. To the scholar and critic Steven Shaviro, her last books are "richer and more powerfully affecting than anything she did before." In his 2006 essay about Acker's work, Gary Indiana concludes, "She wrote too much . . . *Empire*, *In Memoriam* and *Pussy* gave the impression that Acker lost interest in books long before she'd finished them . . . She became something of an assembly line herself." Still, "[a]spects of her final three books suggest that she was preparing to take off in an entirely new direction." "I have no idea," Shaviro recalls, "if she ever pursued this, but I remember her saying she would have liked for *Pussy* to become a virtual world or a video game."

* * *

In May 1989 the feminist Pandora Press published *Young Lust*, a selection of Acker's early work—a short story called "Florida" and the novels *Haiti* and *Toulouse Lautrec*—in the UK. Similar in concept to Grove Press's *Literal Madness* anthology that came out the previous year, the Pandora cover featured a portrait of Acker shot from behind. Naked from the waist up, she stretches her muscle-toned arms over her head and displays her three elaborate tattoos.

Except for Roz Kaveney's thoughtful and positive *Times Literary Supplement* review, the critical reception in London to *Young Lust* was similar to that of *Empire*, although this time it was more cursory. Writing in the *Guardian*, Jonathan Coe found it "all but unreadable for more than a few pages at a time, and her prose can be insanely boring." "It's also curiously naïve: the gang of foul-tongued boy criminals who want Kathy's body come as no surprise, for this is precocious bad-mouthing kiddy literature," Valentine Cunningham wrote in *The Observer*. "This is the easy, self-congratulatorily hedonistic, gratuitously nasty version of the postmodernist chaos of styles choices, selves."

Had she outstayed her welcome?

She couldn't respond directly to these attacks; any response would only empower her adversaries. Given her stature and fame, she couldn't complain to her peers. Since arriving in London, she'd surrounded herself mostly with fans, whom Neil Gaiman referred to as "Ackerlites": "a group of young gay men with ambitions as writers, [who] all had sharp haircuts and better clothes than they seemed able to pay for."

Finally, within weeks of *Young Lust*'s publication, an event occurred that would galvanize Acker's understandable paranoia and rage. A freelance journalist, preparing to write a gossipy exposé piece for the trade journal *Publishing News*, called Acker's Pandora Press editor. Did the editor know that a whole scene of Harold Robbins's *The Pirate* had been lifted almost verbatim into *Toulouse*? Ironically, Robbins himself had been threatened with legal action when he published *The Pirate*. Twenty-four hours before the novel's 1974 UK release, a mysterious "Miss X" appeared before the High Court in London to request an injunction. People, Miss X feared, might think that she was the person on whom Robbins based his adulterous drug-using protagonist, Jordana.

Things at Pandora got out of hand very fast. Depending on which of Acker's several accounts we believe, her editor called Robbins's publisher, or the journalist called Robbins's publisher, and then one of those editors called the director of Unwin Hyman, which was Pandora's parent company. Or then again, according to Robbins's biographer Andrew Wilson, it was the author's overzealous attorney Paul Gitlin who saw the exposé piece when it ran in *Publishing News* on July 28, 1989. Gitlin promptly called Hodder & Stoughton, Robbins's UK publisher, whose director asked Unwin Hyman to withdraw *Young Lust* from circulation. When *Publishing News* reached her for comment for their July 28 piece, Acker, by their account, "replied tetchily: 'I've made a statement about all this to Pandora. If you still don't understand I can suggest several theorists who can fill you in about post-modernism and structural theory.'" Acker's Pandora editor, Kate Figes, a writer herself, treaded a little more lightly: "Kathy plays around with all sorts of styles and ideas. She imitates people to make a point. You have to understand what she's trying to do." And Acker's UK agent, Anne McDermid, added, "She's always used other people's work. It's called appropriation." By all accounts, Pandora asked Acker to sign a public apology to Harold Robbins that would be printed in a trade journal. Acker at first refused. She made furious calls to Figes and

McDermid, who eventually asked her to communicate with them only in writing.

Fred Jordan, Acker's Grove Press editor, found the whole affair laughable. As he recalls, "I thought it was funny! That's what it's all about—getting people to object to what you're doing. The whole point [during Grove's early years] was the controversy. You say something, and some people don't like it, some people like it. So there would be a dispute, maybe, so what? If you're lucky, there's a dispute, if you're not, they ignore it." When Acker called to ask his advice, he suggested that she go to Paris for a few days and then get back to work on her book *In Memoriam*, which was scheduled for Grove's 1990 summer season.

Since the publication of *Empire*, she'd become a snigger-fest target for the London media. Her primary romantic relationship was with an elusive and unavailable sadist. Whatever violation Acker felt during these difficult years crystallized around the outrageous demand that she produce an apology. The following year, 1990, she'd write a long essay, "Dead Doll Humility," in response to the Harold Robbins Affair, in which she details her literary autobiography. In this text, she remembers fleeing to Paris and having a kind of epiphany: *All that matters is work and work must be created in and can't be created in isolation . . . Language is dead . . . Decided that it's stupid living in fear of being forced to be guilty without knowing why you're guilty and, more important, it's stupid caring about what has nothing to do with art. It doesn't really matter whether or not you sign the fucking apology.*

She returned to London and eventually, as she told Sylvère Lotringer, *I did sign the apology. It was a very specific statement and it was published in all the literary magazines.* Meanwhile, Fred Jordan had called William Burroughs, who called Harold Robbins, who told Pandora Press that Acker had his "entire permission" to use his work and that he was "shocked [that] anyone would be so ill-informed as to accuse her of plagiarism." Finally the book wasn't withdrawn, and no legal action occurred.

As specific as Acker's apology may have been, no one can find it. Hand-searching physical copies of all the issues of *Publishing News, Granta, The Guardian, The New Statesman, The Times, NME, TLS, Spare Rib,* and *Melody Maker* published between July and December 1989, my London researcher Hestia Peppe found no further mention of the Robbins affair beyond the original July 28 article. As Roz Kaveney recalls, *Young Lust,* in the end, wasn't withdrawn: "At that point Unwin Hyman was still privately owned and the man who owned it threw a wobbly. I think there was a lot of him making a fuss and being reassured that the book had been pulped rather than that actually happening."

But still, as Acker writes in "Dead Doll Humility," she [*u*]*nderstood that she had lost. Lost more than a struggle about the appropriation of four pages . . . Lost her belief that there can be art in this culture . . . Most of the literati in the country in which the writer was currently living were upper-middle class and detested the writer and her work.*

"The first I knew of any of this," Roz Kaveney wrote in her long essay "Some Years with Acker," "was when Kathy rang to thank me for my review . . . She announced that she had just about had it with London, where her friends did not stick up for her. But, I pointed out, she had not told me, or anyone I knew, what was going on—we could have done something . . . I knew her editor's boss, Phillipa, for example, and indeed Phillipa was a member of Feminists Against Censorship. Kathy was not in a mood to admit she might have handled things differently— London was full of back-stabbing and she was going back to New York."

In October 1989 Acker read at the Kitchen in New York. While she was there, she looked at apartments and made an offer on a Greenwich Village two-bedroom loft on East Twelfth

Street between Broadway and University Place. Back in London, she applied for a loan with a New York mortgage broker. *Publishing News* in London dubbed her Most Old Fashioned Post-Modernist in their end-of-year "Trivial Pursuit of the last decade," but the sale of her new East Twelfth Street apartment closed on December 11, so by then she was back in New York, and she probably missed seeing that.

My decision to come back here, she told Larry McCaffery several months later, *was based on several reasons, some of which are so personal that I didn't really know what the truth is about them. But the more true are certainly personal and not practical reasons. I had a bad summer. It was a personal crisis. A long, two-year relationship I had with someone broke up and I found myself sitting around England waiting for it to happen again. Finally I decided that six months of sitting around waiting was enough . . .*

The other reason was that my own publisher let me know that they were taking one of my books off the market because they had been informed there was some chance that Harold Robbins might sue me over some material I'd appropriated. Anyway, it was a horrendous experience that completely disrupted my life. I couldn't even answer my phone for three weeks . . . I was also feeling very threatened as a writer. I kept thinking to myself, Look, this is a minor, piddling little incident really—it's about a book I wrote twenty years ago about something Robbins wrote thirty years ago. But what if I was ever seriously attacked while I was living in England? Because despite all the bullshit going on right now here in the States about censorship and the NEA . . . there's a Bill of Rights, and artistic communities support their own. That's not true in England at all. There is no Bill of Rights . . . so what if I was in this country and anything seriously political ever happened to me? I could see how vulnerable I'd be to that sort of thing. I'd be screwed. So from a personal and practical standpoint, it was time to get out.

1995

(1989–1995)

the day after
the very long reading,
at the very cool venue,
we, the audience, were
those sluts, those girls—
rats in our hair
vampires in our anus
blood, piss, shit,
spit, bones, vomit—
Kathy Acker's
drunken girls,
she meant us,
that's the way she read
to us . . .

—Pam Brown, "1995"

New York had changed since Acker left in 1983, in ways not to her liking, or maybe she simply forgot what she'd left. *It's so different over here: so careerist . . .* she'd written to Peter Wollen from her Eldridge Street loft at the end of that summer, just as her own career was about to be launched. But by the time Acker returned, in 1990, she was no longer the only one of her down-town New York friends who'd been commercially published.

While she was in London writing *Empire* and posing for glamour photographs of her newly tattooed arms and back, her old friends Catherine Texier and Lynne Tillman were publishing their first novels, *Love Me Tender* and *Haunted Houses*, to much acclaim. Acker had generously blurbed her friends' books, describing Tillman as "the daughter of Jane Bowles," and *Love Me Tender* as "a personal song . . . A welcome antidote to the more trendy and less gutsy . . . accounts of New York City downtown life." Tillman's and Texier's books were both favorably reviewed in *The New York Times*. As Emily Prager wrote of *Love Me Tender*, "Catherine Texier combines, in one woman, questing intellect and guiltless passion. The result is modern, strangely powerful and definitely a turn-on." This was a far cry from James Frakes's 1988 review of Acker's *Literal Madness*, in which he noted her juxtaposition of "the most graphically porno-graphic and stunningly dull sex passages." Tillman's novel was praised in the *Times* for its "spare and compelling style" and "clinical authenticity." In 1988, a year after Tillman's commer-cial debut, Mary Gaitskill's first story collection, *Bad Behavior*, was published. *Bad Behavior* chronicled the aberrant lifestyles of downtown New York in the 1980s. Gaitskill's style was meticulously composed, and her psychological portraits were nuanced with ambivalence. The book was a tremendous critical and commercial success. "In the hands of another writer," Michiko Kakutani wrote in her *New York Times* review, "such unsavory anecdotes might seem merely perverse, but Ms. Gait-skill writes with such authority, such radar-perfect detail, that she is able to make even the most extreme situations seem real." The following year, Grove Press published Gary Indiana's and Dennis Cooper's first novels, *Horse Crazy* and *Closer*. Commer-cially and critically successful, *Spider*, a neo-Gothic novel by their downtown contemporary Patrick McGrath, would appear later in 1990, praised by Michiko Kakutani in *The New York Times* as "a small classic of horror—a model of authorial craft and control."

No one was talking about these writers' tattoos. Had Acker fallen into an image trap partly of her own devising? [*In England*], *I was the token caged animal*, she remarked in an April 1990 interview with Larry McCaffery. *It's quite accurate to say that I was "accepted" there in that I was famous . . . It was as if I had a little sign around me that said "Strange American."* "I feel," William Burroughs had once remarked to Gerard Malanga, "that for a writer to be a novelist, he doesn't have . . . a clear cut image of himself . . . If he cultivates his image too much his work will suffer . . . Involvement with his own image can be fatal to a writer." In London, Acker had fully complied with the notion that branding her image was the best means of advancing her difficult work. Had she made a mistake?

Critics were reading the more conventionally narrative and accessible books of her New York peers seriously. Meanwhile, her own work was being ignored at the expense of her image, and her image was becoming a signifier for '80s excess. By extension, she feared that even her old friends weren't taking her seriously. A year later, after she'd left the city, she wrote to Lynne Tillman about the estrangement she felt when she arrived back in New York. The downtown world had become a society *in which I no longer fitted*. Acker was notoriously absolutist, assuming that anyone who wasn't an unequivocal fan of her work must despise it. Did Lynne Tillman see her just as an image, *some weird, cute sex thing*? *You do not think*, Acker wrote her, *that I can think politically or that my work is at all intellectually responsible*. To Acker, it was a foregone conclusion that she and her old friend were competitors, and she was dismayed that Tillman didn't see it this way.

Acker arrived in time to spend Christmas with her old friends Nancy Reilly and Betsy Sussler. She moved into her new apartment, a luxurious converted loft space at 39 East 12th Street. Purchased at the tail end of the late-1980s New York real estate bubble, before the onset of a massive recession, the apartment was expensive to keep. Her mortgage payment alone was almost $1,700 ($3,189 in today's money), and there were hefty homeowner's dues added to that. Still, for the first time since her childhood, she had a doorman. She bought red leather banquette sofas for the living room and set up her books in double library stacks. But then, after she'd barely unpacked, she fled.

When she arrived back in New York, Acker had expected her old friends and peers to rally behind her real and imagined battles with London's literary establishment during the Harold Robbins debacle. But her friends had their own problems, and she was stunned when they weren't that interested. *I was chatting on the phone with a close friend,* Acker wrote early that February in an unpublished column for *The New Statesman, [and] when he began asking me about my work and the relations between my writing, myself, and media representation . . . I became upset . . . Finally, I had to tell him that I was crying and that I had no idea why . . . I found myself, in a time of personal trouble, isolated, with no one to help me. Until the last fifteen minutes I had blocked out conscious knowledge of what had happened.*

"She needed a soft place to land," her friend and later editor Amy Scholder recalls. "She wanted sympathy, and her New York friends didn't feel sorry for her. I think she wanted some grand gestures; she was insecure and lonely and wanted to be embraced by her community, and New Yorkers, especially at that time, weren't dropping everything to give her what she needed."

Acker's position at Grove Press had been troubled since 1985, when Barney Rosset sold the company to Ann Getty and Sir George Weidenfeld. *They are not putting money into the tour,"* she wrote Ira Silverberg before setting out with *Don Quixote* on a largely self-arranged junket. *[T]hey are not even willing to fly me to New York . . . I'm doing the poetry circuit I'm speaking to the people to whom and with whom I've spoken for the past fifteen years . . . When Barney and Fred bought my books, the implicit understanding was that they were gentlemen and as such were buying both books and the writer. [Now] it's all "dog eat dog."* And then, two weeks after she filed the *New Statesman* piece, Fred Jordan left Grove. When the new owners fired Rosset a year after acquiring his press, Fred Jordan found himself newly restricted. He was forced to drop his longtime author Václev Havel because, the new owners reasoned, their best-selling author Milan Kundera might be offended by the presence of this rival Czech. So when Random House offered Jordan the directorship of their imprint Pantheon Books, he jumped ship.

But Pantheon wasn't a sanctuary. His appointment was widely critiqued in media circles because he'd been hired to replace André Schiffrin. The son of one of Pantheon's original founders, Schiffrin was a publishing *éminence grise*. After a regime change at Random House, he'd been fired for refusing to slash titles and fire editorial staff. Consequently, in publishing circles, and especially among Pantheon's traditionally leftist stable of writers, Jordan was branded a turncoat and scab.

Like others who'd worked with Fred Jordan, Acker defended him passionately: *[Fred Jordan] picked me up, as the phrase goes, when my work was barely known,* she wrote in a letter to The Village Voice, *yet even then regarded, to put it nicely, as controversial. And Mr. Jordan has supported that work for many stormy years. Not only my work. Mr. Jordan is one of the very few editors in the American publishing world who is interested in young, controversial American writers . . . Perhaps some investigative journalism should now be done about the CIA's continuous investigation of Grove Press before the Getty takeover.*

Acker followed Fred Jordan to Pantheon, where he oversaw the 1992 publication of *Portrait of an Eye* (a collection of the early work similar to Pandora's 1989 *Young Lust*) and her 1993 novel *My Mother: Demonology*. He paid a generous advance for the new book, which, at least in her lifetime, would not be earned out. Her 1995 royalty statement showed a negative balance of $26,000. When Pantheon declined to renew Jordan's contract in March 1993, Acker returned to Grove Press alone.

By the late spring of 1990, when Roz Kaveney visited her on a trip to New York, it was clear that Acker wouldn't stay long. New York had been a mistake: "She had been away from the city long enough that it had moved on and she was no longer capable of being flavor of the month or year in the new greedy environment—she was still very angry with London for what it had done to her and let be done to her and there was no real question of her going back there, though she was still thinking about the possibility of living in Brighton. We got a very strong sense that when we next saw her, it would not be in New York."

Acker had already accepted an invitation to teach later that summer at San Francisco Art Institute, and, as portended by Kaveney, she wouldn't return to New York.

Still, at some point—most likely sometime in June 1990, a guess based on fragments of memory shared by her friends Neil Gaiman, Ken Jordan, and Gary Pulsifer, although no one remembers an actual year, let alone date—Acker bought an apartment in Brighton that she'd later abandon without sleeping in once.

She had always liked Brighton, a then still-dilapidated seaside town an hour from London with old-fashioned pubs and sailors' hotels. While she was still living in London, her close friend and later editor Gary Pulsifer had taken her there. Born in the U.S., Pulsifer had attended college in nearby Sussex as an exchange student and then stayed in the UK, finding the atmosphere less homophobic than in his blue-collar hometown, Bath, Maine. He remembers a weekend he and Acker spent in Sussex and Brighton: touring the castle, walking alongside the river, the boardwalk, doing all the usual things. During her painful, protracted involvement with Rainer, Pulsifer remained her ally and close friend. Once, he accompanied her on a mad scheme to ambush the German at a London hotel when she learned that he was there with his wife. Rainer didn't respond to her calls from the desk, so she tipped a porter to deliver one of her enormous signature rings to his room. "It was the kind of friendship where she'd ring you up at like, eight o'clock, and say, *Help me out, I need this kind of thing*," he recalled. "It was crazy . . . But it was still fun, in a way. It was a drama that enlivened life, like Kathy did."

Ken Jordan, a writer and editor who is Fred Jordan's son, house-sat at Acker's East Twelfth Street apartment that summer while she was away. "I was living on Avenue C and Ninth Street, in a total pit, and I ran into Kathy somewhere in the East Village," he recalls. "Surprise! What are you doing here? Oh, I just got an apartment! But she wasn't staying here, I think she was going to London, maybe San Francisco? She arrived in town, bought the apartment very fast, and then decided she didn't like being here and had to leave. I believe she went back to London. And she was going to sell the apartment, right? And at that time the market had already collapsed . . . but . . . she asked if I wanted to house-sit for her. It was really great—it was a really nice apartment. It was amazing and I loved it, because I had no money, I was living in a pit . . . Kathy went to England; then she came back. Then she decided to move to San Francisco."

Gary Pulsifer recalled going to Brighton with her when she viewed the apartment; the owners, two gay men, were still living there. "She only took me to see this one—maybe she'd narrowed it down. It was a basement flat in one of the squares overlooking the west pier. She bought it, and then she went back to San Francisco. And the flat really needed to be renovated a bit. So as a favor, I said I'd paint the whole damn thing for her over the summer. Which I did. And then she decided she didn't want to move there."

"She moved to New York," Neil Gaiman recalls, ". . . and then she moved back and bought a house in Brighton, sight unseen. This was immediately followed by the falling apart of the British housing market and Kathy moving to San Francisco." Gaiman and Roz Kaveney were enlisted to help her get rid of the place. Pleading incompetence, Kaveney declined, and Gaiman "ended with the peculiar task of apparently trying to sell her house and it was something I hadn't quite agreed to do but found myself semi-lumbered with. I made a few phone calls and talked to people and established it was much weirder and more complicated than that . . . I think at some point Kathy . . . decided she was mad at me because I hadn't sold it or something. Then I didn't see her or hear from her for a year or two."

Finally, Pulsifer recalled, she simply stopped paying the mortgage, and that ended that.

She was in free fall. And, for the first time in her adult life, it went unrecorded. There is no correspondence in which she describes these events to a male confidant, nor were they ever transposed into a book.

Before leaving New York, she broke off her author/agent relationship with Ira Silverberg. Acker dated her correspondence only when it pertained to unpleasant business. In a June 9, 1990, letter to Silverberg, she wrote: *[T]wenty years of my work is now dead in the United States for a nonspecific period of time. The plan for foreign rights went awry. As a result of all this, I have gone from a fairly steady income to no income . . . You have said that I'm demanding. All I'm trying to fight for is to keep my work alive. I have failed. All rights on works not yet sold and on works that are freed will revert to me.*

"She went to London," Ken Jordan recalls, "then she came back and decided to move to San Francisco. And when she got an apartment there, she had all of the furniture, the books, everything shipped. I packed it for her. And then she was waiting to sell the apartment. Until she sold the apartment, I could still stay there . . . I camped out there for another three months until she actually sold the place. It was like, three months with furniture, and three months without."

In fact, Acker wouldn't sell the apartment until June 1995. Meanwhile, she had to pay rent on her new San Francisco apartment. Perhaps she'd found someone to sublet her East Twelfth Street loft when she asked Jordan to leave. The sale had been a white lie.

* * *

Acker arrived in San Francisco later that summer of 1990 and began teaching writing at SFAI, a job Scholder arranged, which she kept until the end of 1995. Acker was beloved by her students, but her adjunct position wasn't much of a job. SFAI offered no benefits to its predominantly adjunct faculty, and Acker's net monthly pay wouldn't cover her rent. The first thing she did in San Francisco was buy a Honda 400cc motorcycle, and then she began looking for somewhere to live. She wanted a place near nature, or at least close to a park, where she could step outside and see trees, a place where she could walk. By the end of the summer she found, and settled into, a two-bedroom Cole Valley apartment at 929 Clayton Street. Looking out over a green belt, it was a ten-minute walk from the apartment at 46 Belvedere Street where she'd lived with Peter Gordon almost two decades before.

In San Francisco, she hung out a lot with Amy Scholder, a younger friend whom she'd met when she was touring *Don Quixote* in 1986. Scholder had just finished her B.A. at UC Berkeley and was running the reading series at City Lights Books when Acker read there during the tour. After the reading, Scholder had taken her to dinner and then to Amelia's, a lesbian bar in the Mission, where they drank tequila and danced. The two stayed in touch, exchanging letters between San Francisco and London. By the time Acker moved back to San Francisco, Scholder had become an editor at City Lights Books. In the years since Acker's death, Scholder has been instrumental in representing her writings. In the early 2000s Scholder and Dennis Cooper edited *Essential Acker*, a selected works, and Scholder edited the previously unpublished *Rip-Off Red, Girl Detective*, and *Lust for Life*, a collection of essays on Acker's work. Scholder recalls going through Acker's cassette collection in the warm, dark apartment at 929 Clayton and being surprised that they liked so many of the same artists and bands: not just punk bands, but singers like Rickie Lee Jones, Joni Mitchell, and Kate Bush.

After New York, San Francisco—with its tightly knit activist community of queer, dyke, and radical female artists, musicians, and writers—felt like a reprieve. *I really feel*, she told the poet and artist Nicholas Zurbrugg the following year, *that there is a community here that's working on . . . female sexuality, what the female body is, images of female sexuality, what women really desire . . . and it's totally interesting work.* In New York, the derisive reception to *In Memoriam* that July—"More postmodern blather from the queen of punk fiction" (*Kirkus Review*); "unreadable" (*New York Times*); "predictable, unreadable and clumsy" (*The Observer*)—might have been devastating, but in San Francisco it didn't matter that much. Rereading Acker's work in 2001, Scholder was struck by how her last novel, *Pussy,*

King of the Pirates "seemed to be produced under the spell of the time she spent in SF. It was a time when dykes/radical women were creating public space for themselves, in the creative arts communities and also in the bars and clubs. Kathy would go to queer clubs with me and her SFAI students and friends, and she loved how free these spaces felt."

Acker would allude to this scene in her 1993 novel, *My Mother: Demonology*, describing northern California as *Born out of attempted murder, loneliness, and wildness . . . The cities were born out of riffraff who, unlike those back East, knew no culture . . . In other words: ungovernable.* The city was reeling from the AIDS epidemic, and as Scholder recalls, "you couldn't walk down the street in the Castro district without seeing young men struggling to walk. This was apocalyptic because there was no cure in sight, and there was hardly any visibility of this plague outside our neighborhoods. So, Kathy was living and working in this milieu . . . I'm sure that's why the queer parties were wild and raw and intense, the best and worst of times."

Scholder introduced Acker to the philosopher Avital Ronell, in whom Acker found a true peer. Ronell had just published *The Telephone Book* and was working on *Crack Wars: Literature Addiction Mania*, which would become an immediate classic in 1992 when it appeared. The two became friends. From their first restaurant meeting, Ronell recalls, "We . . . were very spontaneous, excited, talkative. We had read each other, she was working on Bataille and Hegel and wanted me to fill in. She was, generally speaking, interested in my French and German reading lists and probes, we swapped and tested ideas on each other." Until Ronell left for New York in 1995, they enjoyed regular Sunday-afternoon dinners and long conversations at Acker's apartment and on the phone. "She'd give me gifts," Ronell recalls. "The Jewish-German-Bildung-bad girl thing was probably our springboard."

In his notes from a 1991 SFAI writing class with Kathy Acker, Alexander Laurence describes how she "talked about taking a piece of writing and jamming with it, sampling it, altering it. A phrase, a word, a section. The way jazz is made . . . Kathy was pushing me to be more intuitive, raw, exposing the unconscious. . . She wanted us to write every word and every sentence in an interesting way. She wanted us to explore dreams. Dreams were a big deal with Kathy . . . [She] wanted us to break through with writing, to reach some key moment, some epiphany, some crime . . ."

To the writer Anna Joy Springer, who audited the same class, Acker's teaching persona seemed harsh: "She was not polite or friendly at all. She said she was not our mom and she didn't want to be teaching . . . She had a plan to make everyone work a volunteer position among the poor in order to take her class. The ones she seemed to like in the class were the sex workers and drug addicts." Sometimes she'd hold classes off-site at an Irish pub or the Bearded Lady, a famed dyke café. As Springer recalls, "the people who stayed in her classes were a bit like a following. Some of us spent time with her outside of class. Some became close sexually," although "I didn't want that with her, because I wanted a mentor and heroine . . . She was more of a literary parent or godmother than she liked to admit, but she enjoyed the role."

Another ex-student, the writer Jenna Leigh Evans, recalls that though Acker could sometimes be brusque with her students, she was a consummate teacher who didn't repeat a single lesson or exercise in two years. "While it's true that she was clearly more excited by the students who looked/seemed obviously transgressive, she gave everyone's work meticulous individual attention. Plus, she ran a tight ship: she was never late, always showed up prepared." Students were pushed "to write with scorching emotional honesty . . . stuff would come up in the work that was really intimate and painful, experiences of sexual and physical traumas . . . so the vulnerability quotient was off the charts. She treated this . . . with respect and with solemn approval (because we were being honest, her cardinal rule). It set a tone; nothing ever got out of hand or slipped from her control."

Anna Joy Springer was playing in bands and dating Lynn Breedlove of Tribe 8, the iconoclastic dyke punk band whose performance at the 1994 Michigan Womyn's Festival, which included fellatio, castration, and BDSM scenes, was picketed by more traditional feminist attendees. Springer was impressed by how wholeheartedly Acker immersed herself in the SF dyke scene. "She was elated to see punk pits full of women without tops on, being aggressively expressive. She joined the pits. She was still very into working with non–drug-induced altered states, but she was also into troubling notions of femininity and sexiness . . . She was never 'too cool' to say she was learning or that she was excited by the scene—one that was really at least 85 percent women. The women were butches, femmes, tattooed tackle-face types, and smart and high and sometimes suspicious of her." The ethos among them was for women to be unconditionally supportive of one another, and as Springer recalls, "it gave her some hope to see a lot of that competition evaporate when there weren't any men around."

The SF dyke scene was a world apart from Acker's life in the literary worlds of New York and London. Her new friends didn't read the same books, didn't know the same things. None of the women she met in SF would ever think to compete for the mantle of avant-garde intellectual hero that she'd craved since she was fourteen. After ending her agent/author relationship with Ira Silverberg, Acker moved on to the William Morris agent Marcy Posner, but Posner was having a hard time placing her work. Perhaps it was time to dream some new dreams.

I really hate New York, Acker reaffirmed in a 1991 interview with Rebecca Deaton. *Life is so hard there, that all my old friends are very desperate about their careers, and that's a desperation I've felt. It just seemed to me a dreadful place.* Still, she wasn't entirely sold on San Francisco: *I don't know how long I'll remain here . . . It's very protective. It's very nice. What I can do, what I'm doing with the new book, is that I can become more experimental than I've been lately. I can really not be influenced by anybody, do what I want, be left alone, not have any pressures on me. So I'm a bit out of the world, which is good . . .*

Hannibal Lecter, My Father, a collection of her earliest writings, came out from Semiotext(e) in 1991. By now Acker's work was being written about and widely read in the gender studies and postmodern critical theory wings of the academy, and throughout that year she toured a great deal. For two weeks in June she taught at Naropa, where she met Steven Trull, a young writer from San Diego who'd eventually call himself "Janey Smith," after her *Blood and Guts* heroine. She and Trull hung out together, had unsafe sex, and became friends while she taught and maintained her own work schedule, writing four hours a day. As Trull/Smith recalls, "I didn't learn anything in Kathy's classes. I was overwhelmed by what she taught me when we hung out together. To this day, she's the most intelligent person I've ever conversed with." Trull would attain notoriety in the alt/lit world in 2013 when he published his list of "Writers I'd Like to Fuck (or Be Fucked By)" on htmlgiant. "What," wrote Dianna Dragonetti, "was the purpose of this list but to indulge Smith/Trull's own sense of toxic masculine entitlement? . . . Smith/Trull did not seek the consent of those whose names were included prior to publication, or inform anyone of their specific involvement . . . This is not art, but a clear and deliberate example of rape culture, and it must not be tolerated." Channeling Catullus, Acker had famously launched the most scabrous, hyperbolic attacks on both public and private individuals in her earlier work. She had no qualms about revealing the most intimate details of her encounters with named lovers and friends, and no one—at least publicly—minded that much. The Trull/Smith "Fuck List" debacle provides a stunning example of how much mores have changed over two decades. While the use of "the personal" by female writers has been largely redeemed, satirical excess has been pushed off the map.

During the weeks Acker spent at home in San Francisco that year, she slept, wrote, dreamed, and went for long motorcycle rides into the green.

* * *

Published by Pantheon Books in 1993, *My Mother: Demonology* is the most somber and elegiac of all Acker's books, taking the reader into an underworld of tunnels and caverns formed out of memories and dreams. To read it is to go for a long motorcycle ride through the subconscious. Switching between the simple past and present tenses, it's the only one of Acker's books that isn't at least partly composed in real time, the historical present tense. Shorn of the bratty, bad-girl persona that animates her earlier work, the book has none of the abrasion, humor, or shock she'd once been best known for. Narratively confounding and overly long, *Demonology* doesn't lend itself to a continuous read, but the book is compelling in other ways.

The novel begins with a series of letters addressed to a long-ago lover whom she calls "B" or "Bourenine." He's married; a shared life is impossible. Their relationship is as doomed as that of Heloise and Abelard, yet she feels she can tell Bourenine everything. *Dear B . . . I started writing you because I believed that if we told each other everything, there could be only trust between us . . .*

Dear B, the more I try to tell you everything, the more I have to find myself . . . I don't want to tell you anything . . . When I'm lying in your arms, I'm calm . . . At the same time I have to battle you . . .

Here are my most recent thoughts: When I met you, I was drowning because I wasn't going to let another person be close to me. (This frigidity is named "wildness.") I asked you, rather than anyone else, for help because I knew that you're an emotional paralytic. Perverse, as usual, I hollered, "Help!" as you'd beat me over the head so I'd finally drown or fall off a cliff . . . You're just what I want, B: a better death method.

She tells him her dreams: *We're kissing, but I feel nothing. He takes my clothes off me, then picks me naked up off the floor. Carries me into somewhere. In there he cradles me as if I'm a child. I grab what I feel to be safety. At that moment he starts systematically hurting me. After hurting me for a long time, he holds me and the world opens up—*

And then she writes, *You want me to live a lie and you admire me for my honesty. Repeatedly you've said that you respect my intelligence more than that of any woman you've ever met, and you treat me convulsively and continually like less than a dog. Female variety.*

The narrator's letters to B are letters to death—not a literal death, but a death of illusion from which she can revisit scenes of her earlier life from a position of greater clarity. Just as William S. Burroughs did in his 1981–87 *Red Night* trilogy, Acker remixes shards of her earlier autobiographical fiction to a point where these events become more and less real, enmeshing them with stories about historical figures to fashion a narrative myth. She wants to affix the unfixable. Once again channeling Laure and Violette Leduc, she craves "wildness," which she equates with sexuality. *Hello, you wildness. Are you spreading your legs for me again? Inside your vagina is only freedom.*

Just as Burroughs returns to scenes of his St. Louis childhood in *Red Night*, Acker revisits her school days at Lenox: the beloved lesbian English teacher, Miss St. Pierre; the stern headmistress, Mrs. Selby; the horrible Mueller twins, reborn as the Joneses, into whose leopard-skin coats she secretly blows her nose. This time the incidents Acker recalls are more detailed and vivid. She fully projects herself backwards in time. The schoolgirls devise a secret game: *Once a week, without any voting or other democratic procedures, we would unanimously decide on which one among us would be our next victim. The game or law was that for one week none of us could talk to the victim for any reason* . . . She knows she's *excluded, this time forever*, when Miss St. Pierre awards an English prize to one of the Joneses instead of to her. Toward the end of the book, Acker describes the novel's overall enterprise with tremendous lucidity: *Since my childhood is dead, in speaking of it I shall be speaking of something dead, but I shall do so in order to speak of the world of death, of the Kingdom of Darkness, or of Transparency.* Time and again, she finds herself lost in foreign cities. Spiraling water runs down a drain.

In "The Dead Man," the final section, the narrator returns to Germany on a tour whose purpose is to *present new American writing to Germans*, although *I am as much a representative of America and of "new American writing" as I was, and am, in rela-tion to writing practice, close to the other Americans on the tour.* On tour, she re-meets Bourenine and begins an affair with the promoter, "Georg Buchner," or "G." She tells G about her and Bourenine's past and confides, *"Bourenine's wife is scheduled to join the tour tomorrow night." When I began to cry, I realized that I was out of control. Since I wasn't conscious why I was crying, I entered the unknown.*

At the end of the tour, *G had told me three times that he would drive me from the hotel to the airport. He appeared at neither place, nor phoned.*

Of the two dozen letters that Acker preserved in her archive, two are from the promoter "Georg Buchner."

"I didn't go to the airport, cause I hate ggoodbye's [*sic*], he wrote. "In my cranky opinion there's never a way to straighten things out by talking, talking dissolves things. Any hallucination based on memory or affection is better than unburdening by talk(ing), hope that doesn't sound crude."

Demonology was published in the U.S. and the UK in July 1993 and was reviewed respectfully, albeit sparingly. *Publishers Weekly* noted its "hallucinatory amalgam of emotion and desire, held together by a series of abstract events"; the *Library Journal* praised "her formidably talented hand"; and, in a capsule *New York Times* review, Erik Burns observed that "Laure's impressionistic swirl, when it works, takes its power from sheer force of effort, from the skillful use of a writer's only real tool: words."

Weeks later, Acker went into a recording studio with the producer Hal Willner, Tribe 8, and the musicians Ralph Carney and David Cunningham, who'd worked with Tom Waits and the Flying Lizards. Under Willner's direction, they recorded huge swaths of *Demonology* as an avant-operatic spoken-word CD. The work would be titled *Redoing Childhood*. Each take was done virtually nonstop, and Ralph Carney recalls Acker jumping up and down in the booth while Tribe 8 played. When it was finally released two years after her death, *Redoing Childhood* revealed a new dimension to Acker's work. "Her voice in general, there was something so lush and luscious and embracing and sexy," Ira Silverberg told the *Seattle Weekly*. "Kathy had rock star energy about her. [Her performance] had less to do with the punctuation of the actual sentences than with her almost reinterpreting her own work in a lyrical way . . . Kathy just got it."

* * *

Acker met the technology specialist and cyber pioneer R. U. Sirius at an opening for the 1992 movie *Sneakers*, hosted by his magazine, *Mondo 2000*. They became friends right away. When *Demonology* came out, Sirius interviewed her for *Io*, a short-lived literary magazine. Their hilarious, intimate conversation about writing quickly digressed to talk about wild girls and piercings and strap-ons. *The students who come to my class,* Acker told him, *are very closely related to all the evil girls who are very interested in their bodies and sex and pleasure. I learn a lot from them about how to have pleasure and how cool the female body is.* Inspired by one of her students, she'd just gotten two labial piercings—*the little bead on the ring acts like a vibrator*—which enhanced the pleasure of motorcycle riding. In her mid-forties, she was drifting further and further away from her former New York contemporaries—who by now had established themselves as serious writers—into a phantasmic but prescient realm of wild girls, brigands, and pirates: a subculture born from increased family anarchy and personal trauma. On a trip through the desert in *Pussy, King of the Pirates*, Acker's name-shifting protagonist talks to truckers and a fat desert rat woman in pink shorts and a pink halter. She remembers how *an old friend of mine, someone who used to be a friend, a hot-shot media boy, saying in one of his magazine columns that nobody worth anything lives outside New York City. Outside, he said, there's nothing* . . . but here, in the nothing, she cracks antigovernment jokes with a trucker.

During their interview, Acker and Sirius bicker about French intellectuals—*RUS: I'm writing a piece for Wired called "A User's Guide to Trendy French Intellectuals" that thoroughly trashes those people. KA: Oh, evil person. You're so dumb, man. They're cool.*—but they bond around Michael Jackson: *KA: Talk about cyber-identity! It isn't like an older man having sex with a young boy—it's like a Martian having sex with a human.*

Spiraling back to her interest in Pierre Guyotat, whose *Tomb for 500,000 Soldiers* she'd discovered in Paris in the fall of 1979, she tells Sirius how she'd begun writing while masturbating. Guyotat's earliest writings had been composed in this way. "At the time," he told the writer and scholar Noura Wedell, "I wanted to have the masturbatory act find some utility apart from ephemeral pleasure, in the writing of a text marked by desire and imminent ejaculation." *I'm looking*, Acker told Sirius, *for what might be called a body language. One thing I do is stick a vibrator up my cunt and start writing—writing from the point of orgasm and losing control of the language and seeing what that's like.*

A lot of what you heard, she told an audience during a reading from *Pussy, was just, I wanted to see what language just passes through my mind . . . as I'm going through sex. What does that language look like. Don't know anything about cybersex . . . As far as sex goes, I like relationships and I like flesh.*

Sirius's friend and collaborator Jude Milhon, a.k.a. St. Jude, helped Acker connect to the WELL, the Bay Area's pioneer internet service provider. Initiated by the *Whole Earth Catalog* founder Stewart Brand in 1985 as a spin-off enterprise, by the early '90s the WELL had become one of the first public dial-up ISPs. Acker was underwhelmed. "I remember she got bored and disgusted pretty quickly," Sirius recalls. "The WELL had a lot of bourgeois liberals with hippie influences. People who were shocked by *Beavis and Butt Head* and *American Psycho*, who thought they signaled the end of Western civilization. And most of them probably had never heard of her." Soon, she switched service to AOL.

San Francisco was gentle and safe, but after four years Acker knew she was biding her time. Her literary career in the larger world had come to a standstill, she thought. When Marcy Posner didn't reply to a letter, she presumed—maybe rightly—that she'd been dropped. She sent Posner a notice of termination, requesting that she *forward all correspondence and other business matters pertaining to my writings to me at the above address.* She began making alternate plans—forming an "all girl" film company with the producers of *Slackers*, touring with Tribe 8. Although neither of these enterprises came to fruition, others would. Still, she was a famous writer—which she found both a curse and a blessing. The only reason she hadn't already been fired at SFAI, she told younger friends, was because of her fame. She believed everyone hated her. Still, as the filmmaker Michelle Handelman recalls of their friendship during those years, "nearly every conversation I had with her always had a moment where she said . . . *because I'm famous.*"

In September 1993 Acker had another PID flare-up after a first-trimester abortion, although she'd already been warned after an abortion two years before that her next could be fatal. Roz Kaveney called her one night in the summer of 1994 and was shocked when Acker told Kaveney she'd just saved her life: "[S]he had been about to commit suicide—had lined up pills and a glass of water. I had cheered her up enough that she wasn't going to do it now but she was not entirely sure how she felt about me as a result." It was the last time they spoke. She had some readings in the UK in August and early September, and she thought about moving back there but then changed her mind. She'd already agreed to teach that semester at UC San Diego and the University of Idaho (Moscow) as visiting professor.

* * *

In *Pussy*, she writes about attending a Diamanda Galás performance. *Oh yes, I know her, I tell a few girls who're younger than me . . . All of us, girls, are standing outside, on a street.* She goes shopping for sweaters, stands at the threshold of death, rejects a male rocker who wants to fuck her in public, and decides to become a girl pirate. In Brighton, she joins a renegade band who call themselves Girls of Fortune: *we call ourselves fortunate, perhaps because we're talking about our past, know that we come from a long and glorious lineage. Of death . . .*

The Brighton-based publisher Simon Strong heard Acker perform parts of *Pussy* at the spoken-word club Do Tongues during her tour in September 1994. Thrilled by her performance, he quickly arranged for her to record a CD for his new venture, CodeX. "Kathy Acker," he'd later write, "was the most shoplifted female author in the world! Here was a chance to give some five-finger discount options to the kids in the street." She repeated her set the next day in a studio, and the CD was released the following year. By then Acker had already begun a long and productive collaboration with the Mekons, adapting *Pussy* into a trash-rock opera, and she was working with the illustrators Diane DiMassa and Freddie Baer on *Pussycat Fever*, a graphic-novel version of *Pussy* that would be published by San Francisco's anarchist AK Press.

By the mid-1990s the mainstream literary world had become an increasingly improbable context for Acker's work. Picador passed on *Pussy, King of the Pirates*, and the novel would never be published in the UK. But Acker had started to see that the work's episodic, mosaic-like structure was closer in spirit to live performance and the labyrinthine hypertext structure of CD-ROMs than to most of the novels written by her contemporaries.

Banned from AOL for using obscenity in a chat room, she switched to eWorld and logged on to a different MUD or MOO after midnight most nights to converse with strangers. She found a new life there. The fantastic avatars they used most likely bore little relation to their actual selves. Like many others, Acker was already skeptical about the transformative potential of the internet, an information superhighway already littered with commerce and trash. But in the world of online gaming, gender, appearance, and race were hypothetical and fluid. Maybe there, a kind of utopia might be achieved.

If it weren't for teaching and the gym, I might never leave my house! That's how much I got into my computer, she told Cynthia Rose in Seattle. She began to describe herself as *a myth-maker for digital flesh* and wondered if the novel had not become an anachronism. The world of books, she told Rose, *is becoming like the world of opera.*

* * *

At the beginning of 1995, Acker had about $266,000 left in the Merrill Lynch brokerage account set up with her grandmother's trust fund. She was justifiably concerned about finances. Her SFAI paychecks didn't quite cover her rent. Still, for professional or personal reasons, she felt a need to maintain the same lifestyle she'd enjoyed since the '80s. That year she spent $7,500, almost her entire combined royalty income, on clothes. She had to pay for the gym and her trainer and her Reiki appointments. She ate only the best food; she liked nice hotels and didn't hesitate to take taxis. She'd already taken a second mortgage on her New York apartment. Finally, in June, she paid the loans off when it sold. So far, the occasional biopsies she had undergone for irregular breast masses had come back benign, but she feared that her health might be fragile. Was her sense of fragility and precariousness merely somatic? She had regular consultations with naturopaths and homeopaths and turned to Georgina Ritchie, a past-lives regressionist, and the astrologer Frank Molinaro for help.

Acker's expenses were high for a writer who was increasingly working outside the mainstream. By now she was looking for a full-time, tenure-track job virtually anywhere in the U.S. Concern for her cash flow might explain her exhausting 1995 tour schedule. During the first half of the year, she traveled from San Francisco to perform and guest teach in London and Brighton, Dartmouth College, Alfred University, Philadelphia, New York City, and then London again. She traveled to Durham, North Carolina, where Duke University was preparing to acquire her archives. Then again, these invitations may have also provided an escape from the insularity of her life in SF, and a means of affirming her fame. Performing that summer at the Australian Centre for Contemporary Art, she was billed as "Kathy Acker US Superstar Punk Feminist Writer." When young women such as Pam Brown saw her perform, they felt their lives validated. *Kathy Acker's drunken girls, she meant us,* Brown wrote in a poem after seeing her Sydney show. Acker hoped that her long, midwinter trip to New Hampshire to guest lecture at Dartmouth might lead to a job, but it did not. In any event, between January 1 and May 31 she was home for just thirty-eight days.

On July 18 Acker left for an eleven-day, three-city tour of Australia that began with nine days in Brisbane and concluded in Sydney. There, she met the media theorist McKenzie Wark. They hung out in between Acker's performances and publicity duties and spent her last night in Sydney together.

Wark, who is now a professor at the New School for Social Research in New York, was thirty-four when they met. Fourteen years younger than Acker, he was already considered a special-ist in the world of digital media she'd begun exploring intuitively. Wark had just published his firstbook, Virtual Geography, about the emergence of global mediaspace and the transmission of world events as media spectacles. In a manner unthinkable in the United States, Wark was enjoying a precocious career as a national media commentator and advising government ministers on media access while still living a kind of post-student life among artists and activists. He had boyfriends and girlfriends, often concurrently, and wondered about his identity, queerness and straightness, performance, butch/femme-ness and masculinity. Of course he'd read Acker. He'd followed her work since the '80s; he'd underlined passages.

On-tour flirtations, hookups, and romances had long been a part of Acker's touring regime, but something unusual caught between her and Wark. Coming home after the long flight from Sydney, she was delighted to read his first email. *Your message is changing the day*, she replied, and they began an intense round-the-clock email exchange that spanned 119 pages and lasted for twenty-two days. For the first time in a long time, she'd found someone to talk to. Yes, she wrote him, *there's always solitude but . . . I am even more grateful when there are meetings*. Their correspondence, published by Semiotext(e) in 2014, was by turns languid and frantic. Both Acker and Wark knew that an ongoing, real-time romance was unlikely. They lived seventeen time zones away; he had a tenure-track job and various lovers in Sydney, and she toured constantly. At first they approached cautiously. "Do we need to analyze our encounter with each other? Or can we just assume it, and see what kind of dialogue it anchors?" Wark wrote in his next email. And then they began writing in earnest, as often as seventeen times in a day. Connected across time zones by email, the leisurely self-revelation of traditional courtship occurs between them almost instantly. Time is compressed; time escalates. So long as the emails continue, they're in each other's days. They engage in a gentle edge play toward intimacy, discussing music and movies, TV shows and books, mutual friends, each other's feelings and moods, and sex, in general and in particular. When Wark writes about Australia's obsession with all things American, she looks at his life with envy:

[T]he KATHY ACKER *that* YOU WANT . . . *is another* MICKEY MOUSE, *you probably know her better than I do. It's media, Ken. It's not me . . . I'm this: part of a culture that doesn't want me . . . Our only survival card is* FAME *and the other side of the card, the pretty picture, is "homelessness." . . . That's who I am; I overwork most of the time; I come up for air (this is the first time in some years that I'm not running five jobs at once, touring and writing a novel and journalism/theory writing and teaching and what other projects like the Mekons' record, and I come up for air and who am I . . . lonely and scared.) . . .*

No wonder I'm fascinated with . . . by? . . . your relationships. We have the relationships of too many rats in a cage. No, rats who are hungry. No, rats who don't have maps that work. I'm amazed by your culture: you have maps. Culture. Art. Boring dinner parties. RU isn't walking homeless through the streets . . . Oh, sure, we all look glam while traveling . . . we're good at media images . . . You want to see "my" country. Get in a car and drive from little town to little town and talk to people. I do it all the time. It's part of touring. I know my students. I know that over half of them come out of serious child abuse, sexual and other. And they don't by and large, come from poor families . . . I can't bear seeing what I've become.

One week into their correspondence, Acker cautiously extends an invitation for him to stay at her place in September on his way to a Montreal conference: *if you are going to come through SF . . . may I offer one flat, either my bed or a small study with a futon in it . . . and if you tell me . . . what you enjoy, arrangements to meet whoever you want to meet . . . or else a set of keys and you do as you please . . . As you like it—the only policy. You were good to me in Sydney and I would like to respond (and, of course, see you again).* When he responds in kind—"If you're busy I can look after myself but if you have time I'd like to spend time with you"—she's enraged. *[I]t's always in my head that you don't know whether or not you want to have sex with me and you have lots of lovers. That makes a power relation between the two of us. Cause I'm not ambiguous about you and I'm not sleeping with anyone else at the moment . . . So when I say you can either sleep with me or have your own bed in my apartment, etc., I mean that. I mean, I want to be with you and so you set the terms cause that's how the relation so far has been arranged. I'm not fucking playing games . . . My apartment isn't a hotel. I'm trying to be gracious, fuck you . . . You see, I'm really not into these out-of-bed games. Fucking just tell me what you want and I'll go with it. That's what you do when you do s/m scenes. You discuss rules beforehand. Cause otherwise it's all too dangerous and there has to be trust . . . If you don't discuss the rules, then the shit power games are outside the bed and they hurt.*

And then she leaves on a motorcycle trip to L.A. for five days. They read Blanchot's *Le pas au-delà* and discuss Pasolini's film *Theorem* and talk on the phone, but their correspondence never returns to the same intimate pitch. The last email in the series, to Acker from Wark, is dated August 23. Five days later, she leaves for Chicago to finish recording the *Pussy* CD with the Mekons.

Wark arrived in San Francisco on September 14 and stayed with Acker for two nights, as they'd planned. Two weeks later they met up in New York and spent five nights together at her favorite hotel, the Gramercy Park. She showed him the landmarks of her earlier life, both real and imagined. As he'd later recall, "There was something dream-like about the New York she was showing me, like a fable."

Just read this over breakfast, she emailed for the last time, on February 12, 1996. *I too am returning from Zirma: my memory includes dirigibles flying in all directions, at window level; streets of shops where tattoes are drawn on sailors' skin; underground trains crammed with obese women suffering from the humidity. My traveling companions, on the other hand, swear they saw only one dirigible hovering among the city's spires, only one tattoo artist arranging needles and inks and pierced patterns on his bench, only one fat woman fanning herself on a train's platform. Memory is redundant: it repeats signs so that the city can begin to exist.*

Every time you dream I am fucking you, this is what happens. The city.

* * *

Pussy, King of the Pirates came out from Grove Press on January 1, 1996, and the reviews, at least in New York, were atrocious. "In Acker's tiresome world, homeless people, masturbation, body piercing, and S & M are good; patriarchy, rationality and morality are bad. Thus extends the subtleties of her imagination," wrote an anonymous critic for *Kirkus Reviews*. Two months later David Kelly reviewed it in brief for *The New York Times Book Review*: "One of her favorite subjects here is the importance of self-stimulation—appropriately enough, because in this book she has raised literary masturbation to an anti-art form. Them that don't read it will be the lucky ones."

Although the book wasn't published in the UK, Acker went to London and Brighton that March to debut her live performance of *Pussy* with the Mekons, and it was enthusiastically reviewed. Writing for *Melody Maker*, Dave Jennings found it "a glorious exception" to the dire reputation surrounding pop adaptations of literary works. "Sure," he concluded, "Acker's story is about sex and subversion, but then—lest we forget—those things are meant to be fun. Ms. Acker and her Mekons certainly haven't forgotten." *[I]t's not art. It's hot. Oh I'm dying of happiness. I'm never having a book that isn't sung again*, she'd written to Wark after hearing the finished CD for the first time.

On her way home from Brighton she stopped in London, where she met the writer and music critic Charles Shaar Murray at a dinner at a Mexican restaurant in Soho. They went home together. Within twenty-four hours they decided they were in love and resolved to spend the rest of their lives together. They made plans for her to fly back to SF, quit her job, pack, and come back by the end of the spring to live with him in London.

Within weeks of returning, Acker had a routine biopsy of a small lump she'd discovered in her left breast. It was the same unpleasant procedure she'd undergone periodically since her first cancer scare in 1978. But this time it wasn't benign.

FABLE

(1996–1997)

The doctors proposed a lumpectomy followed by radiation, but she demanded a double mastectomy and declined further treatment. She thought, *I'll get rid of it all, just give me a mastectomy.* Which, to her old friend Eleanor Antin, seemed like an act of total self-hate. David Antin talked on the phone to her doctor, who was very concerned about her prognosis without radiation. "She was so afraid," Eleanor Antin recalls. "Her response was very paranoid. Because it was like, to her, radiation meant evil things, invisible rays coming into you, do you know what I mean?" Georgina Ritchie also criticized this decision, feeling that the mastectomy destroyed an essential, defining part of her femininity. *I never liked my breasts*, Acker retorted, *and I'd rather look like a boy.*

Adopting an antioxidant diet designed to eliminate toxins, she consulted healers, acupuncturists, card readers, and astrologers. Charles Shaar Murray had purchased a ticket to see her in San Francisco that April before she joined him in London, so he was with her on the day of the surgery. Later she'd describe routine anesthetization procedures as if they were medical torture:

One of the green figures introduced a pre-anesthetic into the IV fluid that was dripping into veins. As soon as she inserted the

liquid, I felt cold creeping around the base of my skull, eating at
me. My brains were nauseous. I knew that I didn't want to be
here. Then I knew that I couldn't escape because my mind had
been changed . . .

When they discovered that the cancer had spread into some of her lymph nodes, the doctors urged her to start chemotherapy, but she declined. (She was afraid her hair would fall out, she was afraid of losing her teeth, she was afraid her muscles would wither . . .). Eventually she'd come to explain this decision as strictly financial: *At the time, I was working as an adjunct professor at an art college and so did not qualify for medical benefits . . . The price [of the] mastectomy was $7,000. I could afford to pay for that. . . . Chemotherapy begins at $20,000.* Still, she had more than $260,000 left from her trust, and many self-employed people in San Francisco bought their own coverage. Her reasoning here wasn't flawless.

She never spoke to the doctor again. Instead, she consulted Frank Molinaro and Georgina Ritchie. Ritchie referred her to the healer Greg Schelkun. Schelkun told her, *You have to want to be well. You have to learn how to be well. That can take a lifetime, or five lifetimes.* "All her friends," Eleanor Antin recalls, "became enemies. She made enemies of everyone. So no one could talk to her." Georgina Ritchie, the past-lives regressionist, attributed Acker's state of dis-ease, or un-health, to unresolved childhood trauma. Appearing in a cameo role in *Eurydice in the Underworld*, Georgina Ritchie tells Acker's character, *I roto-root the past. When a person goes through regression, childhood or past lives, that person is able to situate the trauma in the whole picture and so, stop obsessing about it.* To overcome cancer, *she had to find out what caused it.* This notion pleased her. Meaning, to Acker, had always meant power. It was a protection against chaos and failure.

You have an abnormal childhood you will have to live childhood over again, the twenty-four-year-old Acker had written in her notebook. With Ritchie, she set out again to retrace her childhood in earnest, to discover what had gone wrong.

Cancer became my whole brain:

She wrote in her notebook that spring.

> *If only I could think enough, if only I*
> *could think hard enough, ...*
> *If I can find out the cause of cancer*
> *then I can change that cause*
> *that's my only chance*
> *then cancer will go away.*

Later, she would transcribe one of her sessions with Ritchie and fold it into *Requiem*, her opera libretto:

GEORGE:
Did Electra's mother try to kill her before she was born?
Yes.
When she was three months in the womb?
When you were seven months in the womb, your mother tried to abort you using something to do with heat, a method common in those days.
ELECTRA: *I know this.*
GEORGE: *The abortion didn't work because you were meant to be born. You were helpless when all this happened. That's why you're scared.*

By July 1996 her healers agreed that she was now cancer-free. She gave up her Cole Valley apartment, packed up her books, and joined Charles Shaar Murray in London. "She was working," Murray wrote later, "on the assumption that she was free of cancer and would do whatever was necessary to stay that way. She maintained a rigorously controlled diet . . . supplemented with all manner of herbs and pills and powders, frequent visits to a gallery of healers, and daily hours of yoga and meditation. Her interest in all things spiritual and esoteric . . . deepened daily. Her healers—the ones she was seeing over here, and the ones in California whom she consulted by phone for several hours a week—all told her that she remained cancer-free, though massively debilitated by both the aftermath of the disease and the high-pressure detoxification of her diet and the various courses of medicines she swallowed daily."

Soon they discovered that living together in Murray's small, cluttered Islington flat wasn't ideal for two self-employed writers. She liked to sleep until noon; he was an earlier riser and wrote in the morning. And there was the question of money. Murray lived modestly, Acker less so. Writing as Eurydice in a short dramatic text, *Eurydice in the Underworld*, she addresses Shaar Murray as Orpheus: *I traveled to your land though I was scared that the trip would kill me . . . legally I was alien; there was no work . . . I was a nobody, a rat, a dowdy housewife . . . in the outside world I was no one; there you were someone.* Which perhaps was a stretch. She was extremely well-known. To younger contemporaries such as the writer Stewart Home, she seemed "so much cooler than Charles. She was a much cooler person, cooler, hip." Still, London was no more hospitable to her than it was six years earlier, when she left it. She couldn't find work. When Home proposed asking her for a blurb for his new Serpent's Tail book, his editor told him not to use Acker. Whatever she wrote would put people off because she was unpopular.

She and Murray decided that things might be better if she found her own place. And so, just two months after arriving in London, she bought a nearby basement apartment near the canals at 14 Duncan Terrace for 130,000 GBP. It was a cramped warren of low-ceilinged rooms, but the house overlooked a thin strip of park with wrought iron fences and benches.

"It was a very prestigious address," recalled Gary Pulsifer. "[But] it was a basement flat. It was dark. It wasn't a particularly big apartment. Books everywhere. Books, books, books. I said to Kathy, You're like a rat living in a maze. I thought, My god, why do you want to live in this place?"

Even in separate quarters, the couple's disagreements continued. As Murray wrote, "We were caught in an endless cycle of breakups and reconciliations. Sometimes two or three a week. Our feelings for each other were far too strong for us to let each other go, but our inability to create a practical emotional structure inhabitable by both of us kept driving us apart."

She was seeing a Chinese herbalist, a cranial-sacral therapist, and a healer. She was constantly tired, but the following month she traveled back to the States to give readings. During that trip she spent several days visiting with William Burroughs at his home in Lawrence, Kansas. *[T]he whole Kansas visit meant so much to me*, she emailed Ira Silverberg, *my lineage . . . William, as I'm sure you know, is happy, and to my surprise open and openly kind (he's always been kind but scary to me on the surface) . . . he hugged me again and made an effort to speak to me despite my ridiculous shyness . . . most of all, for me, I could see how clear he is, how without rancor and all the obterfuscations that blind most people.* Back home in London, the "Charles mess" continued. *He just keeps wanting to play James Dean and Natalie Woods (was that her name) and strangely, I'm too old and too in need of a home.* Allen Ginsberg had just retired from his faculty job in the Creative Writing Department of Brooklyn College, and Acker asked Silverberg to help her apply for it, but he had no clue how to do that. Finally, the department told her they'd consider bringing her in as a visiting writer. *As usual, back on the road . . .* Silverberg suggested that she buy a subscription to AWP (Association of Writers &

Writing Programs)—"a very valuable resource in looking for teaching work"—and apply for jobs, cold. Most of her colleagues and friends knew of her cancer diagnosis, but no one could, or would, help her find more stable employment.

Meanwhile, she'd already accepted a visiting writer position at Hollins University in Roanoke, Virginia, for the spring '97 semester.

* * *

Throughout the late fall of 1996 she worked on "The Gift of Disease," a long essay about cancer and healing commissioned by the *Guardian Weekend* magazine. The essay, she hoped, could eventually be expanded into a book about her encounters with healers.

The piece ran in January, and then she left London for Hollins University. The job was easy enough, but setting up another one-bedroom apartment, buying a motorcycle and a printer, and joining a gym consumed most of her salary. *I can't keep living out of a suitcase and owning a motorcycle in every port*, she emailed to Ira Silverberg. Still, she kept most of her emails to Silverberg—now editor in chief at Grove Press—upbeat and cheery. Sometimes she slipped: *I'm down here til May and the loneliness really stinks. There isn't even a bookstore. A bit worried about the health; have gotten myself run-down what with the strangeness and loneliness here, the break-up with Charles, and moving here. Oh well . . . love to everyone.* A week later she called him and tried to talk with him about her career. *I have been so much in a non-literary world and this, in a way, is a kind of early attempt to make contact with the literary side of things again . . . I have no idea how to move this information [about healing] back to your side of the fence. In fact, I am not sure I know how to move "me" back to your side of the fence. I am a bit nervous . . .* His reply—"career is ever-shifting"—was sagelike but noncommittal.

Back in London in June, she thought about moving to a less depressing apartment and even applied for a mortgage. She was having terrible shooting pains down her back and right arm, which she understood as the somatic effect of her anxiety and perpetual travel. She still had no agent. She'd written two new short pieces, *Eurydice in the Underworld* and *Requiem*, both drawn from her life after cancer. Her old friend Gary Pulsifer had just founded the independent press Arcadia Books. He suggested combining these essays with some of her earlier works that had been published in the U.S. in *Hannibal Lecter, My Father* into a new book for Arcadia. She trusted Pulsifer, and at the time she had no other choices. They agreed that the new book would be titled *Eurydice in the Underworld*. That summer, they met often for lunch at a barge restaurant near her apartment. She didn't look well. As a resident alien in the UK, she could have received free conventional treatment. Pulsifer didn't approve of her medical choices, so they rarely talked about cancer. "Sure, chemotherapy's poison," he told me in London in 2015, "but it's a chance." At the time, he was being treated for cancer, from which he died sixteen months later. "Kathy," he said, "was fascinated by the whole world, or aspects of the whole world. And she pulled the world into herself, which is quite unusual."

As summer progressed, she got sicker. She couldn't eat or digest food or walk more than a few blocks without tiring. *I affirm that every day is a day of wonder. I affirm that though I don't see it, I have more money than I need, I earn more than I need, I live in a house w/ room for all my books next to where I can walk in the woods, I am healthy I love my work, my money & my books are in the hands of the right people & I have time for my work, every day I open more & more to vision*, she wrote in her notebook.

One late afternoon she and Murray went for a walk along the canal. Again, they were arguing. Her hands moving fast as she talked, she dropped her Evian bottle into the water. Murray leaped down the bank, fished it out, and handed it back. She took a long drink of water, not thinking then about how the filthy canal water must have seeped through the cap. By August her liver had swollen to four times its size, but she was convinced that the pain in her gut was a viral infection. Every effect has its cause. Murray had poisoned her.

The next time they fought, it was final.

* * *

Eurydice was about to come out with Arcadia Books in September 1997, but Acker saw no reason for staying in London. She already had tickets to fly to Chicago to perform *Pussy* with the Mekons for three nights in September. She decided not to use her return ticket to London and to move back to California instead. She put her flat on the market and invited the friends she was still in touch with to stop by for a drink and help themselves to the unwanted clothes, books, and Ikea furniture that wasn't worth shipping. When Gary Pulsifer arrived toward the end of the party, nothing was left except a box of financial records. He took them. Someday, he thought, these could be useful, and they have been.

Her Islington flat sold for 160,000 GBP while she was on the plane to Chicago.

For the three *Pussy* performances with the Mekons at the Chicago Museum of Contemporary Art, she wore a gauzy white tunic over black leggings and danced out in front of the band. The cool, clear soprano voice of the singer Sally Timms ranged over Acker's lyrics:

> *The foul breath of the lower mouth*
> *Becomes a jewel*
> *Jewels can't be cut*

Except with special tools
You had to cut me open
I was so closed

She was tired during rehearsals because, she explained, she was getting over a bad case of food poisoning. Sometimes during performances she closed her eyes and just swayed toward the microphone. Everyone in the show knew she was terribly ill and understood that she'd rather not talk about it.

* * *

In San Francisco, she checked into the Market Street Travelodge, an overpriced downmarket motel south of the Tenderloin. She weighed less than a hundred pounds. In her suitcase she had some notebooks and clothes, her favorite stuffed animals, a few books including the *I Ching* and the *Bhagavad Gita*, and an assortment of vitamins, Chinese teas, herbal supplements, and antioxidant compounds. She got back in touch with her healers and called her old friend Bob Glück. Glück was shocked when he saw her condition and urged her to go to a hospital. She didn't call him again.

At age 30, she wrote in an undated notebook that year, *I was working in a cookie shop. There was absolutely nothing in the society that in any way made it seem possible for me to earn my living as a writer. I was, & still am, the most non-commercial of writers. I said, if X doesn't exist you have to make it exist. You just imagine it.*

Now I knew why I was so upset when friends cried over my plight. All of me needed the opposite: joy and light. I would imagine, & those who wouldn't imagine it with me would have to go. I was too weak for any other stance.

Several days later she moved to a boutique bed-and-breakfast in the Mission run by a lesbian couple she'd known from the mid-'90s dyke scene. She hid out in her room, coming down-stairs to make pots of medicinal tea, until finally the owners told her, "You're too sick, you should be in a hospital, you can't stay here." It was then that she called Sharon Grace, Aline Mare, and Matias Viegener. Together, they convinced her to go to a hospi-tal, where she was admitted immediately. A CAT scan revealed that the cancer had spread to her pancreas, lungs, liver, bones, kidney, and lymph nodes.

When he heard news of her illness, Sylvère Lotringer flew from New York to see her immediately. Seventeen years earlier, when she'd asked him if he wanted to live together, he'd been hesitant, never actually answered. And then she left for Seattle. They never formally parted. "I hardly understood at the time that we were breaking up, that I had to make a choice. After that, we kept crisscrossing each other's paths. There was a feeling that something existed between us, but it was never said: a potential that was never realized. I never stopped feeling close to her." He was shocked when he walked into her room at the UC San Fran-cisco Medical Center: "She was extremely thin. I actually sensed she could die any second—she was so green looking, and her skin was like parchment. Her arms looked so pitiful I could hardly touch her, I was afraid of breaking her. And yet she was very excited, at the same time, very lively." The lumps had returned to her breasts. She told him, *I made all the wrong choices, wrong boyfriends, wrong places.*

She knew then that she had cancer—*this little cute girl is not having fun*—but she wanted out of the hospital. In "The Gift of Disease," she'd written about Max B. Gerson's alternative cancer treatment research and the ongoing work of the Gerson Institute in Tijuana. She begged Viegener to bring her down there, but after they saw her X-rays, they told him her cancer was too advanced and they couldn't admit her. Finally, Viegener dis-covered American Biologics, a facility also located in Tijuana.

Founded by a former electronics engineer who added "M.D." to his name when he opened the clinic, American Biologics was the only alternative treatment facility that would accept her.

* * *

Because he knew he'd have to return to L.A. every week for his teaching job at CalArts, Viegener enlisted his brother Valentin to stay at the clinic and help care for Acker. Valentin welcomed the job: he was at a loose end and thinking about going to art school. On Halloween night Viegener ran around San Francisco, through costume parades, renting a van and gathering Acker's possessions. Sharon Grace found a registered nurse, who was also a Buddhist, who could help keep her comfortable during the nine-hour trip. The next day, armed with oxygen tanks, IVs, and Demerol, they embarked on a medical road trip and arrived at the Tijuana clinic on the evening of November 1, the Mexican Day of the Dead. It felt like the final frontier: "We left this hi-tech landscape and arrived at this tiny clinic in a third-world country . . . It was the last stop, there was no going back. And things were good for a week or two. She was happy to get the alternative treatments."

The clinic was located next to an Alliance Française in a formerly middle-class residential neighborhood, one block away from one of Tijuana's best hospitals, the Hospital Del Prado. It was, and still is, frequented by Amish and Mennonite patients whose religious beliefs preclude them from buying commercial medical insurance. "The quality, not quantity, of a life is the basis of our therapy," the staff nurse Guillermina Silva Gigi told me. "We don't give radiation to critical patients. Instead, we build up their overall condition, their weight and their appetite. We take the advanced patients that others don't want to treat. Kathy Acker had pleural effusion with advanced metastasis. She had her lungs drained, but eventually her condition progressed to a point that her heart could not tolerate."

Friends began calling and faxing. Mel Freilicher, Connie Samaras, David and Eleanor Antin, Amy Scholder, Ira Silverberg, Dick Hebdige, and Sylvère Lotringer came down to visit. "The clinic was really the end of the road," Lotringer wrote in his notebook. "Her legs were like sticks. Her arms were so pitifully thin . . . Barely fifty years old, she looked like an old Jewish woman. One afternoon, she asked if I could go out and get a few of those little pale blue notebooks that Mexican schoolchildren use. She wanted to start writing again. It was so sad, seeing her imprisoned in her body, and not yet ready to acknowledge her condition. It was like she was a child, and couldn't accept what was happening. She had this sense of invincibility, in spite of everything.

"When I came back with the notebooks, she sighed. She knew she was too weak to use them. She looked at me and asked, *Do you think they'll make a film about me?*"

"Still," Viegener wrote at the time, "I was hoping the friends in San Diego would be more visible, though Tijuana seems to everyone there so far away, which it is—culturally."

Thanksgiving that year fell on November 27, and by then she was slipping away. Viegener recalls feeling lonely. A few blocks away from the clinic, gunmen from the Tijuana Cartel opened fire on *Zeta* magazine editor Jesús Blancornelas, the "spiritual godfather of Mexican journalism," while he was on his way to the airport. *Zeta* had just published a photograph of cartel leader Ramón Arellano Félix. The editor's driver and bodyguard, Luis Valero Elizalde, was instantly killed. Blancornelas survived and would spend the rest of his life as a virtual prisoner. That Saturday, David and Eleanor Antin and Mel Freilicher came down to visit Kathy. Surrounded by friends, she began to stop breathing, intermittently. She asked Viegener to *look for the list*. What list?

The list to call the animals. Kathy, we didn't make a list. *It's the list to call the animals back home.* Okay. *Would you look for the list?*

During the last two weeks of her life, Viegener and Ira Silverberg worked on a fund-raising letter to help with her clinic expenses. Printed on Grove Atlantic letterhead and signed by Silverberg, it was faxed to a list of her most established colleagues and friends. "Dear X," read the final version, " . . . The crisis looming now is a financial one, and keeping Kathy on a stable course of treatment. $7,000 a week is the cost of her stay, and if she is discharged, she will need help with living expenses and outpatient treatment. I have made arrangements with Giorno Poetry Systems to receive tax-deductible contributions for her health care." The account, closed out two days after her death, totaled $2,440.

In 2007 the Austrian filmmaker Barbara Caspar made a feature-length documentary, *Who's Afraid of Kathy Acker?* Intercut with Acker's performances and interview clips, and the recollections of some of her former colleagues and friends, a chorus of younger women describe what reading her work has been like for them:

She uses real words and words that make people go, oh my god. So I like that about her.

I think I learned a lot about myself, some things I didn't wanna know, and some things I did.

She was able to put it out and say, I don't care what people think about it, it's for me. It's for me to work out my language. It's for me to work out my pain and just find whatever answers I need.

It's just life. It's experience. And the more experience you can have, whether it's good or bad or painful or disgusting or ugly, it's there

. . . I think that's really what makes her so beautiful. That she's naïve, yet she does realize this whole world around her.

She had lost that inner wonder and inner integrity to some sort of addiction or pain . . . And just wanting to be able to experience so much of life and put it into literature? I can relate to that exactly.

They may not read Acker's jokes, her compositional strategies, or her fierce intellect, but something in her work connects deeply with them. Incredibly, critics of all kinds have embraced discursive first-person fiction in the last years as if it were a new, post-internet genre. These contemporary texts owe a great debt to the candor and formal inventiveness of Acker's work and the work of her peers and progenitors.

* * *

"We're all the same in a way, don't you think?" Martha Rosler remarked when we were talking about Acker. "Of course that means we're competitive. But it also means we identify. I could've been Kathy. Kathy could've been me. I don't know. I could've been you, you could've been me. We all could've been Eleanor Antin. It's all the same. And by that I don't mean we're not who we are. But you know what I mean."

Notes

LEGEND (Abbreviated Titles of Sources Frequently Cited)

Archives

UAR: United Artists' Records. MSS 12. Special Collections & Archives, UC San Diego Library.

ISP: Ira Silverberg Papers. MSS 110. Fales Library and Special Collections, New York University Libraries.

JMP: Jackson Mac Low Papers. MSS 180. Special Collections and Archives, UC San Diego Library.

JRP: Jerome Rothenberg Papers. MSS 10. Special Collections and Archives, UC San Diego Library.

KAN: Kathy Acker Notebooks. MSS 434. Fales Library and Special Collections, New York University Libraries.

KAP: Kathy Acker Papers, David M. Rubenstein Rare Book & Manuscript Collection, Duke University.

LPP: Lil Picard Papers. University of Iowa Library, Iowa City, Iowa.

PPA: St. Marks Poetry Project Archives. St. Marks Church-in-the-Bowery, New York.

RSP: Ron Silliman Papers. MSS 75. Special Collections and Archives, UC San Diego Library.

SLP: Sylvère Lotringer Papers and Semiotext(e) Archive; MSS 221. Fales Library and Special Collections, New York University Libraries.

Personal Papers

GPA: Gary Pulsifer Archive. Chris Kraus Personal Papers, Los Angeles.

JGPP: Jeff Goldberg Personal Papers, Los Angeles.

MVPP: Mathias Viegener Personal Papers, Los Angeles.

PBPP: Paul Buck Personal Papers, London.

SLPP: Sylvère Lotringer Personal Papers, Los Angeles.

PWPP: Peter Wollen Personal Papers, London.

NOTES

POLITICS (1971–1973)

25 *There's a black, white, red*: Acker, Kathy. "Continuance." 1971. Box 1, Folder 7. KAN. 13.

26 *The apartment is on*: Neufeld, Len. Interview with the author. Mar. 15 2000; Quasha, George. Interview with the author. Aug. 22 2015.

26 *Down the hall, a staircase*: Description gathered from Kathy Acker. *Xeroxed Diary*. Jan–March 1971. Box 3, Folder 1. JRP. 39.

26 *"the 57th Street prison"*: Acker, *Diary*, 10.

26 *"I'm ugly, I'm not ugly"*: Ibid., 7.

26 *"he lies beside me reading"*: Ibid, 25.

27 *His plan, when they moved*: Neufeld, interview with the author, 2000.

27 *He owes $100 a month*: Acker, *Diary*, 7.

27 *He'd been invited to study linguistics with*: Neufeld, interview with the author, 2000.

27 *In the bedroom together*: Acker, "Continuance," 23.

27 *On weekdays*: Neufeld, interview with the author, 2000.

27 *Fun City, a Times Square emporium*: West, Ashley. "Ghosts of New York Adult Film: Bob Wolfe's Fourteenth Street Studio." *The Rialto Report*, 17 Aug. 2014. www.therialtoreport.com/2014/08/17/ghosts-of-new-york-adult-film-bob-wolfes-14th-st-studio. Accessed 14 Dec. 2015.

27 *They take the subway*: Acker, "Continuance," 27; 6.

27 *Wolfe's Fourteenth Street basement studio*: West, *The Rialto Report*, 2014.

28 *Neufeld and Acker had already*: Neufeld, Len. Email to the author. 28 Sept. 2015.

28 *The two months she'd spent*: Acker, Kathy. "Poems 5/71–6/71." Box 1, Folder 4. KAN. 26.

28 *"'robot' employment"*: Acker, *Diary*, 4.

28 *Besides, unlike in the film loops*: Sitney, Adams P. Interview with the author. 22 Oct. 2014.

28 *The performers were allowed*: Neufeld, interview with the author, 2000.

28 *These scripts could veer off*: Acker, *Diary*, 30.

28 *She banters with customers*: Sitney, interview with the author, 2014.

28 *Should she go back to school*: Acker, *Diary*, 6.

28 *He wants her to be self-supporting*: Acker, *Diary*, 13.

29 *"You have to become a criminal or a pervert"*: Ibid., 35.

29 *"I find I can only"*: Ibid., 23.

29 *At readings, when people ask*: Acker, "Continuance," 11.

29 *"the beginning of a great joy"*: Acker, *Diary*, 10.

29 *"The angels are making me into"*: Ibid., 26.

29 *"The show is like the lowest way"*: Ibid., 22.

29 *The neighbor downstairs complains*: Ibid., 37.

29 *"[O]ur writing is a religious act"*: Ibid., 5.

29 *"2 TO 4 SENTENCES EVERY DAY"*: Acker, Kathy. "Ex Libris Morda." 9 Mar. 1971. Box 1, Folder 12. KAN. 39.

30 *"I can sleep 16 hours a day"*: Acker, *Diary*, 9.

30 *"this writing is getting to be like junk"*: Acker, "Continuance," 4.

30 *"B. Mayer's work list of daily events"*: Acker, Kathy. "DIARIES/DIARY OF THE WORLD." 8 Dec. 1971. Box 1, Folder 7. KAN. 13.

30 *His mentor and friend Jerome Rothenberg*: Quasha, George. Email to the author. 10 Sept. 2015.

30 *He knows all the writers*: Rothenberg address book in Box 81, Folder 7. JRP.

31 *Acker has a huge crush*: Acker, *Diary*, 1971; Rothenberg's Regents Professorship appointment letter found in Box 20, Folder 5. JRP.

31 *"I've never known KA to act shy"*: Quasha, email to the author, 2015.

31 *His friends were an uptown crowd*: Neufeld, interview with the author, 2000.

31 *"I feel like I'm reading my future history"*: Acker, *Diary*, 39.

31 *"Kathy you're always wrong"*: Acker, "Poems 5/71–6/71," 30.

31 *She suffers from pelvic inflammatory disease*: Sitney, interview with the author, 2014.

31 *Exploring their sexuality*: Acker, *Diary*, 39; Neufeld, interview with the author, 2000.

31 *Often she wonders if*: Acker, *Diary*, multiple entries.

31 *"the whole glorious sexual revolution"*: Acker, "Continuance," 12.

31 *"I have no way of meeting her"*: Acker, *Diary*, 12.

32 *"my fucking goddamn grandmother"*: Ibid., 33.

32 *They were still married*: Neufeld, interview with the author, 2000.

32 *Married, like Acker, to his first*: Rosler, Martha. Interview with the author. 9 Mar. 2000.

33 *She stayed in San Diego*: Ibid.

33 *A photograph taken in 1980*: Photograph of Rosler taken from Dawsey, Jill. "Scenes From the Seventies: selections from the Photo Archive of Fred Londonier." *In the Canyon, Revise the Canon*. Ed. Geraldine Gourbe. Paris: Shelter Press, 2014. 191.

34 *The wedding took place*: Acker, Bob. Email to the author. 15 June 2015.

34 *No one expected*: Kaye, Pooh. Facebook message to the author. 3 Mar. 2015.

34 *They were Upper East Side*: Acker, Bob. Interview with the author. 22 Feb. 2000.

34 Thirty years later, walking around New York: Wark, McKenzie. Facebook message to the author. 3 Mar. 2015.

34 *In fact, she and Bob Acker*: Acker, Bob, email to the author, 2015.

34 *A rare family photograph*: Photo provided by Matias Viegener. MVA.

34 *They arrived just in time*: Freilicher, Mel. Interview with the author. 21 May 1998.

34 *"I'm surprised there's any interest"*: Acker, Bob. Email to the author, 2015.

35 *Years later she'd boast*: *Publishers Weekly*. Dec. 11 1995. Cit. in Martin, Douglas A. "When She Does What She Does: Intertextual Desire and Influence in Kathy Acker's Narratives." Diss. City University of New York, 2007. 115.

35 *Even if, as she'd elaborate*: Martin, "When She Does What She Does," 115.

35 *Harvard wouldn't enroll female students*: Walsh, Colleen. *Harvard Gazette*. 26 Apr. 2012. News.harvard.edu/gazette/story/2012/04/hard-earned-gains-for-women-at-harvard. Accessed 18 Jan. 2017.

36 *"very intelligent, eager"*: Sitney, P. Adams. Email to the author. 10 Oct. 2014.

36 *That fall, Sitney left Yale*: Brumbaugh, Robert. Email to the author. 13 Feb. 2015.

36 *"P. Adams made super-8 films"*: Acker, Kathy. "Reasons to Get Happy." *Shift* 15, 1993.

36 *"It had nothing to do with pornography"*: Sitney, P. Adams. Email to the author. 13 Feb. 2015.

37 *Cecily Selby, the Lenox School principal*: Nielsen (name Mueller), Susan. Email to Julien Raffinot. 19 Dec. 2015.

37 *"No sentimentality here either"*: Acker, Kathy. Message to Linda Mueller Vasu, June 1964. Linda Mueller Vasu Personal Papers.

38 *"I had failed in some way"*: Acker, "Ex Libris Morda," 5.

38 *"I hate the Mueller twins"*: Acker, Kathy. *The Childlike Life of the Black Tarantula*. 1973. Rpt. in *Portrait of an Eye: Three Novels*. New York: Grove Press, 1997. 33.

38 *"R. was thinking of poisoning"*:Acker, Kathy. In *Memoriam to Identity*. New York: Grove Press, 1990. 10.

39 *"I thought about the Jones twins"*: Acker, Kathy. *My Mother: Demonology*. New York: Grove Press, 1993. 202.

39 *with her "esoteric" mind*: Lindenbaum Herskovitz, Jean. Interview with Julien Raffinot. 28 Apr. 2015.

39 *A photograph in Acker's class yearbook*: Photograph of Kathy Acker: *The Lenox Lantern*. June 1964. New York City: Birch Wathen Lenox School Archives.

40 *Bilgore recalls that Acker was rarely seen*: Bilgore, Ellen. Interview with Julien Raffinot. 13 Apr. 2015.

40 *"The actual physical pleasure"*: Acker, "Poems 5/71–6/71," 34.

40 *"I don't see Jean in classes"*: Acker, *The Childlike Life of the Black Tarantula*, 33.

40 *"Don't quote me"*: Anonymous. Text message exchange with Julien Raffinot. 13 Apr. 2015.

42 *"Some people think that"*: *The Lenox Lantern*, 1964.

42 *Although she never wrote*: Mueller Vasu, Linda. Interview with Julien Raffinot. 28, 29 Sept. 2015.

43 *"Kathy," she said, "was a rather unhappy"*: Mueller Vasu, interview with Julien Raffinot, 2015.

43 *After Wellesley, Mueller attended graduate school*: Mueller Vasu, interview with Julien Raffinot, 2015.

43 *whom Acker would meet several years later*: Acker, Kathy. Audio transcript of unedited interview transcript with Sylvère Lotringer. 1990. Box 1, Folder 4. SLP.

43 *"Kathy," she said, "was a mess"*: Vasu, interview with Julien Raffinot, 2015.

43 *"she related strongly to"*: Vasu, Linda. Email to Julien Raffinot. 28 Sept. 2015.

44 *"Miss St. Pierre was the youngest"*: Acker, *My Mother: Demonology*, 197.

44 *In 2003, the real Jean St. Pierre*: Chen, Saidi. "English Instructor Jean St. Pierre Receives McKeen Award for Forty Years of Teaching." *The Phillipian* 20 Jan. 2003.

44 *"In the school that I attended"*: Acker, *My Mother: Demonology*, 33.

44 *"I knew that I didn't"*: Acker, Kathy. *Pussy, King of the Pirates*. New York: Grove Press, 1996. 109.

44 *Her friend Mel Freilicher recalls her*: Freilicher, Mel. "One or Two Things That I Know About Kathy Acker." *Rampike* 24.1 (1999); Freilicher, Mel. Interview with the author. May 1998.

45 *David and Eleanor Antin drove out from New York*: Antin, Eleanor. Interview by Judith Olch Richards. "Oral History Interview with Eleanor Antin." 8–9 May 2009. *Archives of American Art*. Smithsonian Institute. www.aaa.si.edu/collections/interviews/oral-history-interview-eleanor-antin-15792. Accessed 25 Apr. 2016.

46 *When David Antin's friend Allan Kaprow*: Antin, David. "California—the nervous camel." *i never knew what time it was*. Berkeley: University of California Press, 2004. 17–18.

46 *"it'll be very good"*: Antin, "California—the nervous camel," 18.

46 *"this is the right place to be"*: Ibid., 21.

46 *The La Jolla campus, built on a tract of land*: Information about UCSD gathered from Wikipedia. "University of California San Diego." Accessed 17 Dec. 2015.

46 *"standing around with an open checkbook"*: Antin, "California—the nervous camel," 17.

46 *To the disgust of the larger San Diego community*: Freilicher, "One or Two Things That I Know About Kathy Acker," 1999.

47 *Later, perhaps attempting to position her work*: See, for example: Acker, Kathy. Interview with Angela McRobbie. "Writers Talk—Kathy Acker with Angela McRobbie." ICA London. 1987. Video recording.

47 *In fact, neither she*: Bob Acker, email to the author, 2015.

47 *"a kind of middle European intellectual"*: Antin, David. "time on my hands." *i never knew what time it was*. Berkeley: University of California Press, 2004. 118.

47 *When a Marcuse acolyte*: Antin, "time on my hands," 123–34.

47 *"it was 1968 when I first visited"*: Antin, "California—the nervous camel," 22.

48 *Shopping for a used fridge*: Antin, Eleanor, "Oral History," 2009.

48 *"I-5 wasn't even completed at the time"*: Antin, "california—the nervous camel," 27.

48 *Once he and his family were settled*: Description of David Antin's early classes gathered from Antin, David. "Talking on Kathy Acker." *Lust for Life: On the Writings of Kathy Acker*. New York University, 8 Nov. 2002. youtu.be/kgcMDnyObSs. Accessed 25 Apr. 2016.

50 *"Kathy was beautiful"*: Neufeld, interview with the author, 2000.

50 *"The first time, we were"*: Ibid.

50 *"Acker came over yesterday"*: Acker, "Poems 5/71–6/71," 30.

51 *"You went to a party"*: Rosler, interview with the author, 2000.

51 *But soon Neufeld and Acker's relationship*: Ibid.

52 *"a big wood house painted green"*: Neufeld, interview with the author, 2000.

52 *"Lenny was madly in love with her"*: Rosler, interview with the author, 2000.

53 *"I move to New York"*: Acker, *The Childlike Life of the Black Tarantula*, 81–82.

53 *"I had to come to New York"*: Acker, Kathy. *I Dreamt I Was a Nymphomaniac: Imagining.* 1974. Rpt. in *Portrait of an Eye: Three Novels.* New York: Grove Press, 1997. 138–39.

54 *She asked her family for help*: Acker, "Poems 5/71–6/71," 35.

54 *"They pissed on me when I was sick"*: Acker, *Diary*, 20.

54 *Thinking about how to get money*: Neufeld, interview with the author, 2000.

54 *The minimum wage in New York*: Hourly wage gathered from New York State Department of Labor. "History of the Hourly Minimum Wage." *Department of Labor.* New York Department of Labor. Accessed 16 Dec. 2015.

55 *"let's see your tits"*: Acker, "Poems 5/71–6/71," 38.

55 *and then for a laugh*: Sitney, interview with the author, 2000.

55 *"Kathy wasn't scared"*: Neufeld, interview with the author, 2000.

55 *"Omar: There are lots of men out here"*: Acker, Kathy. "Algeria." *Hannibal Lecter, My Father.* Ed. Sylvère Lotringer. New York: Semiotext(e), 1991. 135.

56 *"[She] had such a bad ovarian infection"*: Acker, Kathy. *Great Expectations.* New York: Grove Press, 1983. 86.

57 *"the desperate voyeurs who sought"*: Acker, Kathy. *Empire of the Senseless.* New York: Grove Press, 1988. 16.

57 *"Taking my medicine"*: Acker, Kathy. *In Memoriam to Identity*, 131–32.

57 *"the doctor was beginning to control her"*: Ibid., 140.

57 *During the months she was writing*: Kaveney, Roz. "Some Years With Acker." *Roz Kaveney LiveJournal.* 23 June 2007. rozk.livejournal.com/158882.html. Accessed 16 Dec. 2015.

58 *"It's as if there's a territory"*: Acker, *In Memoriam to Identity*, 264.

58 *"The sex during the sex show"*: Acker, *Pussy, King of the Pirates*, 50.

58 *"I want to bring in the total way we experience"*: Acker, *Diary*, 13.

58 *"I maniacally spend everything"*: Ibid., 8.

59 *Late that March, the other shoe dropped*: Neufeld, interview with the author, 2000.

59 *Acker used her right to a call*: Sitney, interview with the author, 2014.

59 *it was Bob Wolfe*: Neufeld, interview with the author, 2000.

59 *"We had to be in court at 9:30"*: Acker, "Ex Libris Morda," 5.

59 *"the hippy male was wearing a Bill Blass suit"*: Acker, *Great Expectations*, 86.

59 *As Neufeld recalls, they weren't especially scared*: Neufeld, interview with the author, 2000.

59 *Unable to actually quit*: Acker, "Ex Libris Morda," 27.

60 *Acker successfully filed for unemployment*: Acker, "Poems 5/71–6/71," 27.

60 *Poorer, but no longer conflicted about doing the sex show*: Ibid., 16.

60 *"I'd like to kick her guts"*: Ibid., 16–23.

60 *Len Neufeld recalls that at the time*: Neufeld, interview with the author, 2000.

60 *"to fuck the women we meet"*: Acker, "Poems 5/71–6/71," 22.

60 *"the political economic and social repercussions"*: Ibid., 22.

60 *Eleanor Antin's* Blood of a Poet Box *included plasmatic samples*: Antin, Eleanor, "Oral History," 2009.

61 *"I decided I wasn't a poet"*: Acker, letter to Jerome Rothenberg. JRP.

61 *"I don't think I want"*: Acker, letter to Jerome Rothenberg, 1971. JRP.

62 *"Does language correspond to reality?"*: Acker, "DIARIES/DIARY OF THE WORLD," 1971. KAN.

62 *Over the years, in New York and London*: Viegener, Matias. Conversation with the author. 19 Feb. 1998.

62 *"I gotta go . . . I just feel so lonely"*: Neufeld, interview with the author, 2000.

62 *and for two years after that*: Neufeld, Len. Letter to Jerome Rothenberg. 29 May 1975. JRP.

63 *"Whereas the very intensity of surface"*: Kotz, Liz. "Why Memory Matters: Notes on Bernadette Mayer's Work." *Concreta* 02 2013. editorialconcreta.org/Why-Memory-Matters-Notes-on. Accessed 4 Aug. 2016.

63 *"After I finished doing it"*: Mayer, Bernadette. Interview with Charles Bernstein. 13 Sept. 2007. writing.upenn.edu/pennsound/xMayer.php. Accessed 18 Jan. 2017.

63 *"I began all this in April, 1972"*: Mayer, Bernadette. *Studying Hunger*. eclipse-archive.org/projects/HUNGER/html/pictures/008.html. Accessed 18 Jan. 2017.

64 *After leaving New York, she wrote postcards and letters*: Letters from Kathy Acker to Bernadette Mayer. UAR; Correspondence with Brodey and Baracks preserved in Kathy Acker Papers.

65 *"I'm sick of fucking"*: Acker, *Diary*, 24.

65 *"I'm sick of fucking not knowing"*: Acker, Kathy. "Politics." 1972. *Hannibal Lecter, My Father*. Ed. Sylvère Lotringer. New York: Semiotext(e), 1991. 35.

65 *"I was working in a sex show"*: Acker, Kathy. "Devoured by Myths: An Interview with Sylvère Lotringer." *Hannibal Lecter, My Father*. Ed. Sylvère Lotringer. New York: Semiotext(e), 1991. 4–5.

THE CHILDLIKE LIFE OF THE BLACK TARANTULA (1971–1974)

66 *"you have abnormal childhood"*: Acker, Kathy. "Journal Black Cats Black Jewels." 1972. *Homage to LeRoi Jones and Other Early Works*. Ed. Gabrielle Cappes. New York: Lost and Found series, CUNY Poetics Documents, 2015. 24.

66 *Solana Beach in 1972 was a sleepy, shabby*: Antin, Eleanor, "Oral History," 2009.

66 *Originally developed in the 1920s*: Information about Solana Beach gathered from Solana Beach Civic & Historical Society. "Solana Beach History." *Solana Beach California*. South Beach Historical Society, n.d. www.ci.solana-beach.ca.us/index.asp?SEC=6BACDB03-96AC-47CC-9F5C-57082740FDAF&Type=B_BASIC Accessed 25 Apr. 2016.

66 *UC San Diego students hitchhiked*: Antin, Eleanor. Interview with the author. 29–30 Mar. 2000.

66 *By the spring of 1972, Acker's relationship with*: Gordon, Peter. Email to the author. 24 Mar. 2015.

67 *" . . . those uptight-about-fame"*: Acker, Kathy. Letter to Jackson Mac Low. 1973. Box 8, Folder 7. JMP.

67 *She had a little money*: Acker, Kathy, *Homage to LeRoi Jones*, 42.

67 *"During the two years"*: Antin, David, "California—the nervous camel," 25.

67 *Solana Beach was where Acker*: Rosler, interview with the author, 2000.

67 *"the shock of going from a really protective environment"*: Acker, *Homage to LeRoi Jones*, 42.

67 *A photograph from Eleanor Antin's*: Photograph of Eleanor Antin from the artist's *King of Solana Beach* series. 1974. Ronald Feldman Gallery, New York.

68 *Mel Freilicher was separating*: Acker, letter to Jerome and Diane Rothenberg, 1972–73. JRP.

68 *"roam over San Diego without purple head"*: Acker, Homage to LeRoi Jones, 25.

68 *"even among freaks am freaks"*: Ibid., 29.

68 *"your stuff isn't personal enough"*: Ibid., 30.

68 *Peter Gordon had just finished*: Gordon, email to the author, 2015.

68 *He graduated a year early*: Gordon, email to the author, 15 May 2016.

69 *Peter Gordon's plan was to take a road trip*: Gordon, Peter. Email to the author. 16 Feb. 2000. Copyright Peter Gordon 2000.

70 *"Coming in crazy"*: Acker, postcard to Bernadette Mayer, 23 Aug. 1972.

70 *"This was the early '70s"*: Gordon, Peter. Email to the author. 25 Mar. 2015.

70 *"I was staying at my parent's house"*: Gordon, email to the author, 2015.

71 *"it was all very fast and intense"*: Gordon, email to the author, 2015.

71 *"I had to get out of New York for personal reasons"*: Acker, Kathy. "Kathy Acker: An Interview," conducted by Barry Alpert. 30 Mar. 1976. *Only Paper Today*, vol. 4, no. 2, November/December 1976, 13–15.

71 *Acker and Gordon would stay together*: Gordon, Peter. Email to the author. 22 June 2015.

71 *"It sure is nice to wake up"*: Acker, letter to Jerome and Diane Rothenberg, 1972–73. JRP.

71 *"I've got a wife named Peter"*: Ibid.

72 *When Eleanor was mailing out*: Antin, Eleanor, interview with author, 2000.

72 *a fugitive narrative*: Fox, Robert Elliot. "Conscientious Sorcerers: The Black Postmodern Fiction of Leroi Jones/Baraka, Ishmael Reed and Samuel R. Delaney." Cit. in Amira Baraka Biography. *Poetry Foundation*. n.d. www.poetryfoundation.org/ poems-and-poets/poets/detail/amiri-baraka. Accessed 25 Apr. 2016.

72 *"the gate was arched like a great hall"*: Acker, *Homage to LeRoi Jones*, 31.

73 *"It was the usual free-form"*: Antin, Eleanor, interview with the author, 2000.

73 *"Prose poems, lyrical images"*: Acker, *Only Paper Today*, 1976.

73 *She and Mel Freilicher*: Acker, letter to Bernadette Mayer, 1972–73. UAR.

73 *"dear Bernadette! dear Ed!"*: Acker, letter to Bernadette Mayer, Aug.–Sept. 1972. UAR.

74 *"Dear Burning Dot"*: Acker, postcard to Bernadette Mayer, 28 Apr. 1974. UAR.

74 *"By the way . . . could you give me"*: Acker, letter to Bernadette Mayer, 22 June 1973. UAR.

74 *"I'm just broke like crazy"*: Acker, letter to Bernadette Mayer, n.d. 1974. UAR.

74 *"I gave a friend of mine"*: Acker, letter to Bernadette Mayer, Apr. 1974. UAR.

75 *The poets Susan Howe and Alice Notley*: See correspondence from Susan Howe, Fanny Howe, Alice Notley to Bernadette Mayer. UAR.

75 *Like Mayer, Notley grew up*: "Alice Notley." *Wikipedia*. en.wikipedia.org/wiki/ Alice Notley. Accessed 25 Apr. 2015.

75 *"I found my old notebook"*: Notley, letter to Bernadette Mayer, 20 June 1977. UAR.

75 *"money" she wrote "is a problem"*: Acker, letter to Bernadette Mayer, Nov.–Dec. 1974. UAR.

75 An off-peak, three-minute long-distance call: "Long Distance Rates For the Late Seventies and Early Eighties." *AskMetaFilter*. 2012. ask.metafilter.com/211826/Long-Distance-Rates-For-the-Late-Seventies-and-Early-Eighties. Accessed 25 Apr. 2016.

75 *two-thirds of the hourly minimum wage*: "History of Federal Minimum Wage Rates Under the Fair Labor Standards Act, 1938–2009." *United States Department of Labor*. United States Department of Labor. www.dol.gov/whd/minwage/chart.html. Accessed 25 Apr. 2016.

75 *while a stamp could be bought for 11 cents*: Dart, Andrew K. "The History of Postage Rates in the United States." *A.K. Dart*. A.K. Dart, 12 July 2016. www.akdart.com/postrate.html. Accessed 25 Apr. 2016.

76 *"[Performing in the Times Square sex show"]*: Acker, Kathy. "An Interview with Kathy Acker" conducted by Larry McCaffery. 12 Apr. 1990. *Some Other Frequency: Interviews with Innovative American Authors*. Philadelphia: University of Pennsylvania Press, 1996. 95.

77 *Their friends among the ex-student crowd*: Freilicher, interview with the author, 1998.

77 *But there were a handful of strip clubs*: Freilicher, "One or Two Things I Know About Kathy Acker," 1999.

77 *She called herself "Target"*: Gordon, email to the author, 2015.

77 *"In San Diego, she rather happily"*: Freilicher, "One or Two Things I Know About Kathy Acker," 1999.

77 *"[San Diego was] a nice place"*: Acker, *Only Paper Today*, 1976.

77 *She danced for a while, and then quit*: Acker, letter to Jerome and Diane Rothenberg, 1972–73. JRP.

78 *The Antins' veterinarian, who*: Antin, Eleanor, interview with author, 2000.

78 *She and Gordon were already planning*: Gordon, email to the author, 2015.

78 *"I can envision my dear late father"*: Gordon, email to the author, 2016.

78 *He was a writer himself*: Ibid.

78 *"I live with Peter, my brother"*: Acker, letter to Jackson Mac Low, 1973. JMP.

79 *"I shared whatever I had with her"*: Gordon, email to the author, 2016.

79 *Among the "stuff" Acker was finding*: Acker, letter to Jackson Mac Low, 1973. JMP.

79 *"I'd love to fuck the whole family"*: Acker, Kathy. *Rip-Off Red, Girl Detective and The Burning Bombing of America*. New York: Grove Press, 2002. 12.

80 *"I have to disintegrate my mind"*: Ibid., 67.

80 *"I was interested in 'fame"*: Acker, *The Childlike Life of the Black Tarantula*, 86.

81 *"There were other women . . . art world women"*: Acker, *Only Paper Today*, 1976.

82 *She worked on it quickly*: Ibid.

82 *"I become a murderess"*: Acker, *The Childlike Life of the Black Tarantula*, 3.

82 *"I'm born poor St. Helen's Isle"*: Ibid., 10.

82 *"I call up D in Los Angeles"*: Ibid., 4.

82 *She showed her new work to*: Antin, Eleanor, interview with the author, 2000; Acker, "Devoured by Myths," interview by Sylvère Lotringer. Unpublished audio transcript. May 1990. SLP.

82 *"incorporating a method of exhibitioning"*: Stull, Ashley, and Chelsea L. Perry. "100 Boots A Continuing Narrative." *100 Boots: a continuing narrative.* 100boots.blogspot.mx. Accessed 25 Apr. 2016.

82 *"It was poor people's art"*: Antin, David, "Talking on Kathy Acker," 2002.

83 *Almost immediately, Acker talked*: Ibid.

83 *She pushed herself hard*: Acker, letter to Jackson Mac Low, n.d. July 1973. JMP.

84 *"I'm born crazy in Barbican"*: Acker, *The Childlike Life of the Black Tarantula*, 23.

84 *"I leave my parents, then my husband"*: Ibid., 25.

84 *"The Black Tarantula series"*: Acker, letter to Jackson Mac Low, July 1973. JMP.

84 *"Dear Kathy Aker [sic]"*: Dawson, Fielding. Postcard to Kathy Acker. 7 July 1973. KAP.

85 *In San Francisco, Acker and Gordon*: Gordon, Peter. Email to the author. 24 Mar. 2014.

85 *"I couldn't bear leaving SD"*: Acker, letter to Jackson Mac Low, July 1973. JMP.

86 *"I think Miss St. Pierre's a lesbian"*: Acker, *The Childlike Life of the Black Tarantula*, 33.

86 *Almost immediately she begins writing*: Acker, letter to Jackson Mac Low, 1 Oct. 1973. JMP.

86 *"I've always feared most that"*: Acker, *The Childlike Life of the Black Tarantula*, 41–62.

86 *Around the same time, she begins drawing*: Gordon, email to the author, 2015.

87 *"I have to stop at the right huts"*: Acker, Kathy. *Blood and Guts in High School.* New York: Grove Press, 1984. These maps didn't appear in TCL. They would not be used until Acker composed the manuscript for *Blood and Guts in High School*, completed in 1978 and first published in 1984.

87 *Ashley—who'd taught at Brandeis in the mid-'60s*: Ashley, Robert. "Robert Ashley: Automatic Writing." *DRAM online.* Feb. 1996. www.dramonline.org/albums/robert-ashley-automatic-writing/notes. Accessed 26 Apr. 2016.

87 *"During the time of composing"*: Ashley, "Automatic Writing," 1996.

88 *At Mills, Gordon and Acker become friends*: Kroesen, Jill. Interview with the author. 19 Mar. 2015; Acker, letter to Bernadette Mayer, 1973. UAR.

88 *Acker and Gordon hosted*: Acker, letter to Jackson Mac Low, 1973. JMP.

88 *Their place at 46 Belvedere*: Kroesen, interview with the author, 2015.

88 *"Age 16: My mother tells me"*: Acker, *The Childlike Life of the Black Tarantula*, 65.

89 *"Everything is incredibly beautiful"*: Ibid., 66–76.

89 *"A cold dry windy day clouds"*: Burroughs, William S. *Exterminator!*. New York: Grove Press, 1973. 55.

90 *"My mother puts on black fur-lined boots"*: Acker, *The Childlike Life of the Black Tarantula*, 62–63.

90 *"Your phenomenology is phenomenal"*: Mac Low, letter to Kathy Acker, 25 Jan. 1974. KAN.

90 *"O Kathy, I'm so lonely"*: Mac Low, letter to Acker, 1974. KAN.

91 *Depressed by what she perceived*: Acker, letter to Jerome Rothenberg, 31 Jan. 1973. JRP.

91 *She was still dependent*: Acker, letter to Jackson Mac Low, Nov. 1974. JMP.

91 *One or two nights a week*: Acker, *Homage to LeRoi Jones*, 36.

91 *"[I] decided this whole country"*: Acker, letter to Jackson Mac Low, 1974. JMP.

91 *"I sort of tried to"*: Acker, letter to Jackson Mac Low, 1974. JMP.

91 *"I slice open the skin"*: Acker, *Homage to LeRoi Jones*, 47.

91 *"it would bore the shit"*: Acker, letter to Jackson Mac Low, Jan. 1974. JMP.

91 *"All of these things"*: Kaveney, Roz. Interview with the author. 16 Jan. 2015.

91 *During the weeks she was deeply depressed*: Acker, letter to Jackson Mac Low, Jan. 1974. JMP.

92 *Her mother's long-ago disappeared lover*: Acker, Kathy, and Alan Sondheim. *Blue Tape*. 1974. Film.

92 *Wildroot Cream Oil, a Buffalo-based family business*: Forgotten Buffalo. "Forgotten Buffalo: Historic and Hip." *Forgotten Buffalo*. 2014. www.forgottenbuffalo.com/forgottenbuffalolost/wildrootfactory.html. Accessed 26 Apr. 2016.

92 *As she was going to read*: Reading Schedule 1974–1976. PPA.

92 *It was during this that trip she met*: Sondheim, Alan. Email to cybermind@listserv.aol. "The Alan Sondheim Mail Archive." *Alan Sondheim*. 20 Sept. 2002. www.alansondheim.org. Accessed 24 Apr. 2016.

BREAKING THROUGH MEMORIES INTO DESIRE (1974–1975)

93 *"How can days and happenings and moments"* Dick, Philip K. *A Scanner Darkly.* New York: Doubleday, 1977. 101.

93 *She and Len Neufeld*: See Acker, Kathy letter to Jerome Rothenberg, .n.d. 1973. JRP.

93 *On February 18, 1974, she and Mel Freilicher*: Reading Schedule 1974–1976. PPA.

93 *The previous year, Mayer and Bowes*: Guggenheim Foundation. "Ed Bowes." John Simon Guggenheim Memorial Foundation. 2010. www.gf.org/fellows/all-fellows/ed-bowes. Accessed. 24 Ap. 2016.

93 *To Mayer, the loft was*: Mayer, Bernadette. Interview by Adam Fitzgerald. "Lives of the Poets—Bernadette Mayer." *The Poetry Foundation.* 4 Apr. 2011. www.poetryfoundation.org/features/articles/detail/69658. Accessed 24 Apr. 2016.

94 *Soon Mayer would move to*: Acker, postcard addressed to Bernadette Mayer, 4 Mar. 1974. UAR.

94 *"Endless meshes incest"*: Acker, postcard to Ron Silliman, Mar. 1974. RSP.

94 *Sondheim, then thirty-one, was a poet/musician*: Information about Alan Sondheim gathered from Sondheim, Alan. "autobiog.txt." *Alan Sondheim.* www.alansondheim.org. Accessed 4 Apr. 2016.

94 *Early in 1974 Sondheim and his wife*: Sondheim, "autobiog.txt."

95 *"[I]nformation as true as I"*: Ibid.

95 *Sondheim heard Acker read*: Acker, Kathy, and Alan Sondheim, *Blue Tape.*

95 *"At this point I thought myself"*: Sondheim, "autobiog.txt."

95 *They didn't fuck then*: Acker, Kathy. Letter to Alan Sondheim. Rp. in *Homage to LeRoi Jones.*

95 *"How close can we get"*: Acker, *Homage to LeRoi Jones*, 37.

96 *"I like (don't know what word"*: Ibid., 37.

96 *Carolee Schneemann filmed herself*: Schneemann, Carolee. "Fuses." *Carolee Schneemann.* Carolee Schneemann. n.d. www.caroleeschneemann.com/fuses.html. Accessed 24 Apr. 2016.

96 in *Vito Acconci's 1972 Seedbed*: Saltz, Jerry. "Vito de Milo." *Artnet.* May 2004. www.artnet.com/Magazine/features/jsaltz/saltz4-28-04.asp. Accessed 24 Apr. 2016.

96 *But neither of these works*: Berne, Eric. *Games People Play.* New York: Grove Press, 1964.

96 *Sondheim replied by sending*: Acker, *Homage to LeRoi Jones*, 38.

96 *"I can't separate this insane"*: Ibid., 39.

97 *"What do I feel about Alan?"*: Ibid., 39.

97 "*I couldn't think what to say*": Ibid., 40.

97 *The next day, February 28*: Ibid., 41.

97 "*I don't know what to say*": Ibid., 40.

98 *She told him about her father's*: Ibid., 40–43.

98 "*my feelings are . . . always too complex*": Ibid., 44.

98 "*I couldn't hardly relate to men*": Ibid., 42.

98 *She leaves out the part*: Gordon, interview with the author, 2015.

98 "*I mean in a way this is crazy*": Acker, *Homage to LeRoi Jones*, 43.

98 "*there's been an incredible run*": Acker, postcard to Ron Silliman, 1974. RSP.

99 "*I mean why should Peter*": Acker, *Homage to LeRoi Jones*, 45.

98 *The new writing, dated March 1*: Ibid., 46.

99 "*pretty straight account of my life*": Acker, letter to Jackson Mac Low, 1974. JMP.

99 "*How close can I get to someone?*": Acker, *Homage to LeRoi Jones*, 46.

99 "*I know who Alan is*": Ibid., 46.

99 *[Kathy] placed me in the position*": Sondheim, "Alan Sondheim Mail Archive," 2002.

99 *He suggested that they make a video together*: Sondheim, "Alan Sondheim Mail Archive," 2002; Sondheim, "autobiog.txt."

100 *The London-based artist Anna-Maria Pinaka*: Pinaka, Anna Maria. "Pornographing: dirty subjectivities & self-objectification in contemporary lens-based art." Unpublished dissertation. University of Roehampton; Pinaka, Anna Maria. Emails to the author. 17–19 Jan. 2016.

100 "*Acconci . . . masturbated eight hours a day*": Saltz, "Vito de Milo," 2016.

100 *In* TV Hijack (1972), *he appeared on* : Boehm, Mike. "Chris Burden's Youthful Edge Grabbed One TV Host by the Throat." *Los Angeles Times*. 12 May 2015.

101 "*You will learn more about yourself*": Lang, Tony. "The History of Synanon and Charles Dederich." Cit. by Paul Morantz. *Paul Morantz*. 2009. www.paulmorantz.com/cult/the-history-of-synanon-and-charles-dederich. Accessed 24 Apr. 2016.

101 "*The game,*" *one survivor reported*: Morantz, "*The History of Synanon and Charles Dederich*," 2009.

101 *Embraced by celebrities and widely accepted*: Dickey, J. D. "The Dark Legacy of a Rehab Cult." *The Fix: Addiction and Recovery Straight Up*. 9 May 2012. Accessed 24 Apr. 2016.

101 "*If you keep people up long enough*": Dederich, Charles. "The People v. Charles Dederich." Cit. by Paul Morantz. *Paul Morantz*. 2009. Accessed 24 Apr. 2016.

101 *"[T]he next day and next few"*: Sondheim, "Alan Sondheim Mail Archive," 2002.

102 *"I met Alan Sondheim when"*: Acker and Sondheim, *Blue Tape*, 1974.

102 *"The next day I went back to California"*: Ibid.

103 *""her own configurated Kathy Acker"*: Schneemann, Carolee. Interview by Barbara Caspar. *Who's Afraid of Kathy Acker?* Dir. Barbara Caspar. 2007.

103 *"And I received a work dated March 1st"*: Acker and Sondheim, *Blue Tape*, 1974.

104 *"You put things in a control situation"*: Ibid.

105 *A philosopher/mathematician, Sondheim*: Sondheim, "Alan Sondheim Mail Archive," 2002.

105 *"I was more attracted to her"*: Sondheim, Alan. Interview by Gary Sullivan. *Alan Sondheim*. N.d. home.jps.net/~nada/sondheim.htm. Accessed 24 Apr. 2016.

105 *"You . . . put me in a position of feeling"*: Acker and Sondheim, *Blue Tape*, 1974.

106 *"I want you to look to the left of the monitor"*: Ibid.

108 *They showed the tape on*: Reading Schedule 1974–1976. PPA.

108 *No one applauded or spoke*: Sondheim, "Alan Sondheim Mail Archive," 2002.

108 *"I just made this tape with Elly Antin"*: Acker, letter to Bernadette Mayer, June 1974. UAR.

108 *"It depended on the first responder"*: Sondheim, Alan. "autobiog.txt: 1977."

109 *"For them, the Whitney was a kind"*: Sondheim, Interview with Gary Sullivan.

109 *"I absolutely love to fuck"*: Acker, Kathy. *I Dreamt I Was a Nymphomaniac: Imagining*. 1974. Rpt. in *Portrait of an Eye: Three Novels*. New York: Grove Press, 1992. 95.

109 *"[I] went to this party"*: Acker, letter to Bernadette Mayer, 1974. UAR.

109 *"When I was sending them out"*: Acker, "Devoured by Myths," interview by Sylvère Lotringer. Unpublished audio transcript, 1990. SLP.

109 *"I never thought I had imagination"*: Ibid.

110 *Perhaps in the wake of her*: Acker, *Only Paper Today*, 1976.

110 *"The world is not in space and time"*: Bergmann, Gustav. Cit. by Guido Bonino. "Space, Time, Concrete, Abstract." *Gustav Bergmann: Phenomenological Realism and Dialectical Ontology*. Ed. by Bruno Langlet. Berlin: Ontos Verlag, 2009. 83.

110 *Time, Bergson wrote, in* Time and Free Will: Bergson, Henri. *Time and Free Will: An Essay on the Data of Consciousness*. New York: Harper and Bros., 1960.

111 *"A horizon is something else other"*: Smithson, Robert. "Incidents of Mirror Travel in the Yucatan." *Artforum*. September 1969.

111 *"radical break from a dominant culture"*: Dooney, Richard. "Repetition in Post-modern Fiction: the works of Kathy Acker, Donald Barthelme and Don DeLillio." Ph.D. thesis abstract. University of Florida, 1993. archive.org/stream/repetitionin-post00doon/repetitioninpost00doon_djvu.txt Accessed 24 Apr. 2016.

111 *"what the reader remember[s] when"*: Friedman, Ellen G. "A Conversation with Kathy Acker." *The Review of Contemporary Fiction*, vol. 9. No. 3, 1989.

111 *"I realized," she told Barry*: Acker, *Only Paper Today*, 1976.

111 *"She and Gordon produced the pamphlets*: Sullivan, Gary. "Ron Silliman Interview." *ReadMe.* 2000. home.jps.net/~nada/silliman.html. Accessed 24 Apr. 2016.

111 *"I told the guy I was living with"*: Acker, *I Dreamt I Was a Nymphomaniac*, 143.

112 *"Dear Bernadette polemic hmmm"*: Acker, letter to Bernadette Mayer, 1974. UAR.

112 *"I don't take criticism very lightly"*: Acker, letter to Bernadette Mayer, 1974. UAR.

113 *"Dear Bernadette, Good to hear"*: Acker, letter to Bernadette Mayer, 1975. UAR.

113 *"I now need the input"*: Acker, letter to Jackson Mac Low, Nov. 1974. JMP.

113 *"I'm not very interested"*: Acker, letter to Jackson Mac Low, Nov. 1974. JMP.

113 *She caught a six-week*: Acker, letter to Jackson Mac Low, Nov. 1974. JMP.

114 *"It sounded too good to be true"*: Acker, letter to Jackson Mac Low, Nov. 1974. JMP.

114 *"Dear Kathy Acker, Since you began"*: Katz, Leandro and Ted Castle. Letter to Kathy Acker. 5 Dec. 1974. KAP.

TASTING AND SPITTING (1975–1979)

115 *"In Times as ours now"*: Picard, Lil. "Tasting and Spitting." 1975. Lil Picard Papers. Box 28, Folder 21. University of Iowa Library, Iowa.

115 *Her friend, the poet Clayton Eshleman, agreed*: Acker, Kathy. Letter to Ron Silliman. Mar. 1975. RSP.

115 *Gordon and Acker didn't know if*: Gordon, email to the author, 2015.

116 *After an intense, brief affair*: Acker, letter to Ron Silliman, Mar. 1975. RSP.

116 *"People have breakdowns and"*: Reines, Ariana. Email to the author. 8 Apr. 2016.

116 *By the time Acker arrived*: Acker, letter to Ron Silliman, Mar. 1975. RSP.

116 *By the end of the year*: Acker, letter to Ron Silliman, June 1975. RSP.

116 *Gordon arrived from Chicago*: Gordon, email to the author, 2015.

116 *Acker's friendship with Mayer*: Acker, letter to Ron Silliman, Mar. 1975. RSP.

117 *Beyond the frisson of:* Acker, letter to Ron Silliman, early June 1975. RSP.

118 *She began looking toward:* Acker, letter to Ron Silliman, mid-June 1975. RSP.

118 *"Thanks for the money and"*: Acker, letter to Ron Silliman, 1974. RSP.

118 *"I even feel like an adult (huh)"*: Acker, letter to Ron Silliman, early June 1975. RSP.

118 *For the next four months:* Gordon, email to the author, 2015.

118 *For a while Acker crashed:* Kaye, Pooh. "A Long List Chris." Letter to the author. 16 Apr. 2016.

119 *Acker used TVRT's East Fourth Street:* Acker, Kathy. Return address on envelopes preserved by Ron Silliman. RSP.

119 *Soon after arriving back in New York.:* Acker, letter to Ron Silliman, Mar. 1975. RSP.

119 *No formal dance steps:* Kaye, letter to the author, 2016.

119 *In Forti's workshops, dancers crawled:* Forti, Simone. Telephone conversation with the author. 19 Apr. 2016.

119 *Acker struck up a sexual friendship:* Acker, letter to Ron Silliman, Mar. 1975. RSP.

120 *"I hate NYC. I totally hate NYC"*: Acker, letter to Ron Silliman, Mar. 1975. RSP.

120 *"NYC calming down, or me"*: Acker, letter to Ron Silliman, early June 1975. RSP.

121 *"By the way, how do I"* : Acker, letter to Ron Silliman, 31 May 1975. RSP.

121 *"The night before I was going to Paris"*: Acker, Kathy. *The Adult Life of Toulouse Lautrec.* Rpt. in *Portrait of an Eye: Three Novels.* New York: Grove Press, 1992. 212–213.

122 *Writing the diaries that would form* Politics: Acker, Kathy. Various correspondence to Jerome Rothenberg. JRP.

122 *for* The Childlike Life*, she chose Jackson Mac Low:* Acker, Kathy. Various correspondence to Jackson Mac Low. JMP.

122 *Her text for Blue Tape was:* Acker, *Homage to LeRoi Jones*, 1974.

122 *Several years later, as she began writing:* Acker, Kathy and Paul Buck. *Spread Wide.* Paris: Editions Dis Voir, 2004.

122 *The New York* Daily News *wouldn't publish:* Van Riper, Frank. "Ford to City: Drop Dead in 1975." New York *Daily News.* 30 Oct. 1975. www.nydailynews.com/new-york/president-ford-announces-won-bailout-nyc-1975-article-1.2405985. Accessed 23 Apr. 2016.

123 *"the sense everyone has"*: Acker, letter to Ron Silliman, early June 1975. RSP.

123 *welfare, unemployment insurance*: See, for example: Breuer, Lee. "How We Work." *Performing Arts Journal* 1, 1976, 29–32.

123 *Molly Crabapple's 2015* Drawing Blood *describes*: Crabapple, Molly. *Drawing Blood*. New York: Harper Collins, 2015. 143–87.

123 *"You know, the '70s were dull"*: Bleckner, Ross. "Inside the Art Bars." *Art in America*. Ed. Elizabeth C. Baker. Dec. 2013.

124 *"We would play this game where"*: Close, Chuck. "Inside the Art Bars." *Art in America*. Ed. Elizabeth C. Baker. Dec. 2013.

124 *In New York, Acker became close friends*: Acker, letter to Ron Silliman, early June 1975. RSP.

124 *and the writer and artist Constance DeJong*: Acker, letter to Ron Silliman, mid-June 1975. RSP.

124 *DeJong had moved to New York*: DeJong, Constance. Interview with the author. 4 Mar. 2014.

124 *She'd already started writing her first book*: DeJong, Constance. *Modern Love*. 1975–1977. *Up Is Up but So Is Down: New York's Downtown Literary Scene, 1974–1992*. Ed. Brandon Stosuy. New York: New York University Press, 2006.

124 *"Everywhere I go I see losers"*: DeJong, "Modern Love," 39.

125 *DeJong was adamant that she wasn't a poet*: DeJong, interview with the author, 2014.

126 *"I was really pleased"*: DeJong, interview with the author, 2014.

126 *"Connie's about the only person"*: Acker, letter to Ron Silliman, late July 1975. RSP.

126 *They talked about starting a press*: DeJong, interview with the author, 2014.

126 *DeJong remembers having long conversations*: DeJong, interview with the author, 2014.

126 *met Acker around the same time*: Kaye, Pooh. letter to the author, 2016.

126 *Years later, they'd discover that*: Kaye, Pooh. Email to the author. 17 Aug. 2015.

126 *Kaye, Acker, and Kroesen went to art openings*: Acker, letter to Ron Silliman, early June 1975.

126 *Barnabus Rex, a 400-square-foot hole-in-the-wall*: Perlman, Cara. "Cara Perlman Bio: Part 1—The 70s." *Sea Perl Productions*, n.d. seaperlproductions.tumblr.com/post/127444134358/caraperlmanbio-part1-1970s. Accessed 23 Apr. 2016.

126 *"Maybe I should go fuck"*: Acker, letter to Ron Silliman, Sept. 1975. RSP.

126 *The Austrian playwright Peter Handke*: Roloff, Michael. "Tribeca—Walkabout: Glimpses of Downtown Manhattan and the Sacarmento Mountains." *Roloff.*. n.d. www.roloff.freehosting.net/custom.html. Accessed 23 Apr. 2016.

127 *The Ramones, the Talking Heads*: "CBGB." *Wikipedia.* en.wikipedia.org/ wiki/CBGB. Accessed 23 Apr. 2016; "Live At CBGBs" Atlantic Records, 1976. CD.

127 *After moving back to New York in 1974*: Kroesen, Jill. Email to the author. 19 Mar. 2016.

127 *Acker became a frequent visitor*: Kaye, letter to the author, 2016.

127 *recruiting Neufeld to run errands*: Kroesen, Jill. Interview with the author. 19 Mar. 2015.

127 *One of the songs Kroesen wrote*: Kroesen, Jill. "Insecure Girlfriend Blues, or Don't Steal My Boyfriend." Copyright 1975.

127 *"I didn't like her"*: Kroesen, interview with the author, 2015.

127 *"She had this way that made you"*: Kroesen, interview with the author, 2015.

128 *"an elaborate morality tale"*: Acker, letter to Ron Silliman, early June 1975. RSP.

128 *"Fuck [philosopher Willard] Quine"*: Acker, letter to Ron Silliman, mid-June 1975. RSP.

128 *No longer much interested in conceptualist*: Acker, letter to Ron Silliman, mid–late June 1975. RSP.

128 *"dirty old man of American letters"*: Parker, Ian. "Making Advances." *The New Yorker*. 1 Apr. 1996.

128 *Robbins's twelfth novel*, The Pirate: Robbins, Harold. *The Pirate*. New York: Simon & Schuster, 1975.

128 *"Robbins turns out to be the main interest"*: Acker, letter to Ron Silliman, mid–late June 1975. RSP.

129 *"He kept looking like he was about to jump me"*: Acker, *Toulouse Lautrec*, 197.

129 *"I'm a totally hideous monster"*: Ibid., 194.

129 *"I don't know how to present"*: Ibid.

129 *"He's putting his arms around me"*: Ibid., 195.

129 *"Reading this early work"*: Indiana, Gary. "Ackerville." *London Review of Books*. 14 Dec. 2006.

130 *"Seems like the 35–45 year old artists"*: Acker, letter to Ron Silliman, early–mid June 1975. RSP.

130 *"I'm interested" Acker wrote*: Acker, letter to Ron Silliman, early–mid June 1975. RSP.

130 *She applied for a CAPS*: Acker, letter to Ron Silliman, early–mid June 1975. RSP.

130 *Still, as DeJong recalls*: DeJong, Constance. Interview with author. 4 Mar. 2014.

130 *When Constance DeJong left*: Gordon, email to the author, 2015.

130 "*I just moved to*": Acker, letter to Ron Silliman, early–mid June 1975. RSP.

131 "*[W]hat's happening here that's interesting*": Acker, letter to Ron Silliman, early–mid June 1975. RSP.

131 "*I got sick of the whole*": Acker, letter to Ron Silliman, mid–late June 1975. RSP.

131 "*more information I can use*": Acker, letter to Ron Silliman, mid–late June 1975. RSP.

132 *A brief romance with the artist*: Acker, letter to Ron Silliman, mid–late June 1975. RSP.

132 "*[I]t just became clear*": Acker, letter to Ron Silliman, late July–early Aug. 1975. RSP.

132 *Reading Govinda's* The Way of the White Clouds: Acker, letter to Ron Silliman, late July–early Aug. 1975. RSP.

132 *The fourth pamphlet, titled* The Creation of the World: Acker, *Toulouse Lautrec*, 226.

132 *From there, she cuts to a scene*: Ibid., 235.

132 "*I was high. The private section*": Acker, *Toulouse Lautrec*, 239–44; Robbins, *The Pirate*, 131–38.

133 *When DeJong returned in early September*: DeJong, interview with the author, 2014.

133 *Sick with the flu*: Acker, letter to Ron Silliman, early Sept. 1975. RSP.

133 *Eventually Gordon found them*: Kroesen, interview with the author, 2015.

133 *Her regime entailed writing*: Lotringer, Sylvère. Interview with the author. 13 Mar. 2000.

133 "*I need a lot of info*": Acker, letter to Ron Silliman, late Sept.–early Oct. 1975. RSP.

134 "*It all ties in*": Acker, letter to Ron Silliman, late Sept.–early Oct. 1975. RSP.

134 *She read Stanislavski's book*: Acker, letter to Ron Silliman, late Sept.–early Oct. 1975. RSP.

134 *Like Ron Silliman, Bruce Andrews, Charles Bernstein*: "The Two Saussures" and "Saussure's Anagrams" had been published in New York by *Semiotext(e)* in 1974 and 1975, respectively; the journal circulated widely in the art world.

134 "*is too narrow for me*": Acker, letter to Ron Silliman, late Sept.–early Oct. 1975. RSP.

134 "*hardly seem to do any work*": Acker, letter to Ron Silliman, late Sept.–early Oct. 1975. RSP.

134 *"issuing non-thought baby pap"*: Acker, letter to Ron Silliman, late Sept.–early Oct. 1975. RSP.

134 *While TVRT helped produce*: Acker, Kathy. "The Adult Life of Toulouse Lautrec [six vol. complete]." New York: TVRT, 1975–1976. *Between the Covers Rare Books Catalogue*. Between the Covers Rare Books. www.betweenthecovers.com/private/Catalogs/C204.pdf. Accessed 23 Apr. 2016.

134 *she wouldn't publish the entire manuscript*: Acker, Kathy. *The Adult Life of Toulouse Lautrec*. New York: Printed Matter Books, 1978.

134 *"enormous respect for people like"*: Acker *Only Paper Today*, 1976.

134 *That fall, Acker and DeJong*: DeJong, interview with the author, 2014.

135 *To this day, deep online*: Acker, Kathy. *The Complete Works of Constance DeJong*. Fantastic Fiction. n.d. www.fantasticfiction.com/a/kathy-acker/complete-works-of-constance-de-jong.htm. Accessed 25 Jan. 2017.

135 *"Kathy, at that point, sort of chose"*: Antin, Eleanor, interview with author, 2000.

136 *DeJong went on first*: DeJong, interview with the author, 2014.

136 *Philip Glass brought his friend*: DeJong, interview with the author, 2014.

136 *"The Novel of Bullshit is dead"*: Pynchon, Thomas. "Book Endorsements." *The Modern Word*. Accessed 12 Oct. 2014.

136 *Embraced by the new Hollywood*: Dixon, Jonathan. "Writer Rudy Wurlitzer's Underappreciated Masterpieces." *Vice*. 26 Feb. 2015.www.vice.com/read/the-inteior-frontier-0000581-v22n2. Accessed 23 Apr. 2016.

136 *"one of the greatest novels ever composed"*: Jacobs, Rodger. "Conversing with Rudy Wurlitzer: 'A Beaten-up Old Scribbler.'" *Pop Matters*. 5 Feb. 2009. www.pop-matters.com/column/69394-conversing-with-rudy-wurlitzer-a-beaten-up-old-scribbler. Accessed 23 Apr. 2016.

136 *After that night, Acker sought Wurlitzer out*: DeJong, interview with the author, 2014.

136 *Wurlitzer's coming-to-culture*: "Rudy Wurlitzer." *Wikipedia*. n.d. en.wikipedia.org/wiki/Rudy_Wurlitzer. Accessed 23 Apr. 2016.

137 *A practicing Buddhist, Wurlitzer was*: Wurlitzer, Rudy. Letter to Kathy Acker. Winter 1976. KAP.

137 *"I'm totally a romantic"*: Acker, letter to Ron Silliman, mid–late June 1975. RSP.

137 *"I guess that's what defines a friend to me"*: Acker, letter to Ron Silliman, mid–late June 1975. RSP.

137 *"Marcia realized she was a bum"*: Acker, *Toulouse Lautrec*, 282–283.

138 *"Suddenly seeing something"*: Ibid., 273.

138 *"Feeling lonely . . . Feeling almost cut"*: Ibid., 289.

139 *"I'm a CAPS finalist"*: Acker, letter to Ron Silliman, Sept. 1975. RSP.

139 *Around the same time, she accepted*: Acker, *Only Paper Today*, 1976.

139 *a former cabaret artist*: Smith, Roberta. "Lil Picard, 94, Artist and Critic Who Was Once a Hat Designer." *New York Times Obituaries. New York Times.* 14 May 1994.

139 *In 1937 she and her husband*: Edwards, Kathleen A. *Lil Picard and Counterculture New York.* New York: Grey Art Gallery, New York University. Apr.–Jul. 2010.

139 *Picard became a key member*: "Boris Lurie Art Foundation." *Boris Lurie Art.* n.d. borislurieart.org/noartists Accessed 23 Apr. 2016.

139 *A fixture at Warhol's Factory*: Edwards, *Lil Picard and Counterculture New York*, 2010.

140 *"a free spirit . . . able to negotiate"*: Schneemann, Carolee. Qtd. In Bloch, Mark. "Lil Picard and Counterculture New York." *Whitehot.* July 2011. whitehot-magazine.com/articles/lil-picard-counterculture-new-york/2327 Accessed 23 Apr. 2016.

140 *"with the idea of destruction and construction"*: Picard, Lil. *1965-2065-2164*: artist's statement written in 1974. Lil Picard Papers. University of Iowa Library, Iowa City, Iowa.

140 *"I had to sit naked right next to"*: Acker, *Only Paper Today*, 1976.

141 *"wind wrapping around the house"*: Wurlitzer, Rudy. Letter to Kathy Acker. 1976. KAP.

141 *"way out of proportion"*: Wurlitzer, letter to Kathy Acker, 1976. KAP.

141 *Acker received a 1976 CAPS grant*: Acker, letter to Ron Silliman, Jan. 1976. RSP.

141 *"I'm far too famous, notorious"*: Acker, Kathy. Email to Ira Silverberg. 16 Nov. 1996. IRS.

142 *"Maybe the party began at Max's"*: Sante, Luc. "The Party." *New York Times Magazine.* 5 Oct. 2003.

142 *Among other 1976 engagements*: Bull, Hank. Email to the author. 12 June 2015.

142 *Still,* Haiti *wouldn't be published*: Acker, Kathy. *Kathy Goes to Haiti.* Rpt. in *Literal Madness.* New York: Grove Press, 1998.

143 *Avalanche editor and general man-about-downtown*: Doyle, Judith. Email to the author. 28 Mar. 2016.

143 *Kushner and Acker met at the early morning meditation*: Kushner, Robert. Email to the author. 23 Aug. 2015.

143 *A photo taken at the A Space house shows Acker*: Judith Doyle Personal Papers, Toronto. Photographer unknown.

143 *Acker's Toronto visit occurred*: Acker, *My Mother: Demonology*, 84.

144 *Eyes closed in a trance*: Photographer unknown. "Robert Desnoes dans l'Atelier de Andre Breton." Reproduced in Breton, André. *Nadja*. New York: Grove Press, 1994.

144 *"yakking like bathrobe after-talk girlfriends"*: Doyle, Judith. Email to the author. 21 Apr. 2016.

144 *Republished by Grove Press*: Acker, *Kathy Goes to Haiti*, 1978.

144 *The headline of James Frakes's* New York Times: Frakes, James. "OOH OOH. AND THEN AGAIN, AH AH." *New York Times*. 17 Jan. 1988.

144 *"a joke . . . a parody of a porn novel"*: Acker, Kathy. "Kathy Acker Interviewed by Rebecca Deaton." *Textual Practice* vol. 6, no. 2, 1992.

145 "[Haiti *was written in*] *73–74*": "A Conversation With Kathy Acker." October 1994. *Another Chicago Magazine*. www.anotherchicagomagazine.net/content/12-03-2010/archive/acm-archive-kathy-acker-interview. Accessed 23 Apr. 2016.

145 *"I want to do a big novel"*: Acker, *Only Paper Today*, 1976.

146 *"I'm becoming a rock & roll lyricist"*: Acker, letter to Ron Silliman, late 1974. RSP.

146 *"this schoolyard nasty-girl desire thing"*: Doyle, email to the author, 2016.

146 The Persian Poems—*her ingenious, maybe real*: Acker, Kathy. "The Persian Poems." *Schizo-Culture*, vol. 3, no. 2 (1978). Ed. Sylvère Lotringer, New York: Semiotext(e).

146 The Persian Poems *appeared again in 1980*: Kushner, email to the author, 2015.

146 *"[In] my life politics don't disappear"*: Acker, Kathy. *Blood and Guts in High School*. New York: Grove Press, 1994. 97.

146 *"Having cancer is like having a baby"*: Ibid., 115.

147 *"[Our marriage] was always"*: Gordon, email to the author, 2015.

147 *Six months later they separated permanently*: Gordon, email to the author, 2015.

147 *"Janey: You're going to leave me"*: Acker, *Blood and Guts in High School*, 7.

148 *"Janey: (searching for a conversation subject"*: Ibid., 11.

149 *"We were basically living separate lives"*: Gordon, email to the author, 2015.

149 *"I think soon things"*: Acker, letter to Ron Siliman, early–mid June. RSP.

149 *During that year, Eric Mitchell, Vivienne Dick*: Stosuy, Brandon. "No New York." *Pitchfork*. 15 Nov. 2005. Accessed 2 Aug. 2016.

149 *Robert Mapplethorpe and Patti Smith had a*: Mapplethorpe, Robert and Patti Smith. *Films and Stills*. 7–24 June 1978. Robert Miller Gallery, New York.

149 *David Wojnarowicz began photographing himself*: Roth, Andrew. Ed. "David Wojnarowicz: Rimbaud in New York 1978–1979. *Artbook Publisher*. Artbook DAP.

149 *The Wooster Group performed* Nayatt School: The Wooster Group. *Nayatt School* (1978). 12 Dec. 2015. Accessed 2. Aug. 2016.

149 *the Mudd Club opened*: "Mudd Club." *Wikipedia*. Wikipedia. n.d. Accessed 2. Aug. 2016.

150 *"We all wanted to do as many things"*: Indiana, Gary. Email to the author. 20 Aug. 2015.

150 *That summer, Acker republished*: Dixon, Claire. "Printed Matter, Inc., The First Decade: 1976–1986." Diss. Virginia Commonwealth University, 2010. *VCU Scholars Compass*. Accessed 21 July 2016.

150 *"Ted Castle and I worked"*: Katz, Leandro. Email to the author. 29 Mar. 2014.

151 *"rewrite first 60 pages [of the new book"*: Acker, letter to Lafayette Young. KAP.

151 *Acker's friend Becky Johnston*: Roloff, Michael. Email to the author. 8 Mar. 2015; 24 Mar. 2015.

151 *"Michael Roloff is a sexist creep"*: Acker, letter to Lafayette Young. KAP.

151 *"I've never had to deal with publishers"*: Acker, letter to Lafayette Young. KAP.

152 *"new novel BLOOD AND GUTS IN HIGH SCHOOL"*: Acker, Kathy. Letter to Douglas Messerli. 1979. UAR.

152 *Stonehill Communications, a New York trade press*: "Jeffrey Steinberg, 34, Innovative Publisher, Founder of Stonehill." *New York Times Obituary*. *New York Times*. 3 June 1981.

152 *"I'm beginning to have some fame success"*: Acker, *Blood and Guts in High School*, 11.

152 *"What looked like the 'greening of America"*: Roloff, email to the author, 2015.

153 *"got the end mixed up"*: Acker, "Devoured by Myths," interview by Sylvère Lotringer. Unpublished audio transcript, 1990. SLP.

153 *"I think your new girlfriend"*: Acker, *Great Expectations*, 25.

A PERSON OF GREAT EXPECTATIONS (1979–1983)

155 *"Happy are those ages"*: Lukács, Georg. *Theory of the Novel*. 1971. Cambridge: MIT Press, 1996. 29.

155 *"On Christmas Eve 1978 my mother committed suicide"*: Acker, *Great Expectations*, 5.

156 *"Consciousness just is: no time"*: Ibid., 57.

156 *"Do I care? Do I care more than I reflect?"*: Ibid., 61.

156 *"I feel much better after I cry"*: Ibid., 15.

157 *"one that appears explicitly personal"*: Kotz, "Why Memory Matters: Notes on Bernadette Mayer's Work," 2013.

157 *"to find out what the structure is"*: Acker and Sondheim, *Blue Tape*, 1974.

158 *"I wanted some kind of enactment"*: Acker, "Devoured by Myths," interview by Sylvère Lotringer. SLP.

158 *"I realize that all my life is is endings"*: Acker, *Great Expectations*, 64.

159 *"Her stepfather Albert Alexander"*: Albert A. Alexander Jr. probate will. filed at the State of New York Surrogate's Court. 21 April 1979.

159 *"He left his widow, Claire Weill Alexander"*: Ibid.

159 *Albert was drafted into the army*: "US Military Service Record." *National Archives Veteran's Service Records*. www.archives.com/search/military. Accessed. 10 June 2015.

160 *"Daddy's drunk and he's still whining"*: Acker, *Great Expectations*, 12.

160 *Pooh Kaye, one of the first*: Kaye, Pooh. Facebook message with the author. 2–3 Mar. 2015.

160 *"When O was 17 years old"*: Acker, *Great Expectations*, 54.

160 *Yet as P Adams Sitney surmised*: Sitney, interview with author, 2014.

160 *"this man who was kind to me"*: Acker, *My Mother: Demonology*, 97.

160 *"my grandmother hates my father"*: Acker, *Great Expectations*, 18.

161 *"so gentle he didn't exist"*: Acker, *My Mother: Demonology*, 10.

161 *Throughout their lives, Florrie, Albert, and Claire*: Viegener, Matias. Email to the author. 31 Jan. 2014.

161 *The Alexander family apartment*: Florence Weill death certificate. New York City Dept. of Vital Records.

161 *"My mother tells me my 'father' isn't"*: Acker, *The Childlike Life of the Black Tarantula*, 199.

162 *"In my writing I am acting as"*: Burroughs, William S. "The Future of the Novel." *Word Virus: The William S. Burroughs Reader*. Ed. James Grauerholz. New York: Grove Atlantic, 1998. 272.

162 *"a cosmonaut of inner space"*: Trocchi, Alexander. The Edwin Morgan Papers. *University of Glasgow Library Wordpress*. University of Glasgow Library. 16 Dec. 2013. universityofglasgowlibrary.wordpress.com/2013/12/16/the-edwin-morgan-papers-alexander-trocchi-cosmonaut-of-inner-space. Accessed 4 Aug. 2016.

162 *"When I write I have trouble"*: Trocchi, Alexander. *Cain's Book*. New York: Grove Press, 1960. 238.

162 *Years later, she would credit him widely*: Acker, "Devoured by Myths" interview by Sylvère Lotringer. SLP; Friedman, "A Conversation with Kathy Acker," 1989.

163 *"I don't write to express anything"*: Acker, Kathy. "Auto-Interview de Kathy Acker." Interview by Gérard-Georges Lemaire. *Dirty* 4/5, Autumn 1980, 57. Trans. Hedi El Kholti. PBPP.

163 *"I never wanted you"*: Acker, *Great Expectations*, 57.

163 *"Three different power groups"*: Ibid., 82.

164 *"George: When you were seven months"*: Acker, Kathy. "Requiem." *Eurydice in the Underworld*. London: Arcadia Books, 1998. 187.

164 *"Since I never knew you"*: Acker, *Pussy, King of the Pirates*, 15.

164 *By the time Albert died*: Freilicher, "One or Two Things I Know About Kathy Acker," 1999.

164 *Luc Sante recalls Acker*: Sante, "The Party," 2003.

165 *"Late in 1978, Kathy called"*: Kaye, email with author, 2015.

165 *Sylvère Lotringer recalls running into Acker*: Lotringer, Sylvère. Conversation with the author. 16 Nov. 1997.

165 *"Mother was a real actress"*: Acker, *Great Expectations*, 60.

166 *Still, the coroner's preliminary*: New York City Bureau of Vital Records.

166 *"I remember that night when I learned"*: Acker, *My Mother: Demonology*, 8.

166 *"it took some time for Kathy"*: Kaye, email to the author, 2015.

166 *"[Kathy] called me up to tell me"*: Goldberg, Jeff. Email to the author. 5 Dec. 2016.

167 *"has always been to fuse the fragments"*: Trocchi, *Cain's Book*, 239.

167 *"Ten days ago (it is now almost Christmas 1979)"*: Acker, *Great Expectations*, 5.

168 *"slice a vegetable or piece of fruit"*: Cruikshank-Hagenbackle, Geoffrey. Email to the author. 12 June 2015.

168 *"Tarot is totemic magic"*: Cruikshank-Hagenbackle, email to the author, 2015.

168 *"New York City is very peaceful"*: Acker, *Great Expectations*, 15.

168 *"There is no time; there is"*: Ibid., 7.

169 *Sometime early that year*: Jeffrey Steinberg, 34, Innovative Publisher, Founder of Stonehill." *New York Times Obituary*. New York Times. 3 June 1981.

169 *In May 1979, Acker told*: Acker, Kathy. Letter to Douglas Messerli. 1979. Sun & Moon Archive.

169 *By January 1981 she'd write Terence Sellers*: Acker, Kathy. Letter to Terence Sellers. Box 1, Folder 13. The Terence Sellers Papers. Fales Collection, New York University.

169 *Messerli had asked Acker*: Acker, letter to Douglas Messerli, 1979.

169 *"Here in New York"*: Kathy Acker, "Algeria," 115–16.

170 *"This is the way THE CUNT"*: Ibid., 118–19.

170 *"Whenever a cock enters me"*: Ibid., 116.

170 *Stuck in New York for the rest of the summer*: "Kathy Acker." Station Hill Press. www.stationhill.org/authors/kathy-acker-2. Accessed 4 Aug. 2016.

170 *Written as and about "Janey Smith"*: Acker, Kathy. "New York City in 1979." Buffalo: Top Stories Press, 1981. Top Stories #9.

172 *"feminine, marvelous and tough"*: Berrigan, Ted. "The Sonnets." *Collected Poems*. Oakland: University of California Press, 2007.

172 *When the British poet and translator Paul Buck*: Buck, Paul. Interview with the author. 11 Jan. 2015.

173 *Acker had recently heard about Guyotat's*: Acker, letter to Douglas Messerli, 1979.

173 *Published by Gallimard, it was hard*: Buck, interview with the author, 2015.

173 *On the festival's marathon opening night*: "One World Poetry Festival Program." 8–14 Oct. 1979. PBPP.

173 *That year, to everyone's*: Buck, interview with the author, 2015.

173 *Before leaving, they visited the artist*: Buck, Paul. Email to the author. 13 Aug. 2015.

174 *Paul Buck had already agreed to read*: Buck, email to the author, 2015.

174 *Acker's first stop in Paris*: Buck, email to the author, 2015.

174 *Acker had met Lemaire in New York*: Grauerholz, James. Email to the author. 15 Aug. 2015.

174 *As the Stonehill saga dragged on*: Acker, letter to Paul Buck and Glenda George, 1980. Rptd. in Acker, Kathy and Paul Buck. *Spread Wide*. London: Encounters, 2004.

174 *"part of the clique-ish Parisian milieu"*: Lotringer, Sylvère. Email to the author. 15 Aug. 2016.

174 *"Lemaire was a fast translator"*: Buck, email to the author, 2015.

175 *She discovered the Ecrits de Laure*: Laure. *Ecrits de Laure*. Paris: Pauvert, 1977.

175 *"Dear Georges, . . . When we first met"*: Acker, Kathy. "Translations of Laure the Schoolgirl." *Hannibal Lecter: My Father*. New York: Semiotext(e), 1991. 105.

175 "*G explained in no way*": Acker, "Translations of Laure the Schoolgirl," *Hannibal Lecter: My Father*, 108.

176 *She would publish this work*: Acker, Kathy. "Translations of the Diaries of Laure the Schoolgirl." *Diana's* (London), 1983.

176 "*She worked hard on the Guyotat*": Buck, interview with the author, 2015.

177 "*My mother often told me*": Acker, *Great Expectations*, 7.

177 *When Paul Buck and his partner*: Buck, email to the author, 2015.

177 *A breakaway group from* Tel Quel: See, for example: Rothenberg, Jerome. "A note and Poem for Jean Pierre Faye and 'Change." *Poems and Poetics*. 15 July 2008. poemsandpoetics.blogspot.com/2015/02/jerome-rothenberg-john-bloomberg. html. Accessed 24 Aug. 2015.

178 "*Feeling your head exploding*": Meinhof, Ulrike. Cit. in Kraus, Chris. *Aliens and Anorexia*. New York: Semiotext(e), 2000. Page 15.

178 *in honor of the Baader-Meinhof*: Buck, email to the author, 2015.

178 Acker told Buck she'd stayed on": Buck, email to the author, 2015.

178 *searching the well-archived schedule*: Festival D'automne A Paris. "Festival D'automne A Paris Archive." n.d. www.festival-automne.com/archive Accessed 6 Aug. 2016.

178 *Still, she made a big impression*: Buck, email to the author, 2015.

178 *She and Jill Kroesen*: Festival D'automne Paris Archive.

178 *They'd either forgotten—or never had*: Buck, email to the author, 2015.

179 "*One fine day, she came to Paris*": Lemaire, Gérard-Georges. "Les Ambiguities des Kathy Acker." *Les Lettres Francaises*. Trans. Hedi El Kholti and author. Feb. 2005. www.les-lettres-francaises.fr/tag/gerard-georges-lemaire. Accessed 24 Aug. 2015.

179 *An artist and cultural entrepreneur, Lebel*: Lotringer, Sylvère. Conversation with the author. Mar. 2000.

179 *During these weeks in Paris*: Buck and Acker, *Spread Wide*, 18.

179 *. . . a writer who then lived with Ingrid Caven*: Schuhl, Jean-Jacques. *Ingrid Caven: A Novel*. San Francisco: City Lights Publishing, 2004.

179 "*I asked the cards*": Acker, *Great Expectations*, 5.

180 *Acker's grandmother Florence Weill died*: Florence Weill probate will. New York City Bureau of Vital Records.

180 "*Florence had a great business head*": Kaye, Pooh. Facebook message with author. 3 Mar. 2015.

180 "*Nana's apartment rooms are tremendous*": Acker, "New York City in 1979."

181 "*Where are the 800 IBM shares?*": Acker, *Great Expectations*, 109.

181 *After Florence's death, Acker became*: Florence Weill probate proceeding. filed at the State of New York Surrogate Court. 7 Dec. 1979.

181 *Paraphrasing a Virginia Holt romance*: Acker, Kathy. Interview with Melvin Bragg. *The South Bank Show*. ITV Mar. 1984.

181 *"My father had left me all his possessions"*: Acker, *Great Expectations*, 68.

182 *"Is my lover trying to murder me?"*: Ibid.. 76.

182 *"I'm going to murder you, honey"*: Ibid., 94.

182 *"My girlfriend] . . . had become sick"*: Ibid., 98.

182 *Florence Weill named Pooh Kaye's father*: Samuel Gordon and Clifford A. Kaye, Order for Advance Payment of Commissions. filed with New York County Surrogate's Court. 24 Sept. 1980.

182 *"Money from my grandmother's will"*: Acker, postcard to Paul Buck. Dec. 1979. *Spread Wide*, 6.

182 *Pooh Kaye recalls a furious string*: Kaye, email to the author, 2015.

183 *Desperate to return to New York*: Kaye, email to the author, 2015.

183 *"Kathy just had to make love"*: Kaye, Pooh. Telephone conversation with author, 18 Aug. 2015.

183 *Florence's furniture, jewelry and personal effects*: Sellers, Terence. Letter to Kathy Acker. 24 July 1980.

183 *She would keep these chairs*: Jordan, Ken. Interview with the author. 3 Mar. 2014.

183 *as she moved from New York to Seattle*: Acker, Kathy. 1995 tax documents. GPA.

183 *"A three-room apartment"*: Acker, *Blood and Guts in High School*, 56.

184 *While she'd been away, a fat sheaf*: Goldberg, Jeff. "Kathy's Legacy," Manuscript in Progress; JGPP.

184 *"here I am back in USA & hot on new book"*: Acker, postcard to Paul Buck and Glenda George. Dec. *Spread Wide*. 6.

184 *Two weeks later, sick with the flu*: Acker, letter to Paul Buck and Glenda George. Jan. *Spread Wide*, 16–20.

184 *Her relation with him remains*: Buck, email to the author, 2015.

185 *Buck saved their correspondence*: Buck, Paul. "Postscriptum." *Spread Wide*. 171–72.

185 *By mid-February 1980 Acker finished*: Acker, mid-February letter to Paul Buck and Glenda George. *Spread Wide*, 32–34.

185 *In a 1977 reading videotaped at the Western Front*: Acker, Kathy. "Reading." 1977. Western Front Archives, Vancouver. vimeo.com/39280856. Accessed 8 Aug. 2016.

185 *"Your explanation that you gave up writing"*: Acker, *Great Expectations*, 28–29.

185 *"my dear husband Mr. Gordon"*: Acker, letter to Paul Buck and Glenda George, Mar. 1980. *Spread Wide*, 38.

186 *"Dear Susan Sontag, Would you please"*: Acker, *Great Expectations*, 27.

186 *"I wish I knew how to speak English"*: Ibid.

186 *"I'm having this weirdo affair with Sylvère"*: Acker, letter to Paul Buck and Glenda George, n.d. Feb. *Spread Wide*, 30.

186 *"My head is gone cause"*: Acker, letter to Paul Buck and Glenda George, n.d. Mar./Apr. 1980. *Spread Wide*, 38.

186 *"It was something else"*: Lotringer, Sylvère. Conversation with the author. 11 Jan. 2016.

186 *"all porn"*: Acker, letter to Paul Buck and Glenda George, N.d. Mar. 1980. *Spread Wide*, 38.

187 *"WHERE DO EMOTIONS COME FROM"*: Acker, *Great Expectations*, 38.

187 *"He shows her his whip"*: Ibid., 39.

187 *"NOT ONLY IS THERE NO ESCAPE"*: Ibid., 41.

187 *"S&M doesn't go beyond the bed"*: Acker, Kathy and McKenzie Wark. *I'm Very Into You*. Los Angeles: Semiotext(e), 2014. 70.

187 *In late March, I Dreamt I Was a Nymphomaniac*: Acker, Kathy. *I Dreamt I was a Nymphomaniac: Imagining*. New York: Traveler's Digest Editions, 1980.

187 *"Everyone loves it"*: Acker, letter to Paul Buck and Glenda George, n.d. Apr. 1980. *Spread Wide*. 44.

187 *"I have been trying to remember"*: Kushner, email to author, 2015.

188 *She'd made tentative plans*: Acker, letter to Paul Buck and Glenda George, n.d. Apr. 1980. *Spread Wide*. 44.

188 *She'd given a reading at Art in Form*: Millin, Laura. Email to the author. 27 Feb. 2015.

188 *The venue's 1980 schedule, with talks and performances*: Hindsight I and Hindsight II. "A Record of Events–1977–1978." Copyright And/Or, Seattle. Annie Grosshans Personal Papers.

188 *While in Seattle, Acker*: Grosshans, Annie. Email to the author. 28 Feb. 2015.

188 *"Aren't going to make it back to NYC"*: Acker, postcard to Jeff Goldberg, 28 May 1980. JGPP.

189 *"He was quite present on the Seattle"*: Grosshans, email to author, 2015.

189 *"a very good artist"*: Acker, *Great Expectations*, 78.

189 *"Okay, first of all your moving out"*: Sellers, letter to Kathy Acker, 1980.

189 *"Jeffrey's no longer talking to me cause . . ."*: Acker, letter to Paul Buck and Glenda George. n.d. approx. early summer 1980. *Spread Wide*. 52.

189 *"I've been absolutely miserable"*: Acker, letter to Jeff Goldberg, 22 Aug. 1980. JGPP.

189 *"[Clifford] lives in Seattle"*: Acker, *Great Expectations*, 78.

190 *"We as women and as Belltown"*: Grosshans, email to the author, 2015.

190 *"We were very excited"*: Millin, email to the author, 2015.

190 *Soon she and Jim Logie*: Acker, letter to Jeff Goldberg, 16 June 1980. JGPP.

190 *"Seattle is bleak and horrible"*: Acker, letter to Paul Buck, n.d. approx. mid-July 1980. *Spread Wide*. 66.

190 *"Seattle is worse than the people"*: Acker, letter to Jeff Goldberg, 10 July 1980. JGPP.

190 *"The love relation here in Seattle"*: Acker, letter to Paul Buck and Glenda George, n.d. summer 1980. *Spread Wide*. 66.

190 *"there's been a violent outbreak"* Acker, letter to Jeff Goldberg, 29 Sept. 1980. JGPP.

190 *"Red everywhere. Red up the river"*: Acker, *Great Expectations*, 94.

191 *"it is very slow"*: Acker, letter to Jeff Goldberg, 16 June 1980. JGPP.

191 *"My mother is the most beautiful woman"*: Acker, *Great Expectations*, 9.

191 *"I realize that all my life is endings"*: Ibid., 64.

192 *Invited that August to teach*: Acker, letter to Jeff Goldberg, 7 Aug. 1980. JGPP.

192 *By the end of September*: Acker, postcard to Paul Buck, September 23 1980. *Spread Wide*. 76.

192 *"I miss you so much I can't bear it"*: Acker, letter to Jeff Goldberg, 22 Sept. 1980. JGPP.

192 *"Rain rain rain right here"*: Acker, postcard to Paul Buck, 19 Nov. 1980. *Spread Wide*. 86.

192 *"One slit wrist & PID as usual"*: Acker, postcard to Jeff Goldberg, Jan. 1981. JGPP.

193 *"decides he doesn't want to fuck"*: Acker, *Great Expectations*, 116.

193 *Beginning in February, she finally rented*: Acker, postcard to Jeff Goldberg, 24 Feb. 1981. JGPP. Return address: 70 Langton Street, SF.

193 *"If you're obsessed for me, bitch"*: Acker, *Great Expectations*, 125–126.

193 *"As I remember our agreement"*: Acker, postcard to Jeff Goldberg, 24 Feb. 1981. JGPP.

193 *Living alone for the first time*: Acker, letter to Paul Buck, n.d. winter 1981. Spread Wide. 108.

193 *"according to me like I'm some Latin"*: Acker, letter to Paul Buck, n.d. January 1981. *Spread Wide*. 98.

193 *"This is my poem to your cunt door"*: Acker, *Great Expectations*, 108.

194 *"I do everything for sexual love"*: Ibid., 109.

194 *"I'm about to collapse"*: Acker, letter to Paul Buck and Glenda George, n.d. approx. late May 1981. *Spread Wide*. 136.

195 *"the book's getting great reviews!"*: Acker, letter to Paul Buck, n.d. approx. Jan. 1982. *Spread Wide*. 154

195 *Acker moved back to New York*: Acker, letter to Paul Buck, early 1982. Return address Ingrid Sischy's 228 Front Street loft.

195 *friends threw a launch*: Acker, letter to Terence Sellers, n.d. approx. Sept. 1981.

195 *By March 1981 she rented her own large*: Acker, letter to Paul Buck, n.d. 1982. Return address 245 Eldridge Street, NY 10002.

195 *Lyon was a close friend and collaborator*: "Robert Mapplethorpe Biography." *Mapplethorpe*. n.d. www.mapplethorpe.org/biography. Accessed 8 Aug. 2016.

195 *A 1982 portrait shows Acker*: Mapplethorpe, Robert. "Kathy Acker." 1982.

195 *"Everything changed. Somehow she'd transitioned"*: Quasha, telephone conversation with author, 2015.

196 *"the most completely unified work of art"*: Robbe-Grillet, Alain. Blurb to *Great Expectations*. Open Book Publications in conjunction with New York: Station Hill Press, 1982.

196 *"Reading Kathy Acker is like playing hopscotch with a genius"*: Seen by author, c. Fall 1982.

197 *"I remember my problem"*: Jordan, Fred. Interview with the author. 7 Mar. 2014.

197 *He decided to lead off in late December*: Jordan, interview with the author, 2014.

197 *"I've been bought up by some dumb publisher"*: Acker, letter to Paul Buck, late spring 1982. *Spread Wide*. 166.

197 *George Quasha recalls*: Quasha, telephone interview with author, 2015.

198 *"I have to work as hard as possible"*: Acker, *Blood and Guts in High School*, 132.

198 *"I lived out in Maidstone"*: Buck, email to author, 2015.

198 *"My mother committed suicide and I ran away"*: Acker, *Great Expectations*, 127.

FICTION (1983–1990)

199 *"What we want to look at"*: Bragg, Melvyn. "Kathy Acker." *The South Bank Show*. ITV, London, 1 Apr. 1984.

199 *Bragg's previous subjects*: "The South Bank Show" *Wikipedia*. en.wikipedia.org/wiki/The_South_Bank_Show. Accessed 31 Aug. 2016.

200 *"a resolution to look for some stability"*: Acker, *The South Bank Show*, 1984.

201 *Todd Haynes would draw a*: Haynes, Todd, director. *Velvet Goldmine*. Newmarket Capital Group, 1998.

201 *"Kathy Acker feels that the disjointed"*: Bragg, *The South Bank Show*, 1984.

201 *"I can't tell you"*: Bracewell, Michael. Interview with the author. 22 Jan. 2015.

202 *Pan/Picador published* Blood and Guts: Acker, postcard to Jonathan Miles, 10 Jan 1983. Jonathan Miles Personal Papers.

202 *Picador's London release dovetailed*: Mehta, Sonny. Email to the author. 10 Aug. 2015; Graham, Jacqueline. Email to author. 27 May 2016.

202 *"the two companies pursued publishing"*: Silverberg, Ira. Email to the author. 31 July 2016.

202 *"Picador is definitely publishing me"* Acker, letter to Jonathan Miles, n.d. Dec. 1982.

202 *Her reputation in London had been*: Poetry Olympics Vol. 1. All Round Records, 1982.

203 City Limits, *a popular London newsweekly*: Rose, Cynthia. "Punk Porn and Plagiarism." *New Musical Express*, 22 Jan. 1983, 8–9.

203 *During that fall 1982 trip*: Rose, "Punk Porn and Plagiarism," 1983.

203 *"abusive toward women"*: Hoffman, Roy. "Blood and Guts in High School." *New York Times*, "Books in Short," 23 Dec. 1984.

203 *"[T]he move to England, as far as"*: Acker, "Devoured by Myths," interview by Sylvère Lotringer. SLP.

203 *Acker's initial entrance to London*: Acker, letter to Jonathan Miles, 26 Dec. 1982; Acker, letters to Peter Wollen, 1 Sept. 1 1983 and 10 Sept. 1983. PWPP.

204 *"ACTING MAD. ARE YOU MARRIED"*: Acker, telegram to Jonathan Miles, 16 Dec. 1982.

204 *"your postcard makes me feel"*: Acker, postcard to Jonathan Miles, 20 Dec. 1982.

204 *"I've never lived in a squat"*: Acker, postcard to Jonathan Miles, n.d. Dec. 1982.

204 *"I have someone to talk to"*: Acker, postcard to Jonathan Miles, n.d. Dec. 1982.

204 *"I try to stay open"*: Acker, postcard to Jonathan Miles, n.d. Dec. 1982.

204 *Channel 4, she tells him, wants to film her*: Acker, postcard to Jonathan Miles, 10 Jan. 1983.

204 *"braised cabbage in juniper berries"*: Acker, letter to Jonathan Miles, 26 Dec. 1982.

205 *The anniversary of her*: Acker, letter to Jonathan Miles, 24 Dec. 1982.

205 *She's trying to finish* My Death, My Life: Acker, letter to Jonathan Miles, n.d. Jan. 1983.

205 *her ulcer is bleeding*: Acker, letter to Jonathan Miles, n.d. Dec. 1982.

205 *"I met him by accident"*: Acker, Kathy. "My Death My Life by Pier Paolo Pasolini" Rpt. in *Literal Madness*. Grove Press: New York 1988. 279.

205 *"I have to make"*: Acker, letter to Jonathan Miles, n.d. early Jan. 1983.

205 *Cynthia Rose's* NME *profile*: Rose, "Punk Porn and Plagiarism," 1983.

206 *"It sounds brutal to say"*: Miles, Barry. Email to the author. 23 Feb. 2015.

207 *"very dramatic sort of"*: Miles, email to the author, 2015.

207 *"was very much someone"*: Miles, email to the author, 2015.

208 *"I believe it is necessary"*: Wollen, Peter. "The Hermeneutic Codes." *Readings and Writings: Semiotic Counter-Strategies*. London: Verso Books, 1982. 41.

208 *"How close can I get to someone"*: Acker and Sondheim, *Blue Tape*, 1974.

208 *In her 1984* Artforum *essay*: Acker, Kathy. "Models of Our Present." *Artforum* Feb. 1984, 62–65.

209 *"Fulsere quondam candidi tibi"*: Acker, Kathy. *Don Quixote*. New York: Grove Press, 1986. 47–48.

209 *"salad and pulpo, thick red"*: Acker, letter to Peter Wollen, 5 Sept. 1983. PWPP.

209 *"particular, not American-like"*: Acker, letter to Peter Wollen, 13 Oct. 1983. PWPP.

209 *"Have to stop being a sentimental"*: Acker, letter to Peter Wollen, 31 Oct. 1983. PWPP.

210 *In her first letter*: Acker, letter to Peter Wollen, 30 Aug. 1983. PWPP.

210 *"Writing, Peter, not only demands"*: Acker, letter to Peter Wollen, 24 Oct. 1983. PWPP.

210 *"Writing is being so calm"*: Acker, letter to Peter Wollen, 27 Aug. 1983. PWPP.

210 *"mental capacities [that are]"*: Acker, *Don Quixote*, 45.

210 *"Want . . . establish or be"*: Acker, letter to Peter Wollen, 29 Aug. 1983. PWPP.

211 *"Everything's again wrong"*: Acker, letter to Peter Wollen, 6 Sept. 1983. PWPP.

211 *"Nothing coheres. No structure"*: Acker, letter to Peter Wollen, 10 Sept. 1983. PWPP.

211 *"The books are coming out"*: Acker, letter to Peter Wollen, 19 Oct. 1983. PWPP.

211 *"lead to all possibilities"*: Acker, letter to Peter Wollen, 30 Aug. 1983. PWPP.

211 *"Having an abortion was"*: Acker, *Blood and Guts in High School*, 33.

212 *"When she was finally crazy"*: Acker, *Don Quixote*, 9.

212 *"having an abortion is a method"*: Ibid., 13.

212 *Like many of her friends*: Acker, "New York City in 1979," 14.

212 *"We have all been there"*: Howard, Maureen. "Don Quixote: Which Was A Dream." *Los Angeles Times*, 9 Nov. 1986.

212 *"When you talk to me"*: Acker, *Don Quixote*, 47.

212 *Appropriating a scene from*: Ibid., 166–71.

213 *"My decision to be with women only"*: Ibid., 126.

213 *"Whatever her (his) confusions"*: Ibid., 138–39.

213 *The leather dykes who*: Novaczek, Ruth. Email to the author. 24 Aug. 2016.

213 *"I have no self"*: Acker, *Don Quixote*, 171.

213 *"go against the truth of my life"*: Ibid., 33.

214 *In a black and white London portrait*: Chris Garnham. *Kathy Acker (nee Lehman)*. Bromide fibre print. 1983. National Portrait Gallery, London. npg.org.uk/collections/search/portrait/mw83423/Kathy-Acker-ne-Lehman. Accessed 31 Aug. 2016.

214 *"the same sort of play I do in my writing with identity"*: Acker, *The South Bank Show*, 1984.

214 *"I remember sitting with her"*: Dick, Leslie. "Seventeen Paragraphs on Kathy Acker." *Lust for Life*. Eds. Amy Scholder, Carla Harryman, Avital Ronell. Verso Books: London, 2006. 112.

214 *In a 1984 profile on Acker, Rosemary Bailey*: Bailey, Rosemary. "The Pornographic Imagination of Kathy Acker." *The Face*, Jan. 1984, 23.

215 *Two years after Acker's death*: Brook, Kaucyila. "Kathy Acker's Clothes." *Art Journal*, vol. 72 no. 2, 2013.

215 *"How to summon the spirit"*: McCormack, Derek. "God's Gaultier." *Fanzine*, 9 Jan. 2006. thefanzine.com/gods-gaultier-2. Accessed 31 Aug. 2016.

215 *Allowing herself to write*: Acker, "Devoured by Myths," interview by Sylvère Lotringer. SLP.

215 *Picador rented her a*: Graham, Jacqueline. Email to the author. 19 Aug. 2015.

215 *She'd already contracted*: Carson, Rebecca. Email to the author. 19 Aug. 2016.

215 "*I went to a party*": Fox, Matt. Email to Ruth Novaczek. 14 Aug. 2016.

216 *In New York, the performance poet*: James, Darius. Email to the author. 22 June 2015.

216 "*THE BOOKS AND MANUSCRIPTS*": Acker, note to Darius James, Jan. 1984. Darius James Personal Papers, Berlin.

216 "*I showed up at the flat*": de Broglio, Nathalie. Interview with the author. 15 Jan. 2015.

217 *Bette Gordon's breakthrough independent feature film*: "Variety." Playing at Screen on Islington Green. *The Guardian* classified ads, 19 May 1984.

217 "*Suddenly here is this astonishing*": Bracewell, interview with the author, 2015.

219 "*I AM, AM I?*": Watson, Don. "I Am Am I?" *New Musical Express*, 25 Aug. 1984.

219 "*What bugs me about Laurie*": Bailey, "The Pornographic Imagination of Kathy Acker," 1984.

220 "*I asked English people*": McPherson, Don. "Great Expectations of Bad Taste." *The Sunday Times*, 26 Feb. 1984, 59.

220 *The play Acker discussed writing*: Bowen, Meirion. "Lulu Unchained." *The Guardian*, 8 July 1985.

220 "*a blazing reinvention of*": ICA Theatre. "Lulu Unchained." Press package, July 2–July 20 1985. ICA archives. Tate Library and Archive, London.

220 *Acker fictionalized her production biography*: Acker, Kathy. Production autobiography from "Lulu Unchained." Press package July 2–July 20 1985. ICA archives. Tate Library and Archive, London.

220 "*ICA in row with writer over script*": "ICA in row with writer over script." *Theatre and Television Today* (London), 18 July 1985.

221 "*THIS IS HYPE CITY!*": Issue, Marc. "Blood & Guts In Hype City." *Blitz* (London), Sept. 1985, 20–22.

221 *She belonged to the Groucho Club*: Fletcher, Sue. Email to Hestia Peppe. 29 Aug. 2016.

222 "*Acker seems most daring*": Webster, Duncan. "Genital on My Mind." *New Musical Express*, 24 May 1986, 11.

222 "*a dead-eyed romance*": Chapman, Robin. "Cervantics." *London Review of Books*, 8. 16, 18 Sept. 1986, 19–21.

222 *"kinky scribbler Kathy Acker"*: *New Musical Express*, 21 June 1986.

222 *she interviewed leading writers*: For example: Conversation between Kathy Acker and Jenny Diski, *New Musical Express*, 20 Sept. 1986; Acker, Kathy. Introduction. *The Power of Theatrical Madness*, by Robert Mapplethorple, ICA London, 1986; Acker, Kathy. "Edinburgh Fringe," *New Musical Express*, 28 June 1986.

222 *Except for a thoughtful discussion*: Davidson, Michael. "Writing at the Boundaries." *New York Times Book Review*, 24 Feb. 1985.

223 *"collapsing with hammer thumps"*: LeClair, Tom. "The Lord of La Mancha and Her Abortion." *New York Times Book Review*, 30 Nov. 1986, 10.

223 *"I write by using other written texts"*: Miller, Lori. "In the Tradition of Cervantes, Sort Of." *New York Times Book Review*, 30 Nov. 1986, 10.

223 *"I think Don Quixote"*: Acker, Kathy. Interview with Angela McRobbie. "Writer's Talk," ICA Video, London 1987.

224 *"I went first to Brandeis"*: Acker, "Writer's Talk," 1987.

225 *"a vividly imagined allegory"*: Doctorow, Cory. Cit. by Cumming, Ed. "William Gibson—The Man Who Saw The Future." *The Guardian*, 28 July 2014.

225 *During the mid-1980s*: Kaveney, Roz. "On Space, and Time, and St. Giles High Street." Unpublished essay. Roz Kaveney Personal Papers, London.

225 *"Because there is no underground movement"*: Acker, "Writer's Talk," 1987.

225 *"You're really an astonishing writer"*: Gibson, William. Letter to Kathy Acker. 6 May 1986. KAP.

225 *"I like to think"*: Gibson, letter to Kathy Acker, 22 June 1986. KAP.

225 *Acker returned the compliment*: Acker, *Empire of the Senseless*, 1988.

226 *Intentionally written in a crude*: Martin, "When She Does What She Does: Intertextual Desire and Influence in Kathy Acker's Narratives," 201.

226 *"After Don Quixote I got sick"*: Acker, "Devoured by Myths" interview by Sylvère Lotringer. SLP.

227 *"Proceeded to tell me to do"*: Acker, *In Memoriam to Identity*, 217.

227 *"Walking back from the restaurant"*: Ibid., 219.

227 *"Now, maybe now, I'm reliving"*: Ibid., 219.

227 *Rainer wrote about things of great interest*: See, for example: Weber, Rainer. "Ich habe Lust zu schreiben." KULTUR *Die Spiegel*, 1 Jan. 1990; "DDR-Minister über neue Kulturpolitik der SED-PDS." *Die Spiegel*, 10 June 1986; "Werdet endlich erwachsen" / Das Ende der Frankfurter Sponti-Exklave" DEUTSCHLAND; "Das ist Wahnsinn, aber es macht Spaß" / Videopirat über Gepflogenheiten seiner Branche." *Die Spiegel*, 12 Dec. 1985. Bibliography compiled by Catalina Escalona.

228 *"Decided she would make"*: Acker, *In Memoriam to Identity*, 221.

228 *"They had a very, very intense"*: Silverberg, Ira. "Who's Afraid of Kathy Acker?" Dir. Barbara Caspar. 2007.

228 *"Expecting. That night, before flying"*: Acker, *In Memoriam to Identity*, 345.

229 *"Where are you left—in a text"*: Acker, "Devoured by Myths," interview by Sylvère Lotringer. SLP.

229 *"At the end of the book"*: Acker, Kathy. Gothenburg Litteraturus, Untitled and uncredited video interview. 1987. Gothenboug Litteraturhus Archives, Gothenburg, Sweden. Courtesy of Sofia Grasberg.

229 *"Myth-dealing," Lotringer observed*: Lotringer, "Devoured by Myths" interview by Sylvère Lotringer. SLP.

230 *Except for Jeanette Winterson's*: Winterson, Jeanette. "Books of the Year." *The Sunday Times*, 27 Nov. 1988, 11.

230 *"Nasty and cantankerous, it is unredeemed"*: Melmoth, John. "Blood, guts and tedium." *The Independent*, 12 May 1988, 13.

230 *"On the surface the book"*: Mackinnon, Lachlan. "The last of the Beats." *The Guardian*, 6 May 1988, 26.

230 *"[T]he main impression is of a performance"*: Karlin, Danny. "Antinomian Chic." *London Review of Books*, vol. 10 no. 11, 1988, 9–10.

230 *"Kathy Acker's new novel"*: Dalley, Jan. "That old black magic." *The Observer*, 8 May 1988, 42.

231 "Empire *trails its Acker-patented*": O'Hagen, Sean. "Blood Wedding." *New Musical Express*, 28 May 1988.

231 *One night she was walking*: Kaveney, "Some Years with Acker," 2007.

231 *"the media had made this huge image"*: Acker, "Devoured by Myths," interview by Sylvère Lotringer. SLP.

231 *"richer and more powerfully affecting"*: Shaviro, Steven. Email to the author. 25 Aug. 2016.

231 *"She wrote too much"*: Indiana, "Ackerville," 25.

231 *"I have no idea"*: Shaviro, email to the author, 2016.

232 *Except for Roz Kaveney's*: Kaveney, Roz. "Darkness on the edge of text." *Times Literary Supplement*, no. 4494, 19 May 1989, 536.

232 *"all but unreadable for"*: Coe, Jonathan. "The lust frontier." *The Guardian*, 5 May 1989, 29.

232 *"It's also curiously naïve"*: Valentine Cunningham, "Betrayed by a kiss." *The Observer*, 7 May 1989, 44.

232 *Since arriving in London*: Kaveney, "Some Years with Acker," 2007.

232 *"a group of young gay men"*: Ibid.

233 *Ironically, Robbins himself had been*: Wilson, Andrew. *Harold Robbins: The Man Who Invented Sex*. London: Bloomsbury Press, 2007. 212–13.

233 *Depending on which of Acker's*: For example, see: Kathy Acker, "Dead Doll Humility," *Postmodern Culture*, vol. 1, no., 1. pmc.iath.virginia.edu/text-only/issue.990/acker.990 Accessed 1 Sept. 2016; Acker, "Devoured by Myths" interview by Sylvère Lotringer. SLP.

233 *Or then again, according to Robbins's biographer*: Wilson, *Harold Robbins: The Man Who Invented Sex*, 260–61.

233 *"I've made a statement"*: Acker, Kathy. *Publishing News, Weekly for People in the Book Trade* 28 July 1989, 1–cont. on 27.

233 *"She's always used other people's work"*: *Publishing News*, 28 July 1989.

233 *By all accounts, Pandora asked Acker*: Acker, "Dead Doll Humility," 20–21.

234 *"I thought it was funny!"*: Jordan, Fred. Interview with the author, 2014.

234 *When Acker called to ask*: Acker, "Dead Doll Humility," 21.

234 *"All that matters is work"*: Ibid., 18.

234 *"I did sign the apology"*: Acker, "Devoured by Myths" interview by Sylvère Lotringer. SLP.

235 *"At that point Unwin Hyman"*: Kaveney, email to the author, 30 Aug. 2016.

235 *"The first I knew of any of this"*: Kaveney, "Some Years with Acker," 2007.

236 Publishing News in *London dubbed her*: Black, Terence. "Trivial Pursuit of the last decade—The Eighties—A Retrospective" *Publishing News*, 15/22 Dec. 1989, 7.

236 *"My decision to come back here"*: Acker, "An Interview with Kathy Acker," conducted by Larry McCaffery, 84–85.

1995 (1989–1995)

237 *"the day after the very"*: Brown, Pam. "1995." *Home By Dark*. Bristol: Shearsman Books, 2013.

237 *"It's so different over"*: Acker, letter to Peter Wollen, 30. Aug. 1983. PWPP.

238 *"Catherine Texier combines, in one woman"*: Prager, Emily. "Red High Heels and Smoke Stockings." *New York Times*, 6 June 1987.

238 *"the most graphically pornographic"*: Frakes, James. "OOH, OOH. AND THEN AGAIN, AH AH." *New York Times*, 17 Jan. 1988.

238 *"spare and compelling style"* New York Times Sunday Book Review of Haunted Houses.

238 *"In the hands of another writer"*: Kakutani, Michiko. "Books of the Times; Seedy Denizens of a Menacing Downtown World." *New York Times*. 21 May 1988.

239 *"a small classic of horror"*: Michiko Kakutani, "Books of the Times; Slowly Dawning Doubt on Narrator's Veracity." *New York Times*. 9 Oct. 1990.

239 *"[In England], I was the token"*: Acker, "An Interview with Kathy Acker" by Larry McCaffery, 85.

239 *"for a writer to be a novelist"*: Burroughs, William. Cit. in Bokris, Victor. *With William Burroughs—A Report From the Bunker*. New York: Seaver Books, 1981. 194.

239 *"in which I no longer fitted"*: Acker, Kathy. Letter to Lynne Tillman. 1991. The Lynne Tillman Papers. Fales Library and Special Collections, New York.

240 *Acker arrived in time*: Williams, Murphy. "Down and out with writers." *New Statesman*, 8 Dec. 1989.

240 *Purchased at the tail end*: Rosenberg, Andrew, et al. *The Mini Rough Guide to New York*. Rough Guides: 2011.

240 *Her mortgage payment alone"*: Kathy Acker financial records 1995. GPA.

240 *hefty homeowner's dues*: Ibid.

240 *She bought red leather banquette*: Jordan, Ken. Interview with the author. 30 Mar. 2014.

240 *"I was chatting on the phone"*: Acker, Kathy. Unpublished column for *The New Statesman*, faxed to Sally Townsend on February 16, 1990. ISP.

240 *"She needed a soft place"*: Scholder, Amy. Email to the author. 24 Oct. 2016.

240 *"They are not putting money"*: Acker, letter to Ira Silverberg, 9 June 1986. ISP.

241 *the new owners fired Rosset*: Jordan, Ken. Email to the author. 7 Nov. 2016.

241 *His appointment was widely critiqued*: Miles, Jack. "Pantheon is Dead, Long Live Pantheon." *Los Angeles Times*, 18 Mar. 1990.

241 *"[Fred Jordan] picked me up"*: Acker, Kathy. Xeroxed typescript of letter to *Village Voice* sent to Ira Silverberg. ISP.

242 *Her 1995 royalty statement showed:*. Kathy Acker financial records 1995. GPA.

242 *"She had been away from the city"*: Kaveney, "Some Years With Acker," 2007.

242 *Acker had already accepted*: Acker, letter to Amy Scholder, n.d. 1989. Amy Scholder Personal Papers, Los Angeles.

242 *Still, at some point*: Gaiman, Neil. "An Interview With Neil Gaiman." Conducted by Jessica Crispin. *Bookslut*. October 2006. www.bookslut.com/features/2006_10_010057.php Accessed 8 Nov. 2016.

242 . . . *Ken Jordan*: Jordan, email to the author, 2016.

242 . . . *and Gary Pulsifer*: Pulsifer, interview with the author, 2015.

242 *She had always liked Brighton*: Strong, Simon. "Kathy Acker Pussy New Gallery Presentation of Her 1994 Work." *Artlyst*, 15 Apr. 2013. www.artlyst.com/articles/kathy-acker-pussy-new-gallery-presentation-of-her-1994-work Accessed 8 Nov. 2016.

243 *"It was the kind of friendship"*: Pulsifer, interview with author, 2015.

243 *"I was living on Avenue C and Ninth Street"*: Jordan, interview with author, 2016.

244 *"She only took me to see"*: Pulsifer, interview with author, 2015.

244 *"She moved to New York"*: Gaiman, "An Interview with Neil Gaiman," conducted by Jessica Crispin, 2006.

244 *Finally, Pulsifer recalled, she simply*: Pulsifer, interview with author, 2015.

244 *"[T]wenty years of my work is now dead"*: Acker, letter to Ira Silverberg, 9 June 1990. ISP.

245 *"She went to London"*: Jordan, interview with author, 2016.

245 *In fact, Acker wouldn't sell*: Kathy Acker financial records 1995. GPA.

245 *She bought a Honda 400cc motorcycle*: Herman, Janine. Unpublished interview with Kathy Acker. Fall 1990. Janine Herman Personal Papers, New York.

246 *In San Francisco, she hung out*: Scholder, email to the author, 2016.

246 *"there is a community here"*: Zurbrugg, Nicholas. "Kathy Acker." *Art, Performance, Media—31 Interviews*. Minneapolis: University of Minnesota Press, 2004. 13.

246 *"More postmodern blather from the queen"*: "In Memoriam to Identity by Kathy Acker." *Kirkus Review*, 2 July 1990.

246 *"unreadable"*: Schiff, Stephen. "Rimbaud and Verlaine, Together Again." *New York Times Book Review*, 22 July 1990.

246 *"predictable, unreadable and clumsy"*: Walker, Christopher. "From lather to black leather." *The Observer*, 22 July 1990.

247 *"seemed to be produced under the spell"*: Scholder, email to the author, 2016.

247 *"Born out of attempted murder"*: Acker, *My Mother: Demonology*, 20.

247 *"you couldn't walk down the street"*: Scholder, email to author, 2016.

247 *Scholder introduced Acker to*: Ronell, Avital. Email to the author. 27 Oct. 2016.

247 *Ronell had just published The Telephone Book*: Ronell, Avital. *The Telephone Book*. Lincoln: University of Nebraska Press, 1989; *Crack Wars: Literature, Addiction, Mania*. Lincoln: University of Nebraska Press, 1992.

247 *"We . . . were very spontaneous"*: Ronell, email to the author, 2016.

248 *"talked about taking a piece of writing"*: Laurence, Alexander. "Reading, Writing: Hell." Customer Review on *My Mother: Demonology*. Amazon, 20 Apr. 2004. www.amazon.com/My-Mother-Demonology-Novel-Acker/dp/0802134033. Accessed 8 Nov. 2016.

248 *"She was not polite"*: Springer, Anna Joy. Email to the author. 29 Oct. 2016.

248 *"While it's true that she was"*: Evans, Jenna Leigh. Email to the author. 16 Dec. 2016.

249 *the iconoclastic dyke punk band*: Chonin, Neva. "Even Within the World of Womyn, Tribe 8 Was A Little Too Punk For Comfort." *SF Gate*, 12 July 2006. www.sfgate.com/entertainment/article/Even-within-the-world-of-womyn-Tribe-8-was-a-2493192.php. Accessed 8 Nov. 2016.

249 *"She was elated to see punk"*: Springer, email to the author, 2016.

249 *William Morris agent Marcy Posner*: Posner, Marcy. Email to the author. 24 Oct. 2016.

250 *"I really hate New York"*: Acker, Kathy. "Kathy Acker Interviewed by Rebecca Deaton." *Textual Practice*, vol. 6. No. 2, 1992, 272.

250 *"I don't know how long"*: Acker, "Kathy Acker Interviewed by Rebecca Deaton," 272.

250 *"I didn't learn anything"*: Trull, Steven. Email to the author. 2 Nov. 2016.

250 *Trull would attain notoriety*: Steven Trull's "Writers I'd Like To Fuck (or Be Fucked By)" on html.giant in 2013 referred to by Diana Dragonetti and various others has since been deleted from html.giant.com.

250 *"was the purpose of this list"*: Dragonetti, Diana. "Diana Dragonetti's Response to Steven Trull/Janey Smith's "Fuck List"—The "Art" of Rape Culture." *htmlgiant*. 5 Sept. 2014. htmlgiant.com/behind-the-scenes/dianna-dragonettis-response-to-janey-smithsteven-trulls-fuck-list-the-art-of-rape-culture. Accessed 8 Nov. 2016.

251 *"Dear B. . . . I started writing you"*: Acker, *My Mother: Demonology*, 22.

252 *"Here are my most recent thoughts"*: Ibid., 23–24.

252 *"We're kissing, but I feel nothing"*: Ibid., 27.

252 *"You want me to live a lie"*: Ibid., 30.

252 *"Hello, you wildness"*: Ibid., 229.

253 *Just as Burroughs returns to scenes*: See, for example, "A whiff of St. Louis, he is

standing on a back porch looking down toward a river. . . ." Burroughs, William S. *The Place of Dead Roads*. New York: Picador/Henry Holt, 1983. 145.

253 *"Once a week, without any voting"*: Acker, *My Mother: Demonology*, 189.

253 *"excluded, this time forever"*: Ibid., 203.

253 *"Since my childhood is dead"*: Ibid., 185.

253 *"present new American writing"*: Ibid., 223.

253 *"Bourenine's wife is scheduled"*: Ibid., 227.

253 *"When I began to cry"*: Ibid., 227.

253 *"G had told me three times"*: Ibid., 238.

254 *"I didn't go to the airport"*: "Georg Buchner." Letter to Kathy Acker. n.d. 1992. KAP.

254 *"hallucinatory amalgam of emotion"*: "My Mother: Demonology." *Publisher's Weekly*, 28 June 1993.

254 *"her formidably talented hand"*: Geary, Brian. "My Mother: Demonology." *Library Journal*, 1 July 1992.

254 *"Laure's impressionistic swirl, when it works"*: Burns, Erik. "Bikers Nightmare." *New York Times* In Short—Fiction, 21 Nov. 1993.

254 *Weeks later, Acker went into*: Reighly, Kurt B. "Spoken Words—A posthumous CD captures the spark of a spirit gone too soon." *Seattle Weekly*, 9 Oct. 2006.

254 *"Her voice in general"*: Ibid.

255 *Acker met the technology specialist*: Sirius, R. U. Email to the author. 28 Oct. 2016.

255 *"The students who come to my class"*: Sirius, R. U. "Kathy Acker: Where Does She Get Off?" *Io* 1993. www.altx.com/io/acker.html. Accessed 8 Nov. 2016.

255 *"an old friend of mine, someone who used"*: Acker, *Pussy, King of the Pirates*, 169.

255 *"RUS: I'm writing a piece"*: Sirius, "Kathy Acker: Where Does She Get Off?," 1993.

256 *"I wanted to have the masturbatory"*: Guyotat, Pierre. "Pierre Guyotat." Interview conducted by Noura Wedell. *Bomb*, Winter 2015.

256 *"what might be called a body language"*: Sirius, "Kathy Acker: Where Does She Get Off?," 1993.

256 *"A lot of what you heard"*: Kathy Acker performance clip. *Who's Afraid of Kathy Acker?* Dir. Barbara Caspar. 2007. Film.

256 *"I remember she got bored"*: Sirius, "Kathy Acker: Where Does She Get Off?," 1993.

257 *"forward all correspondence and other"*: Acker, letter to Marcy Posner, 25 July 1994. ISP.

257 *She began making alternate plans*: Acker, fax to Ira Silverberg, n.d. Feb. 1994. ISP.

257 *"nearly every conversation I had"*: Handelman, Michelle. Letter to the author. 28 May 2015.

257 *In September 1993, Acker had another PID*: Gluck, Bob. Letter to Kathy Acker. n.d. Sept. 1993. ISP.

257 *although she'd already been warned*: Trull, email to the author, 2016.

257 *"she had been about to commit suicide"*: Kaveney, "Some Years With Acker," 2007.

257 *She had some readings in the UK*: Acker, letter to Ira Silverberg, n.d. 1994. ISP.

257 *She'd already agreed to teach that semester*: Acker, Kathy. CV 1996. SLPP.

257 *"Oh yes, I know her"*: Acker, *Pussy, King of the Pirates*, 174.

258 *"we call ourselves fortunate"*: Ibid., 190.

258 *"was the most shoplifted female"*: Strong, "Kathy Acker Pussy New Gallery Presentation of Her 1994 Work," 2013.

258 *Banned from AOL for using obscenity*: Acker, Kathy. "Pussy and the Art of Motorcycle Maintenance—or, how to be a pirate online and channel your energies so as to remember your dreams—Kathy Acker interviewed by Rosie X." *Geocities*, n.d. 1996. www.geocities.ws/nowrite/acker.html. Accessed 8 Nov. 2016.

258 *Like many others, Acker was already skeptical*: Dodge, Trevor. "I Lost My Soul In San Francisco: An Interview/Journal Entry Starring Kathy Acker, Portland and Pussy." *Mekons*, Apr. 1996. www.mekons.de/portland.htm. Accessed 8 Nov. 2016.

259 *"is becoming like the world of opera"*: Rose, Cynthia. "Kathy Acker Is—. . . Hard Goofy Polemical Tough Hilarious Adventurous—. . . And a Writer Who Uses Words As Weapons." *Seattle Weekly*, 12 March 1996.

259 *At the beginning of 1995*: Kathy Acker financial records 1995. GPA.

259 *Her SFAI paychecks didn't quite*: Ibid.

259 *That year she spent $7,500*: Ibid.

259 *She'd already taken a second mortgage*: Ibid.

259 *So far, the occasional biopsies*: Trull, email to author, 2016.

259 *She had regular consultations with naturopaths*: Kathy Acker financial records 1995. GPA.

259 *By now she was looking for a full-time*: Acker, email to McKenzie Wark, 15 Aug. 1995. Acker, Kathy, and McKenzie Wark. *I'm Very Into You*. Los Angeles: Semiotext(e), 2014. 84.

260 *But then again, her agreement*: Kathy Acker financial records 1995. GPA.

260 *Performing that summer at the Australian Centre for Contemporary Art*: Australia Centre for Contemporary Art. *ACCA* 1995 Archive. www.accaonline.org.au/about/first-30-years/1995. Accessed November 8 2016

260 *"Kathy Acker's drunken girls, she meant us"*: Brown, "1995," 2013.

260 *Acker hoped that her long*: Kathy Acker financial records 1995. GPA.

260 *On July 18 Acker left for an eleven-day*: Ibid.

260 *There, she met the media theorist*: Acker and Wark, *I'm Very Into You*, 2014.

260 *Wark had just published his first book*: Wark, McKenzie. *Virtual Geography*. Bloomington: Indiana University Press, 1994.

261 *"there's always solitude but"*: Acker, *I'm Very Into You*, 2.

261 *"Do we need to analyze our encounter"*: Wark, *I'm Very Into You*, 4.

262 *"[T]he KATHY ACKER that YOU WANT"*: Acker, *I'm Very Into You*, 24–25.

262 *"if you are going to come through SF"*: Ibid., 55.

262 *"If you're busy I can look after myself"*: Wark, *I'm Very Into You*, 63.

263 *"[I]t's always in my head"*: Acker, *I'm Very Into You*, 69–70.

263 *The last email in the series*: Wark, *I'm Very Into You*, 70.

263 *Wark arrived in San Francisco*: Viegener, Matias. "Introduction—portishead-space." Acker and Wark, *I'm Very Into You*, xvi.

263 *Two weeks later they met up*: Kathy Acker financial records 1995. GPA.

263 *"There was something dream-like"* : Wark, message to the author, 2015.

263 *"Just read this over breakfast"*: Acker, *I'm Very Into You*, postscript.

264 *"In Acker's tiresome world"*: "Pussy, King of the Pirates." *Kirkus Review*, 1 Jan. 1996.

264 *"One of her favorite subjects"*: Kelly, David. "Pussy, King of the Pirates." *New York Times*, 3 Mar. 1996.

264 *"a glorious exception"*: Jennings, Dave. "Mekons & Kathy Acker—Freedom Café, London." *Melody Maker*, 13 Apr. 1996, 22.

264 *"[I]t's not art. It's hot"*: Acker, *I'm Very Into You*, 42.

265 *On her way home from Brighton*: Murray, Charles Shaar. "Kathy Acker remembered." *Charles Shaar Murray*. 1997. charlesshaarmurray.com/journalism/tha-kulcha/kathy-acker-remembered. Accessed 19 July 2016.

265 *Within weeks of returning*: Shaar Murray, "Kathy Acker remembered," 1997.

FABLE

266 *"She was so afraid"*: Antin, Eleanor and David. Interview with the author. 18 Feb. 2000.

266 *"Georgina Ritchie also criticized"*: Viegener, Matias. "Cannibal Acker." web.archive.org/web/20050309160449/http://www.suspectthoughts.com/viegener.html. Accessed 20 Nov. 2016.

266 *"One of the green figures"*: Acker, Kathy. "Gift of Disease." *The Guardian*, 18 Jan. 1997.

267 *"At the time, I was working"*: Ibid..

267 *Still, she had more than*: Kathy Acker financial records 1995. GPA.

267 *and many self-employed people*: Bellamy, Dodie. Email to the author. 11 Nov. 2016.

267 *"You have to want to be well"*: Acker, "Gift of Disease," 1997.

267 *"I roto-root the past"*: Ibid.

268 *"You have an abnormal childhood"*: Acker, *Homage to LeRoi Jones*, 24.

268 *"Cancer became my whole brain"*: Acker, Kathy. 1997 notebook. MVA.

268 *"GEORGE: Did Electra's mother"*: Acker, *Eurydice in the Underworld*, 186–187.

268 *By July 1996, her healers agreed*: Shaar Murray, "Kathy Acker Remembered," 2016.

268 *"She was working"*: Ibid.

269 *Soon they discovered that*: Ibid.

269 *She liked to sleep until noon*: Kaveney, interview with author, 16 Jan. 2015.

269 *"I traveled to your land though I was"*: Acker, *Eurydice in the Underworld*, 24–25.

269 *"so much cooler than Charles"*: Home, Stewart. Interview with the author. 16 Jan. 2016.

269 *When Home proposed asking her*: Home, interview with the author, 2016.

269 *And so, just two months"*: HM Land Registry. Form 19. Filed 20 Sept. 1996. *Land Registry*. www.gov.uk/land-registry. Accessed 19 Jan. 2017.

270 *"It was a very prestigious address"*: Pulsifer, interview with author, 2015.

270 *"We were caught in an endless"*: Shaar Murray, "Kathy Acker Remembered," 2016.

270 *She was seeing a Chinese herbalist*: Acker, "Gift of Disease," 1997.

270 *"She was constantly tired"*: Shaar Murray, "Kathy Acker Remembered," 2016.

270 *"[T]he whole Kansas visit"*: Acker, email to Ira Silverberg, 8 Nov. 1996. ISP.

270 *"He just keeps wanting"*: Acker, email to Ira Silverberg, 16 Nov. 1996. ISP.

270 *She asked Silverberg to help her*: Ibid.

270 *but he had no clue*: Silverberg, email to Kathy Acker, 18 Nov. 1996. ISP.

270 *"As usual, back on the road"*: Acker, email to Ira Silverberg, 18 Nov. 1996. ISP.

270 *Silverberg suggested that she buy*: Silverberg, email to Kathy Acker, 18 Nov. 1996. ISP.

271 *Meanwhile, she'd already accepted*: Acker, email to Ira Silverberg, 18 Nov. 1996. ISP.

271 *Throughout the late fall*: Acker, email to Ira Silverberg, 7 Dec. 1996. ISP.

271 *"I can't keep living out"*: Acker, email to Ira Silverberg, 14 Feb. 1997. ISP.

271 *"I'm down here til May"*: Acker, email to Ira Silverberg, 3 Mar. 1997. ISP.

271 *"I have been so much"*: Acker, email to Ira Silverberg, 13 Mar. 1997. ISP.

271 *"career is ever-shifting"*: Silverberg, email to Kathy Acker, 14 Mar. 1997. ISP.

272 *Back in London in June*: Acker, email to Ira Silverberg, 28 June 1997.

272 *Her old friend Gary Pulsifer had*: Pulsifer, interview with author, 2015.

272 *"I affirm that every day"*: Acker, Kathy. Notebook 1997. MVA.

272 *One late afternoon she and Shaar Murray*: Pulsifer, interview with author, 2015; this incident also recounted by Matias Viegener, interview with author, 12 Feb. 2000; Eleanor Antin, interview with author; among others.

273 *The next time they fought*: Shaar Murray, "Kathy Acker Remembered," 2016.

273 *When Gary Pulsifer arrived*: Pulsifer, interview with author, 2015.

273 *Her flat sold for 160,000 GBP*: HM Land Registry, 17 Sept. 1997.

273 *For the three* Pussy *performances*: Kathy Acker and The Mekons. Performance video, Chicago 1997. *Selina Scott Show, Super Channel*. www.youtube.com/watch?v=Azh5grNxqIg Accessed 20 Nov. 2016.

273 *Acker was tired during rehearsals*: Langford, Jon. "The Mekons—The Art of Living to the Full" *Puncture*, 43. *The Mekons*. www.mekons.de/pirate.html. Accessed 20 Nov. 2016.

274 *In San Francisco, she checked into*: Gluck, Robert. Interview with the author. 17 Feb. 2015.

274 *She weighed less than a hundred pounds*: Mare, Aline. Interview with the author. 24 Apr. 2015.

274 *"At age 30, I was working"*: Acker, personal notebook, 1997. MVA.

274 *Several days later she moved*: Mare, interview with the author, 2015.

275 *A CAT scan revealed*: Viegener, Matias. Email to Trevor Dodge. 27 Feb. 2000. MVA.

275 *When he heard news*: Lotringer, Sylvère. İnterview with the author. 7 Feb. 2000.

275 *"I made all the wrong choices"*: Acker, cit. in Sylvère Lotringer notebook, Nov. 1997. SLPP.

275 *"this little girl is not having fun"*: Acker, cit. in Sylvère Lotringer notebook, Nov. 1997. SLPP.

275 *In "The Gift of Disease" she'd written*: Viegener, Mathias. Interview with the author. 18 Apr. 2015.

276 *Founded by a former electronics engineer*: Barrett, Stephen. "A Close Look at Robert W. Bradford and His Committee for Freedom of Choice in Medicine." *Quackwatch*. www.quackwatch.org/04ConsumerEducation/Nonrecorg/cfcm.html. Accessed 20 Nov. 2016.

276 *American Biologics was the only alternative*: Viegener, Mathias. Email to Sylvère Lotringer. 14 Feb. 2000. SLPP.

276 *"We left this hi-tech landscape"*: Viegener, interview with the author, 2015.

276 *"The quality, not quantity"*: Silva Gigi, Guillermina. Interview with the author. 13 May 1998.

277 *Friends began calling and faxing*: Viegener, interview with the author, 2015.

277 *"The clinic was really the end of the road"*: Lotringer, notebook, Nov. 1997.

277 *"I was hoping the friends"*: Viegener, email to Trevor Dodge, 2000. MVA.

277 *Thanksgiving that year fell on*: Viegener, email to Trevor Dodge, 2000. MVA.

277 *A few blocks away*: "Jesus Blancornelas." *Wikipedia*. en.wikipedia.org/wiki/Jes%C3%BAs_Blancornelas. Accessed 20 Nov. 2016.

277 *Surrounded by friends*, she began: Viegener, email to Trevor Dodge, 2000. MVA.

277 *She asked Viegener to*: Viegener, Matias. "Cannibal Acker," op. cit.

278 *"Dear X," read the final version*: Silverberg, Ira. Letters faxed to various recipients on Grove Atlantic letterhead. 26 Nov. 1997. ISP.

278 *The account, closed out two days*: Giorno, John. Letter to Ira Silverberg. Faxed 2 Dec. 1997. ISP.

278 *In 2007 the Austrian filmmaker*: *Who's Afraid of Kathy Acker?* Dir. Barbara Caspar. 2007.

278 *Intercut with Acker's performance*: Ibid.

279 *"We're all the same in a way"*: Rosler, interview with the author, Mar. 2000.

Index

0 to 9, 62, 94

10/18, 174
100 Boots, 72, 82
1995, 237

Acker, Bob, 33, 34, 45, 47, 50, 51, 52, 54, 98, 176, 180, 220
Acconci, Vito, 62, 94, 96, 97, 100, 108, 96, 97, 100
Adult Life of Toulouse Lautrec, The ,114, 117, 118, 121, 122, 127, 128, 129, 131, 132, 133, 134, 137, 145, 150, 151, 178, 194, 232, 233
Agee, Philip, 152, 169
AK Press, 258
Akerman, Chantal, 93
Alfred University, 260
Alexander, Albert, 159, 160, 164, 165
Alexander, Claire Weill, 159, 161, 164, 165, 166, 180,182, 184, 220
Alexander, Emily, 159
Alexander, Karen Weill, 42
Alexander, Richard, 159
Alexander Weiss, Wendy, 158, 166, 181
Alexander Bud, 92
Algeria, 55, 170
Allen, Woody, 199
Allende, Salvador, 89
Almeida Theatre, 203, 220
Aloes Books, 170
Alpert, Barry, 71, 77, 81, 111, 134, 140, 145
Amelia's, 246

American Biologics, 275
America a Prophecy, 30
American Legion, 47
American Psycho, 256
Anderson, Laurie, 131, 219
Andrews, Bruce, 134
Antin, David, 33, 45, 46, 47, 48, 49, 50, 60, 64, 67, 68, 72, 73, 74, 75, 78, 82, 83, 223, 266, 277
Antin, Eleanor, 33, 45, 46, 48, 62, 64, 67, 72, 73, 75, 78, 82, 83, 108, 135, 266, 267, 277, 279
Antonioni, Michelangelo, 69, 207
American Biologics, 16
Arcadia Books, 272, 273
Arthur Rimbaud in New York, 149
Artforum, 150
Art in Form, 187
A Scanner Darkly, 89, 93
Ashberry, John, 114
Ashley, Robert, 75, 78, 87, 125, 158
A Space, 143, 144
Art Services, 125
Atwood, Margaret, 161
Australian Centre for Contemporary Art, 260
autobiog.txt, 7, 94, 95, 108
Automatic Writing, 87, 88
Avalanche, 143

B., Beth, 149
B., Scott, 132, 149
Baader-Meinhof Group, 178

Bad Behavior, 237
Bacon, Francis, 199
Bailey, Rosemary, 206, 214, 215, 219
Baldwin, James, 61
Ball, Hugo. 139
Baraka, Amiri, 72, 196
Baracks, Barbara, 64
Bargain Books, 151
Barnabus Rex, 126, 127
Barthelme, Donald, 118
Barthes, Roland, 173
Bataille, Georges, 157, 162, 163, 173, 175, 176, 178, 212
Baum, Louis, 222
Beattie, Ann, 161
Beavis and Butt Head, 256
Beckett, Samuel, 196, 197
Bell, The 213
Bellamy, Dodie, 14, 21, 22, 215
Bergé, Carol, 82, 85
Berger, John, 199
Bergmann, Gustav, 110, 128
Bergson, Henri, 110, 128
Berne, Eric, 96
Bernstein, Charles, 63, 134
Berrigan, Ted, 76, 172
Bhagavad Gita, 274
Bilgore, Ellen, 39, 40
Birch Wathen School, 35, 39
Blackburn, Paul, 30
Black Panther Party, 26
Blanchot, Maurice 173, 263
Blancornelas, Jesús, 277
Bleckner, Ross, 124
Blitz, 221
Blood and Guts in High School, 143, 145, 146, 147, 148, 151, 152, 153, 154, 168, 169, 170, 174, 183, 194, 197, 198, 199, 201 202, 203, 211, 230, 250
Blood of a Poet Box, 45, 60, 62, 83
Blue of Noon, 162, 163, 178
Blue Tape, 92, 99, 100, 102, 105, 108, 109, 122, 157, 164
Boal, Augusto, 151
Bockris, Victor, 149, 187
Bomb, 150, 204
Bourgois, Christian, 174
Bowen, Elizabeth 61
Bowes, Ed, 73, 93, 94, 115

Bowels, Jane, 237
Bowling Alone, 21
Bowie, David, 209
Boz Scagg, 113
Bracewell, Michael, 15, 201, 217, 218
Brach, Paul 46
Bragg, Melvyn, 199, 200, 201, 214
Brakhage, Stan, 36
Brand, Stewart, 256
Brandeis University, 28, 35, 37, 38, 44, 47, 52, 54, 67, 69, 87, 98, 180, 224
Brooklyn College, 270
Brooke, Kaucyila, 215
Brooks, Pete, 220
Brearley School, 39
Breathless, 25
Brecht, 113, 209
Breedlove, Lynn, 249
Brew, Kathy, 16
Brodey, Jim, 64
Brodsky, Michael, 151
Brooks, Rosetta, 203
Brown, Pam, 237
Brown, Steve, 13
Brown, Trisha, 119
Brownstein, Michael, 117
Brumbaugh, Robert, 36
Bryn Mawr College, 37
Buck, Paul, 122, 172, 173, 174, 176, 177, 178, 182, 184, 185, 186, 187, 188, 189, 190, 192, 193, 194, 198
Buchner, Georg, 254
Buddhism, 132
Bull, Hank, 142
Bunker, The, 150
Burden, Chris, 100, 131
Burgess, Anthony, 152
Burning Bombing of America, The, 62
Burns, Erik
Burns, Tim, 149
Burroughs, William S., 30, 43, 89 150, 161, 162, 172, 173, 174, 196, 216, 219, 222, 239 230, 234, 251, 252, 270
Bush, George, 152
Bush, Kate, 246
Butch Whacks and the Glass Packs, 113, 114

Calder, Liz, 222
Lt. Calley, William 31, 97

Cage, John, 111
Cain's Book, 167
CalArts, 276
Cannon, Beth, 94, 101, 102
Capra Press, 113
Capote, Truman, 164
CAPS (Creative Artists Public Service), 130, 139, 140, 141, 142
Carney, Ralph, 254
Carter, Jimmy, 142
Caspar, Barbara, 228, 278
Castle, Ted, 114, 150
Catullus, 209
CBGB, 127
Catullus, 250
Caven, Ingrid, 179
Celan, Paul, 30
Cendrars, Blaise, 128
Center, 82
Cervantes, Miguel, 222, 223
Change group, 175, 177, 201
Channel 4, 203, 204, 221
Chapman, Robin, 222
Chatham, Rhys, 117, 119, 132
Chaucer, Geoffrey, 75
Chelsea House Publishers, 169
Cherie, 180
Chinese Notebook, The, 121
Chomsky, Noam, 27
Christie, Agatha, 128
Cioran, Emil, 209
City Limits, 203, 216
City Lights Books, 246
Clare, John, 209, 211
Close, Chuck, 124
Closer, 237
The Childlike Life of the Black Tarantula, 39, 53, 62, 80, 81, 86, 88, 89, 90, 91, 96, 99, 109, 111, 113, 114, 117, 120, 122, 130, 133, 138, 145, 146, 150, 157, 161, 172, 174, 194
Cocaine Papers, 169
CodeX, 258
Coe, Jonathan, 232
Coe, Sue, 197
Coleman, Ornette, 77
Colette, 180
Columbia University, 162
Comme des Garcons, 201
Compendium Books, 172

Complete Works of Constance DeJong, The, 135
Conrad, Tony, 102
Contortions, The, 149
Cooper, Dennis, 17, 237, 246
Coppola, Francis Ford, 199
Corso, Gregory, 36, 173
Cortázar, Julio, 30, 145
Count Zero, 224
Crabapple, Molly, 123
Crack Wars: Literature Addiction Mania, 247
Crimes of Love, The, 213
Cruickshank-Hagenbuckle, Geoffrey, 167–168
Cunningham, David, 254
Cunningham, Valentine, 232
Curtains magazine, 172
Curtis, Jackie, 13
Cut Piece, 140

D'Allesandro. Sam, 22
Dalley, Jon, 230
Dartmouth College, 260
Davidson, Michael, 222
Dawson, Fielding, 84
"Dead Doll Humility," 235
Deaton, Rebecca, 144, 250
de Broglio, Nathalie, 216
Debord, Guy, 114
Deep Throat, 28
DeJong, Constance, 118, 124, 125, 126, 130, 132, 135, 136
Der Spiegl, 227
de Sade, Marquis, 88, 213
Descartes, René, 210, 211
Desnos, Robert, 144
Dederich, Charles, 101
DiMassa, Diane, 258
DeVille, Mink, 127
DIARIES } DIARY OF THE WORLD, 61
Dial Press, 61
Dick, Leslie, 214
Dick, Philip K., 89, 93
Dick, Vivienne, 149
Dickens, Charles, 157, 167, 181, 184
di Prima, Diana, 21, 23
Dixon, Jonathan, 7
Doctorow, Cory, 225
Doobie Brothers, 113

Don Quixote, 122, 201, 208, 211, 212, 213, 214, 220, 221, 223, 224, 225, 226, 241, 246
Dorn, Ed 173
Dostoyevski, Fyodor, 43, 159
Do Tongues, 258
Doyle, Judith, 143, 144, 146
DNA, 149
Dragonetti, Dianna, 250
Drawing Blood, 123
Duke University, 260

Écrits de Laure, 175
Eden Eden Eden, 168, 173, 176, 177
Edinburgh Writers' Conference, 162
Edinburgh Fringe Festival, 222
Eins, Stefan, 139
Empire of the Senseless, 57, 225, 226, 229, 230, 231, 234, 237, 238
Empty Elevator Shaft, 111
Eno, Brian, 149
Eshleman, Clayton, 115
Essential Acker, 246
Eurydice in the Underworld, 18, 267, 268, 269, 272, 273
Evans, Jenna Leigh, 248
Evergreen Review, The, 196
"Excerpts From: Entrance into Dwelling in Paradise," 72
Exterminator, 89
Eyre, Jane, 222

Face, The, 203
Factory, The, 139, 142
Fassbinder, Rainer Werner, 179
Faulkner, William, 25, 57
Faye, Jean-Pierre, 11, 177, 178, 201
Fear of Flying, 89
Félix, Ramón Arellano, 277
Figgs, Kate, 233
File, 43
Film Comment, 14, 36
Film Culture and Film Makers' Cooperative, 36
Fisher, Joel, 132
Flanders, Moll, 56
"Florida," 232
Flying Lizards, 254
Foreman, Richard 196
Forti, Simone, 119, 126, 188

Fowles, John, 96
Fox, Robert Elliot, 72
Fox, Matt, 215
Frame, Janet, 161
Frakes, James, 144
Freilicher, Mel, 22, 44, 64, 67, 68, 73, 77, 93, 277
Freud, Sigmund, 169
Fried, Howard, 192, 193
Friedman, Ed, 131
Friedman, Ellen, 111
Froese, Dieter, 140
Fun City, 27, 28, 29, 58, 59, 65, 67, 77 212
Fuses, 96

Gaiman, Neil, 225, 232, 242, 244
Gaitskill, Mary, 237
Galás, Diamanda, 257
Gallimard, 173
Games People Play, 96
Garnham, Chris, 214
Gauguin, Paul, 127, 128
Gaysek, Fred, 143
Geek Maggot Bingo, 203
Genet, Jean, 36, 199, 230
General Pinochet, 89
General Structure of the World, 105
Gentle, Mary, 225
Gerson, Max B., 275
George, Glenda 177, 184, 186, 187, 189, 190, 192, 194
Georgia Fame, 222
Getty, Ann, 240
Gibson, William, 224, 225
Gift of Disease, The, 18, 271, 275
Gigi, Guillermina Silva, 276
Ginsberg, Allen, 174, 270
Giorno Poetry Systems, 278
Girls of Fortune, 257
Gitlin, Paul, 233
Giuliani, Rudolph, 23
Glass, Philip, 126, 132, 136
Glück, Bob 13. 19, 21, 22, 192, 194, 274
Godard, Jean-Luc, 25
Gogol, Nikolai, 43
Gold, Rich, 91
Goldberg, Jeff, 149, 166, 184, 187, 189, 190, 191, 192, 193

Goldman, Emma, 30, 102
Gold's Gym, 15, 200
Gombrich, Sir Ernest, 201
Gordon, Bette, 149, 217, 220
Gordon, Peter, 15, 68, 69, 70, 71, 72,
75, 76, 77, 78, 79, 83, 85, 87, 88, 91,
95, 98, 99, 103, 109, 111, 113, 114,
115, 116, 118, 127, 130, 131, 132,
145, 146, 148, 153, 173, 185, 245
Gordon, Samuel, 182, 184
Gosselin Caroline, 173
Govinda, 132
Grace, Sharon, 16, 19, 22, 275, 276
Graham, Dan, 74, 75, 81, 95, 131
Graham, Jacqueline, 202
Granta, 235
Grauerholz, James, 150, 174
Graves, Robert, 137
Great Expectations, 56, 59, 122, 151,
153, 154, 155, 156, 157, 158, 159, 160,
161, 163, 165, 166, 167, 168, 177, 179,
181, 183, 184, 185, 186, 188, 189, 190,
191, 192, 193, 194, 197, 198, 201
Grosshans, Annie, 188, 190
Groucho Club, 221
Grosz, Georg, 197
Grove Press, 144, 152, 153, 196, 197,
198, 202, 203, 222, 223, 225, 232,
234, 237, 240, 241, 242, 264, 271, 278
Guardian, The, 203, 220, 230, 232,
234, 271
Guattari, Félix, 179
Guernica, 97
Guyotat, Pierre, 162, 168, 173, 176,
177, 184, 256
Gysin, Brion, 30, 172, 173, 174

Halloween Party, 128
Hallwalls, 143
Handelman, Michelle, 13, 257
Handke, Peter, 126, 151
Hannibal Lecter, My Father, 250, 272
Hardy, Thomas, 43
Harryman, Carla, 134
Harvard University, 35, 37
Haunted Houses, 237, 238
Havel, Václev, 241
Haynes, Todd, 201
Hayward, Julia, 126
Hearst, Patty, 113
Heartbreakers, The, 127

Hebdige, Dick, 224, 277
Hennings, Emmy, 139
Herskovitz, Jean Lindenbaum, 39
Higgins, Dick, 36, 118, 126
Highsmith, Patricia, 139
Hitler, Adolf, 48
Hobbes, Thomas, 222
Hodas, Marty, 27, 59
Hodder & Stoughton, 223
Hollins University, 18, 271
Holt, Virginia, 181
Holzer, Jenny, 195, 208
Homage to LeRoi Jones, 72, 73
Home, Stewart, 269
Honegger, Arthur, 88
Hopkins, Gerard Manley, 35
Horovitz, Michael, 202
Horse Crazy, 237
Howard, Maureen, 212
Howe, Fanny, 335
Howe, Susan, 75
HP Radio Show, 142
htmlgiant, 250
Huelsenbeck, Richard, 11
Husserl, Edmund, 184, 209, 211
Huxley, Aldous, 152, 169

I Ching, 274
*I Dreamt I Was a Nymphomaniac:
Imagining,* 53, 57, 111, 118, 122, 133,
145, 187, 193, 213
Indiana, Gary, 129, 149, 150, 185,
200, 231, 237
Infobase Publishing, 169
Independent, The, 230
In Memoriam to Identity, 57, 58, 226,
231, 234, 246
Inside the Company, 169
Institute of Contemporary Art, Lon-
don 219, 220, 221, 223
International Exhibition of New
America Cinema, 36
Interview, 150
In the Realm of the Senses, 56
Io, 255
Issue, Marc, 221
ITVS, 199, 200

Jackson, Michael, 255
Jagger, Bianca, 164

Jakobson, Roman, 35
James, Darius, 216
Jennings, Dave, 264
Joan of Arc, 28
Johnston, Becky, 149, 151
Johnson, Mimi, 125
Jonathan Livingston Seagull, 89
Jonas, Joan, 91
Jones, LeRoi, 30
Jones, Rickie Lee, 246
Jong, Erica, 89
Jonson, Ben, 157
Jordan, Fred 196, 197, 202, 234, 241, 242
Jordan, Ken, 242, 243, 245
"Journal Black Cats Black Jewels," 66, 68
Joyce, James, 209
Judd, Donald, 157
Judson Theater, 45
Juliette, 213

Kakutani, Michiko, 238, 239
Karlin, Danny, 230
Kaprow, Allan, 46, 139
Kathy Goes to Haiti, 142, 143, 144, 145, 146, 232
Kathy Acker's Clothes, 215
Katz, Leandro, 114, 150
Kaveney, Roz, 91, 232, 235, 242, 244, 257
Kaye, Clifford, 165, 182
Kaye, Pooh, 124, 126, 160, 165, 166, 180, 181, 182, 183
Kelly, David, 264
Kennedy, Robert F., 45
Kennedy Onassis, Jackie, 164
Kern, Richard, 203
Kerouac, Jack, 196
Killian, Kevin, 21, 22
Kimberley, Nick 172
King, Kenneth, 119
King of Solana Beach, The, 67
Kirkus Review, 246, 264
Kissinger, Henry, 212
Kitchen, The, 119, 135, 136, 235
Knowles, Alison, 119, 126
Komater, Chris, 21
Kotz, Liz, 63, 157
Kristeva, Julia, 151
Kroesen, Jill, 88, 113, 120, 126, 127,

178, 183
Kropotkin, Peter, 127
Kundera, Milan, 241
Kusama, Yayoi, 139
Kushner, Robert, 143, 146, 152, 187

Lady Pink, 208
La Princesse des Clèves, 189
Language School, 134
Lasky, Burton 67
Laure, 173, 175, 176, 184, 212, 252, 254
Laurence, Alexander, 248
Lawrence, D. H., 31
Lazare, Jane, 178
Lebel, Jean-Jacques, 139, 179
LeClair, Tom, 223
Leduc, Violette, 146, 252
Lehmann, Donald, 92, 159
Leiris, Michel, 173
Lemaire, Gérard-Georges, 174, 178, 179
Lenox School, 35, 37, 38, 39, 40, 42. 43, 54, 86, 98, 146
Le pas au-delà, 263
LeRoi, Jones, 72
Les Lettres Françaises, 178
Letter from a Prisoner in the Isolation Wing June 16, 1972–February 9, 138
LeWitt, Sol, 150, 152
Lezak, Iris, 60, 90
Leventhal, Liz, 39
Library Journal, 254
Lindisfarne, 222
Lippard, Lucy, 150
Lisa Lyon's Body Magic, 195
Literal Madness, 144, 205, 232, 237
Locale, The 126
Logie, Jim 188, 189, 190
London Review of Books, 222, 230
Londonier, Fred, 33
Los Angeles Times, 212
Lotringer, Sylvère, 13, 20, 43, 65, 146, 149, 162, 165, 174, 176, 185, 186, 203, 226, 229, 231, 234, 275, 277
Lovelace, Linda, 28
Love Me Tender, 237, 238
Lukacs, Georg, 155
Lulu Unchained, 220, 221
Lunch, Lydia, 149, 203

Lurie, Boris, 139
Lust for Life, 246
Lyon, Lisa, 195

Mackinnon, Lachlan, 230
Mac Low, Jackson, 36, 60, 67, 78, 84, 85, 90, 91, 93, 98, 99, 108, 113, 114, 122, 184
Madame de Lafayette, 189
Magus, The, 96
Mailer, Norman, 61
Malanga, Gerard 239
Manson, Charles, 26
Mapplethorpe, Robert, 149, 195, 200, 222
Marcuse, Herbert, 14, 46, 220, 224
Mare, Aline, 16, 19, 22, 23, 275
Marlatt, Daphne, 30
Marioni Tom, 188
Mars, 149
Mass, Steve 184, 185
Massachusetts Institute of Technology, 27
Mastro, Winifred, 68
Mathews, Harry, 162
Matter, 93
Mayer, Bernadette, 30, 62, 63, 64, 70, 73, 74, 75, 76, 93, 94, 108, 109, 112, 113, 115, 116. 117, 157
Mayer, Rosemary, 94
McCaffery, Larry, 76, 236, 239
McCormack, Derek, 215
McCartney, Paul, 199
McClure, Michael 172
McDermid, Anne, 233, 234
McGrath, Patrick, 239
McGough, Roger, 202
McRobbie, Angela, 223, 224, 225
Mehta, Sonny, 202
Meinhof, Ulrike, 138, 178
Mekons, The, 19, 258, 263, 264, 273
Melmouth, John, 230
Melody Maker, 235, 264
Melville, Samuel, 209, 211
Memoirs of a Beatnik, 79
Memory exhibition, 62, 63, 64, 157
Merleau-Ponty, Maurice, 157
Messerli, Douglas, 152, 169
Metaphors on Vision, 36
Methuen Books, 196
Michaux, Henri, 30

Michigan Womyn's Festival, 249
Milhon, Jude (St. Jude), 256
Miles, Barry, 206 , 207
Miles, Jonathan, 202, 204, 214
Miller, Lori, 223
Millin, Laura 190
Mills College, 87, 88, 113
"Miss X," 233
Mitchell, Eric, 149
Mitchell, Joni, 246
Modern Love, 124
Molinaro, Frank, 19, 22, 23, 259, 267
Moore, Alan, 225
Mona Lisa Overdrive, 225
Mondo 2000, 255
Montag, Haoui, 13
Moré, Marcel, 175
Morris, Michael, 221
Mudd Club, 149, 171, 184, 185, 195
Mulvey, Laura, 206, 209
Mueller, Cookie, 13
Mueller, Susan ,37, 38, 43, 44
Mueller-Vasu, Linda, 37, 38 42, 43, 44
Muktananda, Swami, 143
Munchen Café, 225
Munro, Alice, 161
Murray, Charles Shaar, 265, 266, 268, 269, 272, 273
My Death, My Life, by Pier Paolo Pasolini, 202, 205
My Mother, Demonology, 38, 44, 166, 168, 176, 242, 247, 251, 254, 255

Nares, James, 149
Naropa, 250
National Defense Fund fellowship, 33
National Endowment for the Arts, 236
Nayatt School, 149
Neufeld, Len, 26–33, 37, 38, 44, 50–55, 57, 59, 60–62, 64, 66, 67, 70, 71, 93, 95, 98, 108, 111, 127, 195
Neuromancer, 224, 225, 226
New Langton Arts, 193
New Musical Express, 203, 205, 219, 222, 231, 235
News from Home, 93
New School for Social Research, 63, 260
Statesman, New, 235, 240, 241
Newton, Helmut, 169
New York City in 1979, 59, 170, 172, 180

New York *Daily News*, 122
New York Times, 120, 144, 203, 222, 223, 230, 237, 246, 254, 264
NO! art group, 139
Nog, 136
No New York, 149
Notley, Alice, 75
Nova Convention, 174

Oates, Joyce Carol, 118
Oblowitz, Michael, 149
Observer, The, 203, 230, 232, 246
Oedipus Rex, 43, 222
Ofili, Chris, 23
Onassis, Jacqueline, 132
Only Paper Today, 134
Oshima, Nagisa, 56
Oulipo, 48
Olson, Charles, 35
One World Poetry Festival, 172, 173
Ono, Yoko, 140
Oppen, George, 30
Oppenheim, Denis, 157
Oxford University, 209

Padgett, Ron, 76
Paladin Books, 221
Palestine, Charlemagne, 188
Pandora Press, 232, 233, 234, 242
Pantheon Books, 241, 242, 251
Patterson, Andy, 143, 144, 170
Papyrus Press, 65
Parra, Nicanor, 114
Passenger, The, 208
Pasolini, Pier Paolo, 230, 263
Pat Garrett and Billy the Kid, 136
Patti Smith Group, The, 127
Pearlman, Boris, 126
Peignot, Jérôme, 175
Peppe, Hestia, 235
Performance, 96
Performing Garace, 149
Persian Poems, The, 146, 151, 187
Picador, 152, 153, 202, 203, 206, 215, 230
Picard, Lil, 115, 139, 140, 141
Picasso, Pablo, 97
Pinaka, AnnaMaria, 100, 103
Pinter, Harold, 209
Piper, Adrian, 81

Pirate, The, 128, 132, 233
P-Orridge, Genesis, 222
Plaza Hotel, 34
Phillips Academy, 44
Phillips, Jayne Anne, 161
Poems 5/71–6/71, 60, 61
Poetry Olympics, 203
Politics, 65, 68, 122
Pompidou Center, 174, 178
Portrait of an Eye, 242
Posner, Marcy, 249, 256, 257
Pound, Ezra, 35, 174
Powell, Sheppard, 21, 22, 23
Printed Matter, 134, 150
Proust, Marcel, 157
PublishersWeekly, 254
Publishing News, 233, 235 236
Pulsifer, Gary, 15, 242, 243, 244, 269, 272, 273
Pushcart Press, 170
Putnam, Robert, 21
Pussy, King of the Pirates, 44, 58, 160, 161, 164, 197, 231, 232, 246, 255, 256, 257, 258, 263, 264, 273
Pynchon, Thomas, 136

Quasha, George, 30, 31, 195, 197
Quake, 136
Queneau, Raymond, 145
Quine, Willard, 128

Radcliffe University, 35, 37
Raffinot, Julien, 39, 40, 41, 43
Railroad Collage, 139
Rainer, 226, 227, 231, 243
Rainer, Yvonne, 60
Ramones, The, 127
Random House, 241
RAW, 197
Readings and Writings: Semiotic Counter-Strategies, 209
Réage, Pauline, 44, 157, 187
Red Night trilogy, 252, 253
Redoing Childhood, 254
Reed, Lou, 173
Reich, Steve, 111
Reilly, Nancy, 240
Reines, Ariana, 116
RE/Search, 195
Resnick, Marcia, 149

Rexroth, Kenneth, 113
Rhode Island School of Design, 94, 108
Riding, Laura, 75
Rifka, Judy, 140
Riley, Terry, 88, 111
Rimbaud, Arthur, 230
Rip-Off Red, Girl Detective, 78, 79, 80, 83, 133, 145, 246
Ritchie, Georgina, 163, 259, 266, 267, 268
Robbe-Grillet, Alain 196
Robbins, Harold, 56, 128, 132, 134, 145, 233, 234, 236, 240
Robert Miller Gallery, 149
Roeg, Nicholas, 96
Rolling Stone Magazine, 169
Roloff, Michael, 151, 152
Ronell, Avital, 247
Rose, Cynthia, 203, 205, 259
Rosset, Barney, 196, 197, 240, 241
Rossetti, Christina, 152, 169
Rosler, Martha, 32, 33, 47, 50, 51, 52, 53, 67, 127, 279
Rothenberg, Jerome, 11, 30, 61, 71, 73, 122, 177, 184, 195
Rothenberg, Diane, 30, 71
Roth, Philip, 200
Rubell, Steve, 164
Rumour Publications, 143, 170
Rushdie, Salman, 15, 222
Ruskin, Mickey, 126
Ryman, Geoff, 225

Salle, David, 200
Saltz, Jerry, 100
Samaras, Connie, 277
San Francisco Art Institute, 15, 16, 192, 244, 247, 248, 257, 259
Sante, Luc, 142, 164
Sarah Lawrence College, 37
Schapiro, Miriam, 33
Schelkun, Greg, 267
Schiff, Harris, 64
Schiffrin. André, 241
Schizo-Culture, 146
Scholder, Amy, 22, 23, 24, 246, 247, 277
Schneemann, Carolee, 36, 60, 96, 103, 140
Schrager, Ian, 164

Schuhl, Jean-Jacques, 179
Schulz, Wieland, 151
Scorpions, The, 145
Scott, Sir Walter, 151
Seattle Weekly, 254
Seberg, Jean, 25
Seedbed, 96, 100
Sekula, Alan, 33
Selby, Cecily, 37
Sellers, Terence, 149, 169, 189
Semiotext(e), 146, 149, 162, 250, 261
Série Noire, 172
Serpent's Tail, 269
Serra, Richard, 126
Sexless, 93
Shaar Murray, Charles, 18, 19
Shapiro, Sue, 44
Shakespeare, William, 222
Sharpe, Willoughby, 131, 143, 144
Shaviro, Steven, 231
Shepard, Sam, 151
Sherry, James, 134
Sherman, Stuart 188
Shoot, 100
Silliman, Ron, 94, 98, 116, 117, 118, 119, 120, 121, 122, 123, 126, 128, 130, 131, 132, 133, 134, 135, 137, 139, 146, 148, 184
Silverberg, Ira, 20, 141, 202, 228, 241, 244, 249, 254, 269, 270, 271, 277, 278
Sirius, R. U., 15, 255, 256
Sischy, Ingrid, 150
Sitney, P. Adams, 35, 36, 37, 54, 55, 59, 97, 160
Slackers, 257
Sleep, 97
Smith, Jack, 36
Smith, Janey, 250
Smith, Lindzee, 150
Smith, Patti, 31, 149
Smithson, Robert, 110, 157
Sneakers, 255
Soldado, Juan 20
Sollers, Philippe, 173, 209
Solomon, Holly, 62
Sondheim, Alan, 7, 92, 94, 95, 96, 97, 98, 99, 101, 102, 103, 104, 105, 106, 107, 108, 109, 110, 122, 157, 164, 184, 208

Sontag, Susan, 185
South Bank Show, The, 199, 200, 214, 218
Spare Rib, 235
Spence School, 39
Spider, 237
Spitting Image, 199
Sprawl, 224
Spread Wide, 185
Springer, Anna Joy, 248, 249
Stanislavski, Constanin, 134
Station Hill Press, 195
Stein, Gertrude, 211
Steinberg, Harold, 169
Steinberg, Jeffrey, 169
Stevenson, Robert Louis, 151
St. Mark's Poetry Project, 31, 61, 64, 67, 74, 75, 76, 92, 93, 95, 108, 112, 115, 117, 139
Stonehill Communications, 152, 169, 174
Story of the Eye, 163
St. Pierre, Jean, 44
Strindberg, August, 209
"Stripper Disintegration," 77
Strong, Simon, 258
Studio 54, 124, 164
Studying Hunger, 63
Subculture: The Meaning of Style, 224
Sun and Moon, 152, 169
Sussler, Betsy, 150, 204, 240
Synanon, 100, 101
System of Dante's Hell, The, 72

Talking Heads, The, 127
Tasting and Spitting, 115, 140
Telephone Book, The, 247
Telling, The, 75
Teenage Jesus and the Jerks, 149
Texier, Catherine, 237, 238
Tillman, Lynne, 200, 238, 239
Times Square, 200
Timms, Sally, 273
Thatcher, Margaret, 152
Theatre News, 220
Theorem, 263
Thérèse and Isabelle, 85
They Eat Scum, 203
Thinking Body, The, 119
Third Mind, The, 30, 216

Time and Free Will: An Essay on the Immediate Data of Consciousness, 110
Times Literary Supplement, 232, 235
Times of London, The, 235
Todd, Mabel Elsworth, 119
Tomb for 500,000 Soldiers, 256
Top Stories, 143, 170
Translations of the Diaries of Laure the Schoolgirl, 49, 176
Traveler's Digest, 187
Tribe 8, 249, 254
Trinity College, 35, 36
Trocchi, Alexander, 79, 162, 167
Trudeau, Pierre Elliott, 142
Trull, Steven, 250
Toulouse-Lautrec, Henri de, 128
Turyn, Anne, 170
TV Hijack, 100
TVRT (The Vanishing Rotating Triangle Press), 114, 118, 119, 120, 134, 142, 150, 194
Turgenev, Ivan, 43
Turyn, Anne, 143
Two-Lane Blacktop, 136

UC Berkeley, 246
University of Idaho, 257
University of California, San Diego, 33, 44, 45, 46, 49, 66, 68, 69, 75, 81, 224, 257
UC San Francisco Medical Center, 16
University of Illinois, 32
Unwin Hyman, 233, 235
Urizen Books, 151, 153, 162
U.S. Department of Defense, 46

Vallejo, César, 114
van Gogh, Vincent, 128
Variety, 217, 220
Vauxhall Tavern, 213
Velvet Goldmine, 201
Viegener, Matias 275, 276, 277, 278
Viegener, Valentine, 276
Village Voice, 27, 54, 55, 56, 62, 241
Virgil, 35
Viegener, Matias, 16, 17, 18, 19, 20, 21, 22, 23, 24
Vietnam Nurse, 79
Virtual Geography, 260
V.Vale, 195

Waite, Chrissie, 207
Waldrop, Keith and Rosemarie, 94
Waldman, Anne, 116, 117
Waits, Tom, 254
Wallace, Irving, 128
Warhol, Andy, 36, 45, 164
Wark, McKenzie, 34, 187, 260, 261, 262, 263, 264
Warsh, Lewis, 116, 117
Watson, Don, 219
Way of the White Clouds, The, 132
Webster, Duncan, 222
Wedekind, Frank, 220
Wedell, Noura, 256
Wegman, William, 150
Weidenfeld. Sir George, 240
Weil, Simone, 75, 179
Weill, Florence, 159, 161, 165, 166, 180, 181, 182, 183, 184
Weiner, Hannah, 112, 115
Weiner, Lawrence, 75
Weiss, Wendy, 180
WELL, 256
Wellesley College, 37
Western Front, 142, 185
Whole Earth Catalog, 256
Who's Afraid of Kathy Acker?, 278
Wild Palms, The, 25, 57
Wildroot Cream Oil, 92
William Morris, 249
Williams, Heathcote, 172, 202
Willner, Hal, 254
Wilson, Andrew, 233
Wilson, Martha, 81
Winterson, Jeanette, 230
Wired, 255
Whitney Museum of American Art, 108
Wojnarowicz, David, 149
Wolfe, Bob, 27, 28, 54, 59
Wollen, Peter, 122, 206, 207, 208, 209, 210, 237
Woolf, Virginia, 75
Wooster Group, 149
Writers I'd Like to Fuck (or Be Fucked By), 250
Wurlitzer, Rudy, 7, 136, 137, 140, 141, 185, 200
Wylie, Andrew, 187

Yale University, 35, 36, 108
Young, Lafayette, 151
Young, Noel, 113, 114
Young Lust, 232, 233, 234, 242

Zabriskie Point, 69
Zedd, Nick, 203
Zeta, 277
ZG, 204
Zurbrugg, Nicholas, 246

Acknowledgments

This book wouldn't have been possible without the help of the writer and artist Matias Viegener, director of the Kathy Acker Literary Trust. He took care of Acker at the end of her life and has continued to take great care of her work. He trusted me with the material before I knew what I was doing. I'm grateful for his insight, collaboration, and support.

Thank you to the dozens of people who spoke generously and candidly about the friendships and time they shared with Kathy Acker: Bob Acker, David Antin, Eleanor Antin, Dodie Bellamy, Michael Bracewell, Kathy Brew, Natalie de Broglio, Ellen Bilgore, Robert Brumbaugh, Hank Bull, Constance DeJong, Leslie Dick, Judith Doyle, Morgan Entrekin, Jenna Leigh Evans, Mel Freilicher, Robert Gluck, Jeff Goldberg, Peter Gordon, Jacqueline Graham, James Grauerholz, Annie Grosshans, Michelle Handelman, Stewart Home, Gary Indiana, Darius James, Fred Jordan, Ken Jordan, Leandro Katz, Roz Kaveney, Pooh Kaye, Kevin Killian, Jill Kroesen, Robert Kushner Liz Leventhal, Sylvère Lotringer, Aline Mare, Douglas Martin, Sonny Mehta, Barry Miles Jonathan Miles, Laura Millin, Arthur Nusbaum, Len Neufeld, Marcy Posner, Sheppard Powell, Gary Pulsifer, George Quasha, Linda Mueller Rasu, Michael Roloff, Avital Ronell, Joel

Rose, Martha Rosler, Amy Scholder, Susan Shapiro, Steven Shaviro, Will Shutes, Ira Silverberg, R. U. Sirius P. Adams Sitney, Alan Sondheim, Steven Trull, and McKenzie Wark dug deep into their papers and memories of Acker and her artistic eras.

Special thanks to Paul Buck for sharing his rich archives and explaining the crossovers between the British, French, and American avant-gardes of the 1960s and '70s.

Thank you to Geoffrey Cruickshank-Hagenbuckle for tarot instruction, and for reading the cards; and to Ariana Reines for sharing some of her knowledge about astrology.

Thank you to fellow biographer Jason McBride for sharing materials and a helpful, ongoing exchange of ideas and information.

Thank you to the librarians and archivists who pointed me in the right direction and responded to dozens of queries: Colleen Garcia and Heather Smedburg at the Mandeville Special Collections Library, University of Californa, San Diego; Lisa Darms, Sophie Glidden-Lyon, Brent Phillips and Marvin Taylor at the Fales Library & Special Collections, New York University; Elizabeth Dunn, Laura Micham and Kelly Wooten at the David M. Rubenstein Rare Book & Manuscript Library, Duke University; Laura Henriksen at the St. Marks Poetry Project; and Alonso Avila at the Special Collections and University Archive, University of Iowa Libraries.

I'm grateful to the lead researchers Hestia Peppe (London) and Julien Raffinot (New York) for their diligent, inspired investigations that led to new insights and lines of inquiry. Thanks to private investigator Denise Witzeman and philosopher Rebecca Carson for digging through municipal records in New York and London, and to scholar Carolina Escalona for additional research in Berlin.

Thank you to first readers Amy Scholder, Sylvère Lotringer, Jeff Goldberg, Hestia Peppe, Mark von Schlegell, Emily Gould, Erik Morse, Tamar Brott, Kevin Vennemann and Ariana Reines for their helpful suggestions.

Other people helped, too: Ruth Novaczek, Marco Vera, Sergio Haro, Kevin Vennemann, Matt Fishbeck, Natasha Soobramanian, copy editor Maxine Bartow, notation compiler and indexer Janique Vigier, transcriber Carlo Craig, additional archival researchers Helena Bassett, Laura Jaramillo and Caroline Wallace; Rebecca Waldron, Emily Gould, Heidi Julavits, and Laurence Laluyaux.

Grateful acknowledgment to the John Simon Guggenheim Foundation for their support of this project; and to Alex Sainsbury and the staff at Raven Row London, for a residency that made the London research possible.

Finally, thanks to my editor, friend, and longtime collaborator Hedi El Kholti, and to my partner, Philip Valdez, for "protecting the bubble" and his constant belief.